CW01096182

Security Certification
FOR
DUMMIES®

Security + Certification For Dummies®

Key Acronyms

3DES (Triple DES). An enhancement to the original DES algorithm that uses multiple keys to encrypt plaintext.

AES (Advanced Encryption Standard). A block cipher based on the Rijndael cipher which is expected to eventually replace DES.

CA (Certificate Authority). In a PKI infrastructure, the CA issues certificates, maintains and publishes status information and Certificate Revocation Lists (CRLs), and maintains archives.

CHAP (Challenge-Handshake Authentication Protocol). A remote access control protocol that uses a three-way handshake to authenticate both a peer and a server.

CRC (Cyclic Redundancy Check). A simple mathematical calculation or checksum used to create a message profile.

DAC (Discretionary Access Control). An access policy determined by the owner of a file or other resource (see also **MAC**).

DBMS (Database Management System). Restricts access by different subjects to various objects in a database.

DCE. Data Communications Equipment. Consists of devices at the network end of a user-to-network interface.

DES (Data Encryption Standard). A commonly used symmetric key algorithm that uses a 56-bit key and operates on 64-bit blocks.

DNS. Domain Name Service. Uses UDP port 53.

EAP (Extensible Authentication Protocol). A remote access control protocol that implements various authentication mechanisms including MD5, S/Key, generic token cards, and digital certificates. Often used in wireless networks.

EBCDIC. Extended Binary-Coded Decimal Interchange Mode.

EES (Escrowed Encryption Standard). Divides a secret key into two parts and place those two parts into escrow with two separate, trusted organizations. Published by NIST in FIPS PUB 185 (1994).

ESP (Encapsulating Security Payload). In IPSec, provides confidentiality (encryption) and limited authentication.

FDDI (Fiber Distributed Data Interface). Token-passing network protocol for fiber optic networks operating at data rates of up to 100-Mbps. Consists of two fiber optic rings for high availability. Sometimes used in WAN backbones.

ICMP. Internet Control Message Protocol.

IDEA. International Data Encryption Algorithm. A symmetric algorithm that operates on 64-bit plaintext blocks using a 128-bit key.

IKE (Internet Key Exchange). Provides key management in IPSec using three complementary protocols: the Internet Security Association and Key Management Protocol (ISAKMP), the Secure Key Exchange Mechanism (SKEME), and the Oakley Key Exchange Protocol.

IPSec (Internet Protocol Security). An IETF open standard for secure communications over public IP-based networks.

IPX (Internetwork Packet Exchange). A connectionless protocol used primarily in NetWare networks for routing packets across the network.

MAC (Mandatory Access Control System). Access policy is determined by the system rather than the owner (see also **DAC**).

MOSS (MIME Object Security Services). Provides confidentiality, integrity, identification and authentication, and non-repudiation using MD2 or MD5, RSA asymmetric keys, and DES.

OSPF (Open Shortest Path First). A link-state routing protocol that uses a variety of metrics for determining the best route to a network destination.

PAP (Password Authentication Protocol). A remote access control protocol that uses a two-way handshake to authenticate a peer to a server when a link is initially established.

Security + Certification For Dummies®

Cheat Sheet

PEM (Privacy Enhanced Mail). Provides confidentiality and authentication using 3DES for encryption, MD2 or MD5 message digests, X.509 digital certificates, and the RSA asymmetric system for digital signatures and secure key distribution.

PGP (Pretty Good Privacy). A freely available, open source e-mail application that provides confidentiality and authentication using the IDEA Cipher for encryption and the RSA asymmetric system for digital signatures and secure key distribution.

PKI (Public Key Infrastructure). Enables secure E-commerce through the integration of digital signatures, digital certificates, and other services necessary to ensure confidentiality, integrity, authentication, non-repudiation, and access control.

PPP (Point-to-Point Protocol). Used in remote access service (RAS) servers to encapsulate IP packets and establish dial-in connections over serial and ISDN links.

PPTP (Point-to-Point Tunneling Protocol). A VPN protocol standard developed by Microsoft to enable the Point-to-Point Protocol (PPP) to be tunneled through a public network. PPTP uses native PPP authentication and encryption services (such as PAP, CHAP, and EAP).

RA (Registration Authority). In a PKI infrastructure, the RA is responsible for verifying certificate contents for the CA.

RADIUS (Remote Authentication Dial-In User Service). An open-source, UDP-based client-server protocol used to authenticate remote users.

RIP (Routing Information Protocol). A basic distance-vector routing protocol that uses hop count as a metric for determining the best route to a network destination.

S-HTTP (Secure Hypertext Transfer Protocol). An Internet protocol that provides a method for secure communications with a web server.

S/MIME (Secure Multipurpose Internet Mail Extensions). Provides confidentiality and authentication for e-mail using the RSA asymmetric key system, digital signatures, and X.509 digital certificates.

SMTP. Simple Mail Transfer Protocol. Uses TCP port 25.

SNMP. Simple Network Management Protocol. Uses UDP port 161.

SPI (Security Parameter Index). In IPSec, the SPI is a 32-bit string used by the receiving station to differentiate between SAs terminating on that station.

SSH (Secure Shell). A terminal emulation program that provides secure remote access. Uses TCP port 22.

SSL/TLS (Secure Sockets Layer/Transport Layer Security). A transport layer protocol that provides session-based encryption and authentication for secure communication between clients and servers on the Internet.

SSO (Single Sign-On). Allows a user to present a single set of logon credentials, typically to an authentication server, which then transparently logs the user onto all other enterprise systems and applications for which that user is authorized.

TCP (Transmission Control Protocol). A full-duplex, connection-oriented protocol that provides reliable delivery of packets across a network.

VPN (Virtual Private Network). A secure tunnel over a public network such as the Internet.

WAN (Wide Area Network). A data network that operates across a relatively large geographic area.

WAP (Wireless Access Point). Radio transceivers that provide the wireless connection to a wired network.

WTLS (Wireless Transport Layer Security). A protocol that provides security services for the Wireless Application Protocol (WAP) commonly used for internet connectivity by mobile devices.

For Dummies: Bestselling Book Series for Beginners

by Lawrence Miller and Peter H. Gregory

Wiley Publishing, Inc.

Security+ Certification For Dummies®

Published by
Wiley Publishing, Inc.
909 Third Avenue
New York, NY 10022
www.wiley.com

For general information on our other products and services or to obtain technical support, please contact our Customer Care Department within the U.S. at 800-762-2974, outside the U.S. at 317-572-3993, or fax 317-572-4002.

Wiley also publishes its books in a variety of electronic formats. Some content that appears in print may not be available in electronic books.

Library of Congress Control Number: 2002114827

ISBN: 0-7645-2576-X

Manufactured in the United States of America

10 9 8 7 6 5 4 3 2 1

1O/RZ/QS/QT/IN

WILEY   is a trademark of Wiley Publishing, Inc.

About the Authors

Lawrence Miller, CISSP, MCSE+I, CCNP, and Sun Certified Systems Administrator, has worked in systems administration and information security for over nine years. His other certifications include CNA, A+, Network+, and i-Net+. He is currently working as the Information Technology Operations Manager for a major U.S. law firm. Previously, he has worked as the Internetworking Security Engineer for a service provider in the U.S. retail sector and as a consultant for various multinational clients in Tokyo, Japan. He also served as a Chief Petty Officer in the U.S. Navy in various roles, including as an Information Systems Security Manager, Technical Services Department Head, and Meteorologist/Oceanographer.

Peter H. Gregory, CISSP, is the author of *Solaris Security, Sun Certified System Administrator for Solaris 8 Study Guide,* and *Enterprise Information Security.* He has been the technical reviewer/editor for more than 20 business computing books over the past eight years, including *Secure Electronic Commerce, Halting the Hacker, Essential Guide to Intelligent Optical Networks,* and several of the Sun Microsystems Press system administration references and guides for Solaris. Peter is the Logical Security Strategist at a wireless telecommunications carrier in Seattle, Washington. Prior to this, he was the Manager for Enterprise Security Architecture, and in the five years before that, he held less-glamorous IT management titles there. When he pries his hands off the keyboard, Peter and his wife, Corinne, can be found raising their three young girls and getting dirt under their fingernails in the garden. Peter's Web site can be found at www.hartgregorygroup.com, and he can be reached at peter.gregory@hartgregorygroup.com.

Dedication

From Lawrence Miller to my family.

From Peter H. Gregory to those who have been heroes all along — the police, firefighters, and paramedics in New York City and everywhere.

Author's Acknowledgments

Larry Miller would like to thank everyone at Wiley Publishing for making this a very pleasant and rewarding experience, especially Melody Layne, Pat O'Brien, and Diana Conover. I would also like thank Pat O'Day for your friendship and professional guidance. Finally, a very special thank you to Thad Stoner and Mica Johnson for your friendship, encouragement, and for introducing me to this wonderful opportunity!

Publisher's Acknowledgments

We're proud of this book; please send us your comments through our online registration form located at `www.dummies.com/register/`.

Some of the people who helped bring this book to market include the following:

Acquisitions, Editorial, and Media Development

Project Editor: Pat O'Brien

Acquisitions Editor: Melody Layne

Senior Copy Editor: Diana Conover

Technical Editor: James E. Kelly

Editorial Manager: Kevin Kirschner

Permissions Editor: Carmen Krikorian

Media Development Specialist: Megan Decraene

Media Development Manager: Laura VanWinkle

Media Development Supervisor: Richard Graves

Editorial Assistant: Amanda Foxworth

Cartoons: Rich Tennant, `www.the5thwave.com`

Production

Project Coordinator: Ryan Steffen

Layout and Graphics: Stephanie D. Jumper, Jacque Schneider, Jeremey Unger

Proofreaders: Laura Albert, John Greenough, Susan Moritz, TECHBOOKS Production Services

Indexer: TECHBOOKS Production Services

Publishing and Editorial for Technology Dummies

Richard Swadley, Vice President and Executive Group Publisher

Andy Cummings, Vice President and Publisher

Mary C. Corder, Editorial Director

Publishing for Consumer Dummies

Diane Graves Steele, Vice President and Publisher

Joyce Pepple, Acquisitions Director

Composition Services

Gerry Fahey, Vice President of Production Services

Debbie Stailey, Director of Composition Services

Contents at a Glance

Table of Contents

Part II: General Security Concepts *39*

Chapter 3: Access Control **41**

Chapter 4: Attacks and Malicious Code **67**

Introduction

CompTIA's Security+ is an exciting new certification for computer and networking professionals interested in getting a great start in the information security world. And *Security+ Certification For Dummies* is your no-nonsense blueprint for success on the Security+ exam!

This introduction describes the book's purpose, style, organization, and conventions.

About This Book

Information security covers a broad spectrum of computer skills and experiences. This book, as with the Security+ certification, *introduces* you to many of these requisite skills. It is not an in-depth, desk-side reference replete with answers and explanations for every conceivable security topic or issue you will encounter in your career. This book provides you with the basic understanding of information security concepts to pass the Security+ exam.

How This Book Is Organized

Security+ Certification For Dummies is organized into easy-to-read, modular chapters to help you prepare for the Security+ exam. You can read it from beginning to end (recommended), end to beginning, or pick and choose chapters at random! The topics presented in each chapter, for the most part, do not require an understanding of material presented in other chapters. If so, we'll point you back to the appropriate section!

This book is organized into eight parts.

Part I: Exam Basics

Part I provides you with some general information about taking the exam and a brief overview of the content domains for the Security+ test. This includes information on how to register for and schedule the exam, what to expect at the testing center and on the exam, and some basic networking and security terms and concepts.

Part II: General Security Concepts

Part II covers topics in the General Security Concepts content domain, including access control, authentication, nonessential services and protocols, attacks, malicious code, social engineering, and auditing.

Part III: Communication Security

Part III covers topics in the Communications Security content domain, including remote access, e-mail, Web, directory, file transfer, and wireless security issues.

Part IV: Infrastructure Security

Part IV covers topics in the Infrastructure Security content domain, including devices, media, security topologies, intrusion detection, and security baselines.

Part V: Cryptography

Part V covers topics in the Cryptography content domain, including algorithms, concepts of using cryptography, PKI, standards and protocols, and key management/certificate lifecycles.

Part VI: Operational/Organizational Security

Part VI covers topics in the Operational/Organizational Security domain, including physical security, disaster recovery, business continuity, privilege management, forensics, risk identification, education, and documentation.

Part VII: The Part of Tens

Part VII includes test preparation and test taking tips, study resources, and information to help guide your professional development as a security professional.

Part VIII: Appendixes

Part VIII includes a 100-question practice exam and information about what's on the CD in the back of this book and how to use the CD.

CD-ROM

The CD-ROM included in this book contains various study aids and practice tests to help you prepare for and pass the Security+ exam.

How the Chapters Are Organized

Every study chapter in this book follows a simple, standard format based on a complex, time-tested, proven *For Dummies* model for testing success, which includes:

- ✔ Preview questions (to see what you already know)
- ✔ Detailed coverage (to teach you what you need to know)
- ✔ Review questions (to make sure that you know what you need to know)

First page

Each chapter begins with a preview of what's coming soon to a theater near you — well, at least what's coming in the pages to follow. This includes:

- ✔ A brief introduction
- ✔ Study subjects

Quick Assessment

Right after the first page, you'll find a quick assessment test covering the exam objectives for the chapter. This test will help you quickly determine how much you already know about the topics covered in the chapter.

- ✔ **If you get every question right,** skip to the end of the chapter and see how you do on the prep test. If you score 100 percent on the prep test, you may want to skip the chapter altogether or give it a quick, cursory read.

- ✔ **If you get every question wrong,** you should definitely spend time reading the chapter carefully to make sure that you understand the topics presented.

- ✔ **If you get some right and some wrong,** you should flag any of your weak areas and spend some extra time on those topics as you read through the chapter.

Study Subjects

The heart of each chapter extensively covers the topics you will need to know to pass the Security+ exam. Tables or illustrations are provided whenever helpful. However, because this is a vendor-neutral certification, you will not find screen captures or simulation-type graphics. More room for good, old-fashioned information!

Prep Tests

Most chapters finish with a quick multiple-choice test to help you determine how well you understand and retain the information just presented. The tests at the end of each chapter contain questions similar to the ones you'll find on the actual Security+ exam.

Icons Used in This Book

Instant Answer icons highlight important information that will help you answer questions on the actual exam. These are not brain dumps, but they will help you remember critical points and succeed on the Security+ exam.

Remember icons identify general information and core concepts that you may already know but should certainly understand and review before the Security+ exam.

Tip icons include short suggestions and tidbits of useful information.

Warning icons identify potential pitfalls, including easily confused or difficult-to-understand terms and concepts.

Let's Get Started!

Turn the page and begin the journey, grasshopper!

Part I
Exam Basics

In this part . . .

The road to knowledge begins with . . . Part I! If you're a fan of prequels, then this part is for you! It belongs on your bookshelf next to *The Hobbit* and *The Phantom Menace* to be cherished for many generations to come!

In this part we'll provide the backdrop for the Security+ examination. Use this part of the book to learn about the Security+ exam — its format, types of questions, test objectives, registration, and cost. You'll also get a *very brief* overview of some networking basics and an introduction to some basic security concepts and terminology.

If you're familiar with CompTIA exams and the testing experience, you may be inclined to skip this part. I recommend at least a quick read. We promise it won't take as long as reading *The Hobbit*. We can also give you a 100 percent money-back guarantee that the book will be much better than the movie (we're reasonably certain this book will not spawn any lucrative movie deals!).

Chapter 1

CompTIA and the Security+ Certification

*T*he demand for skilled information security professionals has never been greater. This need is in every industry and occupation where computers are found.

To answer that need for highly skilled information security professionals, CompTIA — the wonderful folks that brought us the cornerstone of IT certifications, A+ (as well as Network+, Server+, and others) — introduces Security+!

As with all other CompTIA certifications, Security+ is a vendor-neutral exam. Although security exams and certifications from such vendors as Checkpoint, Microsoft, and Cisco provide in-depth technical certifications, they are typically highly specialized (geared toward their specific product) and limited in scope (for example, firewall design as only one facet of information security). Other vendor-neutral certifications, such as SANS or ISC2, require extensive knowledge and experience, may be less-readily available (not available through VUE or Prometric testing centers), and can be prohibitively expensive.

By comparison, the Security+ certification provides a broad-based, foundation-level security exam that enables networking professionals to join forces against the dark side in this epic battle between good and evil!

Who (Should Take the Exam)?

The target candidate for the Security+ certification is a networking professional with at least two years of experience in at least one of these network areas:

- ✔ Help desk
- ✔ Network administration
- ✔ Junior-level system engineering

Ideally, the candidate also has the A+ and/or Network+ certification (although this is not a requirement).

What (Can You Expect on the Exam)?

The Security+ exam (#SY1-101) is a 125-question, multiple-choice exam. You will have two hours to complete the exam and must score 75 percent (94 questions) or better to pass. The exam covers five security content domains, as follows:

- ✔ General Security Concepts (30 percent)
- ✔ Communications Security (20 percent)
- ✔ Infrastructure Security (20 percent)
- ✔ Basics of Cryptography (15 percent)
- ✔ Operational/Organizational Security (15 percent)

Fortunately, CompTIA exams are more straightforward than other certification exams — you either know the answer or you don't.

- ✔ You do not have to drag and drop answer choices, simulate a task, click a crosshair on a diagram, or pore through an overblown, wordy, unrealistic scenario scattered across five tabs of information beginning with "You are the network administrator for a large company . . . " and ending 20 minutes later when you finally get to the point of the question and the only 2 relevant pieces of information needed to answer the question.
- ✔ There are no fill-in-the-blank or true/false questions. The answer choices are, for the most part, unambiguous, and they have one, and only one, correct choice — no multiple answers. And that choice will be the *correct* answer, not the *most correct* or *best* answer.

If you find a question or answer choice confusing or subject to interpretation, CompTIA provides you with the opportunity to comment on any question during the exam. The clock is still ticking, so keep your comments brief.

✔ The exam is not *adaptive*. You can move forward and backwards throughout the exam and mark questions you are unsure of for later review (at the end of the exam's time period). This feature is helpful if you get stuck on a question because you may find the answer or helpful information from an earlier (or later) question.

The Security+ exam is currently available in English only. However, I am assuming this will not be a problem for you because you are reading this book, which is currently available in English only!

When (Should You Take the Exam)?

The answer to this question, of course, varies greatly, depending on the individual. In general, the answer will be sometime after reading this book and before the end of your professional career. However, because you were smart enough to choose this book to help you prepare, you can expect to take (and pass) the exam soon after you've read this book (unless you're retiring next week).

✔ The sample questions at the end of each chapter and the practice exams in Appendix A and on the CD-ROM can also help you prepare. If you consistently answer from 85 to 90 percent of the practice questions in this book, you can expect to do well on the actual Security+ exam.

✔ Chapters 20 and 21 list many excellent security books and Web sites. Use these resources to further enhance your learning and study experience. You can also find discussion groups and study guides on the Internet (such as those at `www.cramsession.com`) that can help you prepare for the Security+ exam.

✔ You can also purchase exam simulations from such vendors as

  • **Boson** at `www.boson.com`

  • **Transcender** at `www.transcender.com`

Avoid brain dumps! Brain dumps are a big no-no for IT certifications, in general, but especially so for CompTIA certifications. CompTIA has sued Web sites posting brain dumps, and the folks at CompTIA take the nondisclosure agreement (the one you agree to before taking the exam) *very* seriously.

Where (Do You Take the Exam)?

CompTIA exams are administered by two organizations. You need to contact one of these two organizations to register for and schedule your Security+ examination. You can do this via the Internet or phone:

- ✔ **Prometric** at www.prometric.com or www.2test.com; 800-977-3926
- ✔ **VUE** at www.vue.com; 877-551-PLUS (7587)

Registering on the Internet has the following advantages:

- ✔ You don't have to wait on hold to speak with a customer representative.
- ✔ You can easily search for a list of all testing centers in your area (based on zip code) and find the one that is most convenient for you.
- ✔ You can print a map with directions to that testing location while you're online (www.mapquest.com).
- ✔ You can easily search for a list of all available dates and times for your preferred testing center.

Your choice of testing center doesn't change the exam's cost or format. But other factors that may affect which testing organization you choose include the following:

- ✔ You can schedule an exam with VUE for the same day or even do a walk-in registration, if they have space for you.
- ✔ VUE exams are delivered *online* at the testing center. Exam results are delivered immediately to CompTIA when you finish your exam. (Prometric exam results must be manually uploaded.) This minimizes the chances that your exam results can somehow disappear into a black hole somewhere, and it also means that you can get your certificate from CompTIA a little quicker.
- ✔ You should probably have an easier time finding a Prometric testing center near you.

  You may have previously known your local Prometric center as one of these:
    - Sylvan Testing Center
    - Sylvan Prometric
    - Thomson Prometric

Arrive early and be prepared

Everyone's human. But not everyone gets cut slack every time they need it. Although testing centers (whether Prometric or VUE) may relax their rules, don't count on it. Stick to these guidelines and you won't go wrong:

- ✔ **Arrive early.** Plan to be in the testing center at least 15 minutes early. This ensures that you have sufficient time to sign in, relax, and meditate before your exam. It also gives you some breathing room for unforeseen contingencies (getting lost, getting stuck in traffic, finding no parking space, attending to sudden calls of nature, and the like).

  If you're late, you may lose your seat and forfeit your exam fee.

- ✔ **Bring ID.** You will have to prove your identity to the test administrator. You probably won't have time for "Six Degrees of Kevin Bacon," and the test administrator probably wouldn't go for it anyway. To be safe, bring the following:

  - A picture ID (such as your driver's license or passport)

  - A major credit card (with the same name on it)

- ✔ **Bring your confirmation letter.** After you register and pay for your exam, you receive a confirmation letter (normally via e-mail). Print it out and bring it with you. If, for some reason, the testing center does not have your exam properly scheduled (it happens), you can save yourself valuable time and needless hassles by presenting the confirmation letter (so you don't have to convince the test administrator that you are in the right place at the right time for the right exam).

- ✔ **Surrender all your worldly possessions.** Plan to leave your cell phone, PDA, pager, voice-processing product, computer video game, wireless e-mail product, and other gadgets and toys with the test administrator or in your car.

Use scratch paper

The test administrator will offer you scratch paper (some places may have an erasable whiteboard instead) to use during the exam. Use it!

Right before you go into the exam room, review the cheat sheet at the front of this book and anything else you may need to remember. As soon as you enter the exam room, write it on your scratch paper before you begin the exam. This is perfectly legal and completely recommended. Just remember: You have to give the scratch paper back after the exam.

To agree or not to agree

That is the question they shall ask of thee! In order to continue on to the Security+ exam, you must first agree to comply with the testing firm's nondisclosure agreement (NDA). This is a standard legal agreement that says you will not disclose any questions from the exam. I can't authoritatively tell you what happens if you click No or I do not agree, but I suspect that it is the quickest way to fail a CompTIA exam (or any other certification exam). However, I've never known anyone that had $200 to burn by trying! Don't waste any brain cells on this one, click I agree and get on with the hard stuff.

Instant gratification (or not)

After you complete and submit your exam, you receive an instant score report notifying you of whether you have passed or failed. Try to control your emotions until after you have departed the courtroom, uhhh . . . exam room. The test administrator gives you a printed copy of your exam report with a raised seal of authenticity and an important rubber-stamped notice that says "Do not lose this report." My advice — do not lose this report. It can, and does occasionally, happen that your results are not correctly processed or you do not receive your certificate in the mail. The official exam report is then your only proof of certification until you can get everything sorted out.

How (Much Will It Cost)?

As mentioned earlier, the Security+ exam costs you $200. You must pay in advance with a major credit card or by personal check. (You will receive an exam voucher after your check clears.)

If you don't want to pop for the exam out of pocket, there may be a few ways to recover the money:

- ✔ Ask whether your employer will pick up the tab. A few still do.

- ✔ U.S. veterans may qualify for reimbursement under the Montgomery G.I. Bill.

- ✔ You may also be able to claim the exam as a job-related expense on your federal income tax return (unless you don't pay U.S. Income Tax).

Why (Should You Take the Exam)?

If you've read this far, I'm assuming that you've already purchased *Security+ Certification For Dummies* and, at the very least, have made some investment of time in reading up to this point. So why not take the exam?

But more important, the Security+ certification serves a significant role by helping to identify the basic skills required of security professionals and those individuals that possess these requisite skills.

Responding to the need for a knowledgeable security workforce in the IT industry, CompTIA developed the Security+ certification. In CompTIA's words, "The need is there. The jobs are there. Both employees and employers benefit from an educated information security workforce." Many major industry players, including the following, agree and have cosponsored the Security+ certification:

- ✔ The Information Systems Security Association (ISSA)
- ✔ Microsoft
- ✔ Novell
- ✔ RSA Security
- ✔ Sun Microsystems
- ✔ The U.S. Federal Bureau of Investigation (FBI)
- ✔ The U.S. Secret Service
- ✔ VeriSign

So do your part to help make the world a safer, more secure place — get Security+ certified!

Chapter 2

Networking and Security Basics

*T*ime to dust the old noggin and knock out some cobwebs! In this chapter, I review some of the basics. None of the information presented here should be new to a seasoned network professional, so you should be able to breeze through it with no problems! Although you're not likely to be directly tested on information in this chapter, it forms an important foundation for the rest of the Security+ exam.

Quick Assessment

1   List the seven layers of the OSI Model.

2   The two sublayers of the Data Link Layer are _____ and _____.

3   A LAN data transmission in which packets are sent from the source to a single destination device using a specific destination IP address is referred to as a _____ transmission.

4   A problem associated with bridges in which broadcast traffic is automatically forwarded and floods the network is known as a _____ .

5   A _____ is implemented on switches to logically segregate a network and limit broadcast domains.

6   _____ translates private, nonroutable IP addresses on internal network devices to registered IP addresses when communication across the Internet is required.

7   _____ are intelligent devices that link dissimilar networks and forward data packets based on logical or physical addresses to the destination network.

8   FTP operates on TCP ports _____ and _____.

9   The three fundamental aspects of information that must be protected are _____, _____, and _____.

10   A concept that is closely related to confidentiality and is most often associated with personal information is _____.

Answers

1 Application, Presentation, Session, Transport, Network, Data Link, Physical. *See "The OSI Reference Model."*

2 Logical Link Control (LLC) and Media Access Control (MAC). *Review "Data Link Layer (Layer 2)."*

3 Unicast. *Review "LAN protocols and transmission methods."*

4 broadcast storm. *See "Networking equipment at the Data Link Layer."*

5 Virtual LAN (VLAN). *See "Networking equipment at the Data Link Layer."*

6 Network Address Translation (NAT). *See "Internet Protocol (IP)."*

7 routers. *See "Routers."*

8 20 and 21. *See "Application Layer (Layer 7)."*

9 Confidentiality, Integrity, Availability. *See "The Goal of Information Security."*

10 Privacy. *See "Confidentiality."*

The OSI Reference Model

In 1984, the International Standards Organization (ISO) adopted the Open Systems Interconnection (OSI) reference model (or simply, the *OSI model*) to facilitate interoperability between network devices independent of the manufacturer. The OSI model defines standard protocols for communication and interoperability by using a layered approach. This approach divides complex networking issues into simpler functional components that help the understanding, design, and development of networking solutions, and it provides the following specific advantages:

- ✔ Clarifies the general functions of a communications process rather than focusing on specific issues
- ✔ Reduces complex networking processes into simpler sublayers and components
- ✔ Promotes interoperability by defining standard interfaces
- ✔ Aids development by allowing a vendor to change individual features at a single layer rather than rebuilding the entire protocol stack
- ✔ Facilitates easier (and more logical) troubleshooting

The OSI model consists of seven distinct layers that describe how data is communicated between systems and applications on a computer network. (See Figure 2-1.)

In the OSI model, data is passed from the highest layer (Application; Layer 7) downward through each layer to the lowest layer (Physical; Layer 1) and is then transmitted across the network medium to the destination node where it's passed upward from the lowest layer to the highest layer. Each layer communicates only with the layer immediately above and below it (adjacent layers). This communication is achieved through a process known as *data encapsulation*. Data encapsulation wraps protocol information from the layer immediately above in the data section of the layer immediately below. Figure 2-2 illustrates this process.

Physical Layer (Layer 1)

The Physical Layer sends and receives bits across the network. It specifies the electrical, mechanical, and functional requirements of the network, including topology, cabling and connectors, and interface types, as well as the process for converting bits to electrical (or light) signals that can be transmitted across the physical medium.

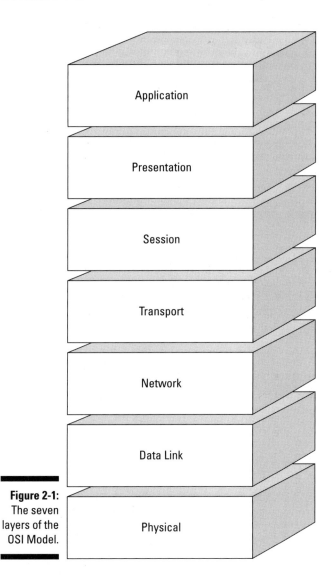

Data Link Layer (Layer 2)

The Data Link Layer ensures that messages are delivered to the proper device across a physical network link and defines the networking protocol (for example, Ethernet and token-ring) used for sending and receiving data between individual devices. It formats messages from layers above into frames for transmission, handles point-to-point synchronization and error control, and can perform link encryption. The Data Link Layer consists of two sublayers: the Logical Link Control (LLC) and Media Access Control (MAC) sublayers.

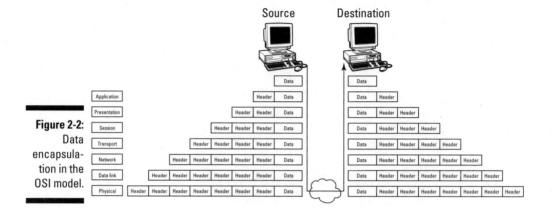

Figure 2-2:
Data
encapsula-
tion in the
OSI model.

The Logical Link Control (LLC) sublayer is defined in IEEE standards 802.1 (Internetworking) and 802.2 (Logical Link Control). See Table 2-1 for more information about the IEEE 802 standards. The LLC sublayer operates between the Network Layer above and the MAC sublayer below. The LLC sublayer performs the following three functions:

✔ Provides an interface for the MAC sublayer.

✔ Manages the control, sequencing, and acknowledgement of frames being passed up to the Network Layer or down to the Physical Layer.

✔ Bears responsibility for timing and flow control. Flow control monitors the flow of data between devices to ensure that a receiving device, which may not necessarily be operating at the same speed as the transmitting device, is not overwhelmed.

Table 2-1	The IEEE 802 Standards
Standard	**Description**
802.1	Internetworking
802.2	Logical Link Control (LLC)
802.3	Ethernet
802.4	Physical Bus
802.5	Token Ring
802.6	Metropolitan Area Networks (MANs)
802.7	Broadband Technical Advisory Group

Standard	Description
802.8	Fiber Optic Technical Advisory Group
802.9	Integrated Voice/Data Networks
802.10	Network Security
802.11	Wireless Networks
802.12	High-Speed Networks

The Media Access Control (MAC) sublayer is defined in these IEEE standards:

- 802.3 (Ethernet)
- 802.4 (Physical Bus)
- 802.5 (Token Ring)
- 802.12 (High-Speed Networks)

The MAC sublayer operates between the LLC sublayer above and the Physical Layer below. It is primarily responsible for framing and performs the following three functions:

- **Performs error control:** It performs error control by using a cyclic redundancy check (CRC). A *CRC* is a simple mathematical calculation or checksum used to create a message profile. The receiving device recalculates the CRC. If the calculated CRC doesn't match the received CRC, the packet is dropped, and a request to resend is transmitted.

- **Identifies hardware device (or MAC) addresses:** A *MAC address* (also known as a *hardware address* or *physical address*) is a 48-bit address that is encoded on each device by its manufacturer. The first 24 bits identify the manufacturer or vendor. The second 24 bits uniquely identify the device. The MAC address is usually written in hexadecimal format, such as 00-06-F4-00-73-F7.

- **Controls media access:** The three basic types of media access are as follows:

  - **Contention:** In contention-based networks, individual devices must vie for control of the physical network medium. This type of network is ideally suited for networks characterized by small, bursty traffic. Ethernet networks use a contention-based method, known as *Carrier-Sense Multiple Access Collision Detect* (CSMA/CD), in which all stations listen for traffic on the physical network medium. If the line is clear, any station can transmit data. However, if more than one station attempts to transmit data at the same time, a collision occurs, the traffic is dropped, and both stations must wait a random period of time before attempting to retransmit. Another slight variation of the CSMA/CD method, used in Apple LocalTalk networks, is known as *Carrier-Sense Multiple Access Collision Avoidance* (CSMA/CA), in which a station broadcasts a warning that it is about to send data before actually sending the data.

- **Token passing:** In token-passing networks, individual devices must wait for a special frame, known as a *token*, before transmitting data across the physical network medium. This type of network is considered *deterministic* (transmission delay can be reliably calculated, and collisions don't occur) and is ideally suited for networks with large, bandwidth-consuming applications that are delay-sensitive. Token-ring and FDDI networks, described in the following section, use various token-passing methods for media access control.

- **Polling:** In polling networks, individual devices (secondary hosts) are polled by a primary host to see whether they have data to be transmitted. Secondary hosts can't transmit until the primary host grants permission. Polling is typically used in mainframe environments.

LAN protocols and transmission methods

Common LAN protocols are defined at the Data Link (and Physical) Layer and include

- ✔ **ARCnet:** The ARCnet protocol is one of the earliest LAN technologies developed. It uses the token-passing media access method that I discussed in the preceding section to transport data to the physical LAN medium. You can use coaxial cable to implement it in a star topology. ARCnet provides slow but predictable network performance.

- ✔ **Ethernet:** The Ethernet protocol transports data to the physical LAN medium by using CSMA/CD (which I discuss in the preceding section) and is designed for networks characterized by sporadic, sometimes heavy traffic requirements. Ethernet is the most common LAN protocol used today and is implemented in a bus topology over coaxial or twisted pair cabling. Ethernet operates at speeds up to 10 Mbps. Two recent enhancements to the Ethernet protocol include Fast Ethernet (speeds up to 100 Mbps over CAT-5 twisted-pair or fiber-optic cabling) and Gigabit Ethernet (speeds up to 1000 Mbps over CAT-6 twisted pair or fiber-optic cabling).

- ✔ **Token-Ring:** The token-ring protocol transports data to the physical LAN medium by using the token-passing media access method that I discuss in the preceding section. Originally developed by IBM, *token-ring* refers to both IBM Token-Ring and IEEE 802.5. All nodes are attached to a Multistation Access Unit (MSAU) in a logical ring (physical star) topology. One node on the token-ring network is designated as the *active monitor* and ensures that no more than one token is on the network at any given time. (Variations permit more than one token on the network.) If the token is lost, the active monitor is responsible for ensuring that a replacement token is generated. Token-ring networks operate at speeds of 4 and 16 Mbps.

✔ **Fiber Distributed Data Interface (FDDI):** The FDDI protocol transports data to the physical LAN medium by using the token-passing media access method that I discuss in the previous section. It's implemented as a dual counter-rotating ring over fiber-optic cabling at speeds up to 100 Mbps. All stations on a FDDI network are connected to both rings. During normal operation, only one ring is active. In the event of a network break or fault, the ring wraps back through the nearest node onto the second ring.

LAN data transmissions are classified as:

✔ **Unicast:** Packets are sent from the source to a single destination device by using a specific destination IP address.

✔ **Multicast:** Packets are copied and sent from the source to multiple destination devices by using a special multicast IP address that the destination stations have been specifically configured to use.

✔ **Broadcast:** Packets are copied and sent from the source to every device on a destination network by using a broadcast IP address.

WAN technologies and protocols

WAN technologies function at the lower three layers of the OSI reference model (the Physical, Data Link, and Network layers), primarily at the Data Link Layer. WAN protocols define how frames are carried across a single data link between two devices. These technologies and protocols include the following:

✔ **Point-to-point links:** Provides a single, pre-established WAN communications path from the customer's network, across a carrier network (such as a Public Switched Telephone Network [PSTN]), to a remote network. These links and protocols include the following:

• **Leased lines:** A transmission line reserved by a communications carrier for the exclusive use of a customer.

• **Serial Line IP (SLIP):** The predecessor of Point-to-Point Protocol (PPP), SLIP was originally developed to support TCP/IP networking over low-speed asynchronous serial lines (such as dial-up modems) for Berkeley Unix computers.

• **Point-to-Point Protocol (PPP):** The successor to SLIP, PPP provides router-to-router and host-to-network connections over synchronous and asynchronous circuits. It is a more robust protocol than SLIP and provides additional built-in security mechanisms. PPP is far more common than SLIP in modern networking environments.

✔ **Circuit-switched networks:** In a circuit-switched network, a dedicated physical circuit path is established, maintained, and terminated between the sender and receiver across a carrier network for each communications session (the *call*). This network type is used extensively in telephone company networks and functions similarly to a regular telephone call. Examples of circuit-switched networks include the following:

- **Integrated Services Digital Network (ISDN):** ISDN is a communications protocol that operates over analog phone lines that have been converted to use digital signaling. ISDN lines are capable of transmitting both voice and data traffic. ISDN defines a *B-channel* for data, voice, and other services, and a *D-channel* for control and signaling information.

- **Digital Subscriber Lines (xDSL):** xDSL uses existing analog phone lines to deliver high bandwidth connectivity to remote customers.

✔ **Packet-switched networks:** In a packet-switched network, devices share bandwidth (by using statistical multiplexing) on communications links to transport packets between a sender and receiver across a carrier network. This type of network is more resilient to error and congestion than circuit-switched networks. Examples of packet-switched networks include

- **X.25:** The first packet switching network, *X.25* is a CCITT (Comité Consultaif International Téléphonique et Télégraphique) (formerly ITU-T) standard that defines how point-to-point connections between a DTE and DCE (which I discuss in the next section) are established and maintained. X.25 specifies the *Link Access Procedure, Balanced* (LAPB) protocol at the Data Link Layer and the *Packet Level Protocol* (PLP; also known as *X.25 Level 3)* at the Network Layer. X.25 is more common outside of the United States but is being superseded by frame relay.

- **Frame relay:** *Frame relay* is a packet-switched, standard protocol that handles multiple virtual circuits using High-Level Data Link Control (HDLC) encapsulation (which I discuss later in this section) between connected devices. Frame relay utilizes a simplified framing approach with no error correction and Data Link Connection Identifiers (DLCI) addressing to achieve high speeds across the WAN. Frame relay can be used on *Switched Virtual Circuits* (SVCs) or *Permanent Virtual Circuits* (PVCs). An *SVC* is a temporary connection that's dynamically created (circuit establishment phase) to transmit data (data transfer phase) and then disconnected (circuit termination phase). PVCs are permanently established connections. Because the connection is permanent, a PVC doesn't require the bandwidth overhead associated with circuit establishment and termination.

- **Switched Multimegabit Data Service (SMDS):** *SMDS* is a high-speed, packet-switched, connectionless-oriented, datagram-based technology available over public switched networks. Companies that exchange large amounts of bursty data with other remote networks typically use it.

- **Asynchronous Transfer Mode (ATM):** *ATM* is a very high-speed, low-delay technology that uses switching and multiplexing techniques to rapidly relay fixed-length (53-byte) cells containing voice, video, or data. Cell processing occurs in hardware that reduces transit delays. ATM is ideally suited for fiber-optic networks with bursty applications.

- **Voice-Over IP (VOIP):** *VOIP* transports various data types (such as voice, audio, and video) in IP packets providing major cost, interoperability, and performance benefits.

✔ **Other WAN protocols:** Two other important WAN protocols defined at the Data Link Layer are the following:

- **Synchronous Data Link Control (SDLC):** The *SDLC protocol* is a bit-oriented, full-duplex, serial protocol that was developed by IBM to facilitate communications between mainframes and remote offices. It defines and implements a polling media-access method in which the *primary* (front-end) polls the *secondaries* (remote stations) to determine whether communication is required.

- **High-Level Data Link Control (HDLC):** The *HDLC protocol* is a bit-oriented, synchronous protocol that was created by the ISO to support point-to-point and multipoint configurations. Derived from SDLC, it specifies a data encapsulation method for synchronous serial links and is the default for serial links on Cisco routers. Unfortunately, various vendor implementations of the HDLC protocol are incompatible.

Asynchronous and synchronous communications

Asynchronous communication transmits data in a serial stream with control data (start and stop bits) embedded in the stream to indicate the beginning and end of characters. Asynchronous devices must communicate at the same speed, which is controlled by the slower of the two communicating devices. Because no internal clocking signal is used, parity bits are used to reduce transmission errors.

Synchronous communications utilize an internal clocking signal to transmit large blocks of data, known as *frames*. Synchronous communication is characterized by very-high-speed transmission rates.

Networking equipment at the Data Link Layer

Networking devices that operate at the Data Link Layer include bridges, switches, DTEs, and DCEs.

A *bridge* is a semi-intelligent repeater used to connect two or more (similar or dissimilar) network segments. A bridge maintains an Address Resolution Protocol (ARP) cache containing the MAC addresses of individual devices on connected network segments. When a bridge receives a data signal, it checks its ARP cache to determine whether the destination MAC address is on the local network segment. If it's determined to be local, the data signal isn't forwarded. However, if the MAC address isn't local, the bridge forwards (and amplifies) the data signal to all other connected network segments. A serious networking problem associated with bridges is a *broadcast storm*, in which broadcast traffic is automatically forwarded by a bridge, thus effectively flooding a network.

A *switch* is essentially an intelligent hub that uses MAC addresses to route traffic. Unlike a hub, a switch transmits data only to the port connected to the destination MAC address. This creates separate collision domains (network segments) and effectively increases the data transmission rates available on the individual network segments. Additionally, a switch can be used to implement Virtual LANs (VLANs) to logically segregate a network and limit broadcast domains. Switches are traditionally considered to be Layer 2 (or Data Link Layer) devices, although newer technologies allow switches to function at the upper layers, including Layer 3 (the Network Layer) and Layer 7 (the Application Layer).

Data Terminal Equipment (DTE) is a general term used to classify devices at the user end of a user-to-network interface (such as computers). A DTE connects to *Data Communications Equipment* (DCE; also known as a Data Circuit-Terminating Equipment), which consists of devices at the network end of a user-to-network interface. The DCE provides the physical connection to the network, forwards network traffic, and provides a clocking signal to synchronize transmissions between the DCE and DTE. Examples of DCEs include NICs, modems, and CSU/DSUs (Channel Service Unit/Data Service Units).

Network Layer (Layer 3)

The Network Layer (Layer 3) provides routing and related functions that enable data to be transported between systems on the same network or on interconnected networks or *internetworks*. *Routing protocols,* such as the Routing Information Protocol (RIP), Open Shortest Path First (OSPF), and Border Gateway Protocol (BGP), are defined at this layer. Logical addressing of devices on the network is accomplished at this layer by using *routed* protocols, including the Internet Protocol (IP) and Internetwork Packet Exchange (IPX).

Internet Protocol (IP)

Internet Protocol (IP) contains addressing information that enables packets to be routed. IP is documented in RFC 791 and is part of the TCP/IP protocol suite, which is the language of the Internet. IP has two primary responsibilities:

- ✔ Connectionless, best-effort delivery of datagrams
- ✔ Fragmentation and reassembly of datagrams

IP Version 4 (IPv4; currently the most commonly used) uses a 32-bit logical IP address that's divided into four 8-bit sections (octets) and consists of two main parts: the network number and the host number.

IP addressing supports five different address classes indicated by the high-order (leftmost) bits in the IP address, as listed in Table 2-2.

Table 2-2	IP Address Classes			
Class	*Purpose*	*High-Order Bits*	*Address Range*	*Maximum Hosts*
A	Large networks	0	1 to 126	16,777,214
B	Medium networks	10	128 to 191	65,534
C	Small networks	110	192 to 223	254
D	Multicast	1110	224 to 239	N/A
E	Experimental	1111	240 to 254	N/A

Several IP address ranges are also reserved for use in private networks. These private addresses are

- ✔ **Class A.** 10.0.0.0
- ✔ **Class B.** 172.16.0.0 through 172.31.0.0
- ✔ **Class C.** 192.168.0.0

These addresses aren't routable on the Internet and are thus often implemented on firewalls and gateways by using *Network Address Translation* (NAT) to conserve IP addresses, mask the network architecture, and enhance security. NAT translates private, nonroutable addresses on internal network devices to registered IP addresses when communication across the Internet is required.

IP Version 6 (IPv6) uses a 128-bit logical IP address and incorporates additional functionality to provide security, multimedia support, plug-and-play compatibility, and backward compatibility with IPv4. IPv6 hasn't yet been widely implemented on the Internet.

Internetwork Packet Exchange (IPX)

Internetwork Packet Exchange (IPX) is a connectionless protocol used primarily in NetWare networks for routing packets across the network. It's part of the IPX/SPX (Internetwork Packet Exchange/Sequenced Packet Exchange) protocol suite, which is analogous to the TCP/IP protocol suite.

The Network Layer is also responsible for converting logical addresses into physical addresses. The Address Resolution Protocol (ARP) and Reverse Address Resolution Protocol (RARP) accomplish this.

Address Resolution Protocol (ARP)

The *Address Resolution Protocol* (ARP), defined in RFC 826, maps Network Layer IP addresses to MAC addresses. ARP discovers physical addresses of attached devices by broadcasting ARP query messages on the network segment. IP address to MAC address translations are then maintained in a dynamic table that is cached on the system.

Reverse Address Resolution Protocol (RARP)

The *Reverse Address Resolution Protocol* (RARP) maps MAC addresses to IP addresses. This is necessary when a system, such as a diskless machine, needs to discover its IP address. The system broadcasts a RARP message providing its MAC address and requests to be informed of its IP address. A RARP server replies with the requested information.

The Network Layer also defines a management protocol for IP known as the *Internet Control Message Protocol (ICMP)*.

Internet Control Message Protocol (ICMP)

The *Internet Control Message Protocol* (ICMP) reports errors and other information back to the source regarding the processing of transmitted IP packets. ICMP is documented in RFC 792.

Common ICMP messages include Destination Unreachable, Echo Request and Reply, Redirect, and Time Exceeded. The Packet Internet Groper (PING) is a popular utility that uses simple ICMP messages to test the connectivity and availability of network devices.

Networking equipment at the Network Layer

The primary items of networking equipment defined at Layer 3 are routers and gateways.

Routers

Routers are intelligent devices that link dissimilar networks and forward data packets based on logical or physical addresses to the destination network only (or along the network path). Routers consist of both hardware and software components and employ various routing algorithms (for example, RIP, OSPF, and BGP) to determine the best path to a destination based on different variables, including bandwidth, cost, delay, and distance.

Gateways

Gateways are created with software running on a PC (workstation or server) or router. Gateways link dissimilar programs and protocols by examining the entire data packet to translate incompatibilities. For example, a gateway can be used to link an IP network to an IPX network or a Microsoft Exchange mail server to a Lotus Notes server (a mail gateway).

Transport Layer (Layer 4)

The Transport Layer (Layer 4) provides transparent, reliable data transport and end-to-end transmission control. The Transport Layer hides the details of the lower layer functions from the upper layers.

Specific Transport Layer functions include the following:

- **Flow control:** Manages data transmission between devices, ensuring that the transmitting device doesn't send more data than the receiving device can process.

- **Multiplexing:** Enables data from multiple applications to be transmitted over a single physical link.

- **Virtual circuit management:** Establishes, maintains, and terminates virtual circuits.

- **Error checking and recovery:** Implements various mechanisms for detecting transmission errors and taking action to resolve any errors that occur, such as requesting that data be retransmitted.

Two important host-to-host protocols defined at the Transport Layer are the following:

- **Transmission Control Protocol (TCP):** TCP is a full-duplex, connection-oriented protocol that provides reliable delivery of packets across a network. A *connection-oriented* protocol requires a direct connection between two communicating devices before any data transfer occurs. In TCP, this is accomplished via a *three-way handshake*. The receiving device acknowledges packets, and packets are retransmitted if an error occurs. The following characteristics and features are associated with TCP:

- **Connection-oriented:** Establishes and manages a direct virtual connection to the remote device.

- **Reliable:** Guarantees delivery by acknowledging received packets and requesting retransmission of missing or corrupted packets.

- **Slow:** Because of the additional overhead associated with initial handshaking, acknowledging packets, and error correction, TCP is generally slower than other connectionless protocols, such as User Datagram Protocol (UDP).

✔ **User Datagram Protocol (UDP):** *User Datagram Protocol* is a connectionless protocol that provides fast, best-effort delivery of datagrams across a network. A connectionless protocol doesn't guarantee delivery of transmitted packets (datagrams) and is thus considered unreliable. It doesn't attempt to establish a connection with the destination network prior to transmitting data, acknowledge received datagrams, perform resequencing, and perform error checking or recovery. UDP is ideally suited for data requiring fast delivery, which is not sensitive to packet loss and doesn't need to be fragmented. Examples of applications using UDP include domain name system (DNS), Simple Network Management Protocol (SNMP), and streaming audio or video. The following characteristics and features are associated with UDP:

  - **Connectionless:** Doesn't pre-establish a communication circuit with the destination network.

  - **Best effort:** Doesn't guarantee delivery and is thus considered unreliable.

  - **Fast:** No overhead associated with circuit establishment, acknowledgement, sequencing, or error checking and recovery.

Several examples of connection-oriented and connectionless protocols are identified in Table 2-3.

Table 2-3   Connection-Oriented and Connectionless Protocols

Protocol	Layer	Type
TCP (Transmission Control Protocol)	4	Connection-oriented
UDP (User Datagram Protocol)	4	Connectionless
IP (Internet Protocol)	3	Connectionless
IPX (Internetwork Packet Exchange)	3	Connectionless
SPX (Sequenced Packet Exchange)	4	Connection-oriented

Transport Layer security protocols include the following:

- **Secure Shell (SSH and SSH-2):** SSH provides a secure alternative to Telnet for remote access. SSH establishes an encrypted tunnel between the client and server and can also authenticate the client to the server.

- **Secure Sockets Layer/Transport Layer Security (SSL/TLS):** The SSL protocol, developed by Netscape in 1994, provides session-based encryption and authentication for secure communication between clients and servers on the Internet.

- **Simple Key Management for Internet Protocols (SKIP):** SKIP is similar to SSL but doesn't require prior communication to establish a connection or exchange keys.

Session Layer (Layer 5)

The *Session Layer (Layer 5)* establishes, coordinates, and terminates communication sessions (service requests and service responses) between networked systems.

A communication session is divided into three distinct phases, as follows:

- **Connection establishment:** Initial contact between communicating systems is made, and the end devices agree upon communications parameters and protocols to be used, including the mode of operation:

  - **Simplex mode:** In simplex mode, a one-way communications path is established with a transmitter at one end of the connection and a receiver at the other end. An analogy is an AM radio on which a radio station broadcasts music, and the radio receiver can only receive the broadcast.

  - **Half-duplex mode:** In half-duplex mode, both communicating devices are capable of transmitting and receiving but not at the same time. An analogy is a two-way radio in which a button must be pressed to transmit and then released to receive a signal.

  - **Full-duplex mode:** In full-duplex mode, both communicating devices are capable of transmitting and receiving simultaneously. An analogy is a telephone with which you can transmit and receive signals (but not necessarily communicate) at the same time.

- **Data transfer:** Information is exchanged between end devices.

- **Connection release:** After data transfer is completed, end devices systematically end the session.

Some examples of Session Layer protocols include

- ✔ **Network File System (NFS):** Developed by Sun Microsystems to facilitate transparent user access to remote resources on a Unix-based network using TCP/IP.
- ✔ **Structured Query Language (SQL):** Developed by IBM to provide users with a simplified method for defining its data requirements on both local and remote database systems.
- ✔ **Remote Procedure Call (RPC):** A client/server network redirection tool. Procedures are created on clients and performed on servers.

Presentation Layer (Layer 6)

The Presentation Layer (Layer 6) provides coding and conversion functions that are applied to data being presented to the Application Layer. These functions ensure that data sent from the Application Layer of one system are compatible with the Application Layer of the receiving system.

Tasks associated with this layer include

- ✔ **Data representation:** Use of common data representation formats (standard image, sound, and video formats) enables application data to be exchanged between different types of computer systems. Some examples include Graphics Interchange Format (GIF), Musical Instrument Data Interface (MIDI), and Motion Picture Experts Group (MPEG).
- ✔ **Character conversion:** Information is exchanged between different systems using common character conversion schemes, such as Extended Binary Coded Decimal Interchange Code (EBCDIC) or American Standard Code for Information Interchange (ASCII).
- ✔ **Data compression:** Common data compression schemes enable compressed data to be properly decompressed at the destination.
- ✔ **Data encryption:** Common data encryption schemes enable encrypted data to be properly decrypted at the destination.

Application Layer (Layer 7)

The Application Layer (Layer 7) is the highest layer of the OSI model. It supports the components that deal with the communication aspects of an application requiring network access and provides an interface to the user. That is, both the Application Layer and the end user interact directly with the application.

The Application Layer is responsible for the following:

- ✔ Identifying and establishing availability of communication partners
- ✔ Determining resource availability
- ✔ Synchronizing communication

Don't confuse the Application Layer with software applications, such as Microsoft Word or WordPerfect. Applications that function at the Application Layer include operating systems (such as Windows 2000 Server and NetWare), OSI applications (File Transfer, Access, and Management [FTAM] and Virtual Terminal Protocol [VTP]), and TCP/IP applications, including the following:

- ✔ **HyperText Transfer Protocol (HTTP):** The language of the World Wide Web (WWW). Attacks typically exploit vulnerabilities in Web browsers or programming languages, such as CGI, Java, and ActiveX. HTTP operates on TCP port 80.
- ✔ **File Transfer Protocol (FTP):** Used for file transfers between remote systems. Attacks exploit incorrectly configured directory permissions and compromised passwords, which are always sent in clear text. FTP operates on TCP ports 20 and 21.
- ✔ **Trivial File Transfer Protocol (TFTP):** A lean, mean version of FTP without directory browsing capabilities or user authentication. Generally considered less secure than FTP. TFTP operates on TCP port 69.
- ✔ **Simple Mail Transfer Protocol (SMTP):** Used to send and receive e-mail across the Internet. This is an inherently insecure protocol with numerous well-known vulnerabilities. SMTP operates on TCP port 25.
- ✔ **Simple Network Management Protocol (SNMP):** Used to collect network information by polling stations and sending *traps* (or alerts) to a management station. This has many well-known vulnerabilities, including default community strings (passwords) transmitted in clear text. SNMP operates on TCP port 161.
- ✔ **Telnet:** Provides terminal emulation for remote access to system resources. Passwords are sent in clear text. Telnet operates on TCP port 23.

Application Layer security protocols include the following:

- ✔ **Secure Multipurpose Internet Mail Extensions (S/MIME):** *S/MIME* is a secure method of sending e-mail; it is incorporated into several popular browsers and e-mail applications.
- ✔ **Privacy Enhanced Mail (PEM):** *PEM* is a proposed IETF (Internet Engineering Task Force) standard for providing e-mail confidentiality and authentication.

✔ **Secure Electronic Transaction (SET):** MasterCard and Visa developed the *SET* specification to provide secure e-commerce transactions by implementing authentication mechanisms while protecting the confidentiality and integrity of cardholder data.

✔ **Secure HyperText Transfer Protocol (S-HTTP):** *S-HTTP* is an Internet protocol that provides a method for secure communications with a Web server. S-HTTP is a connectionless-oriented protocol that encapsulates data after security properties for the session have been successfully negotiated.

✔ **Secure Remote Procedure Call (S-RPC):** *S-RPC* is a secure client-server protocol that's defined at the upper layers of the OSI model, including the Application Layer. RPC is used to request services from another computer on the network. S-RPC provides public and private keys to clients and servers using Diffie-Hellman (see Chapter 13). After initially authenticating, S-RPC operations are transparent to the end user.

The Goal of Information Security

Well, duh! It's to protect information, right? Actually, it's not quite that simple. The goal of information security *is* to protect information, but from what and whom?

Three fundamental aspects of information must be protected:

✔ **Confidentiality:** The secrecy or privacy of information

✔ **Integrity:** The accuracy of information

✔ **Availability:** Being able to get to the information when needed

These three goals of information security are commonly referred to as the C-I-A triad (as shown in Figure 2-3).

Confidentiality

Confidentiality prevents the unauthorized use or disclosure of information. It ensures that information cannot be accessed by anyone without proper authorization. *Privacy* is a closely related concept that's most often associated with personal information about an individual, such as medical records.

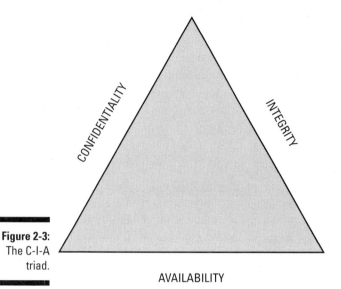

Figure 2-3:
The C-I-A
triad.

AVAILABILITY

Integrity

Integrity safeguards the accuracy and completeness of information. It
ensures that

- ✔ Unauthorized users (or processes) cannot modify data.
- ✔ Authorized users (or processes) cannot make unauthorized modifications to data.
- ✔ Data is internally and externally consistent: That is, a given input
  produces an expected output.

Availability

Availability ensures that authorized users have reliable and timely access to
information and the necessary information systems when required. This is
perhaps one of the most difficult aspects of information security to ensure
because the threats to availability include human threats (such as a distributed denial of service attack against your systems or an authorized user accidentally deleting critical files) and nonhuman threats (such as a natural
disaster or a system hardware failure).

Prep Test

1 The process of wrapping protocol information from one layer in the data section of another layer describes:

A ○ Data encryption

B ○ Data encapsulation

C ○ Data hiding

D ○ TCP wrappers

2 The LLC and MAC are sublayers of what OSI model layer?

A ○ Data Link

B ○ Network

C ○ Transport

D ○ Session

3 The Ethernet protocol is defined at what layer of the OSI Model and in which IEEE standard?

A ○ Data Link Layer, 802.3

B ○ Network Layer, 802.3

C ○ Data Link Layer, 802.5

D ○ Network Layer, 802.5

4 All the following are examples of packet-switched WAN protocols, except:

A ○ X.25

B ○ Frame Relay

C ○ ISDN

D ○ SMDS

5 Routing protocols, such as RIP and OSPF, are defined at what layer of the OSI Model?

A ○ Layer 1

B ○ Layer 2

C ○ Layer 3

D ○ Layer 4

6 Which of the following is an example of a Class B IP address?

A ○ 17.5.5.1

B ○ 127.0.0.1

C ○ 192.167.4.1

D ○ 224.0.0.1

7 All of the following are examples of private IP addresses, except:

A ○ 10.0.0.0
B ○ 172.16.0.0
C ○ 172.30.0.0
D ○ 224.0.0.0

8 The _____ maps IP addresses to MAC addresses.

A ○ Address Resolution Protocol
B ○ Internet Control Message Protocol
C ○ Reverse Address Resolution Protocol
D ○ Internetwork Packet Exchange (IPX) Protocol

9 S-RPC, S-HTTP, and S/MIME are all defined at what layer of the OSI Model?

A ○ Layer 4
B ○ Layer 5
C ○ Layer 6
D ○ Layer 7

10 The three goals of information security are to protect all of the following except:

A ○ Confidentiality
B ○ Integrity
C ○ Authentication
D ○ Availability

Answers

1 **B.** Data encapsulation. Data encapsulation wraps protocol information from one layer in the data section of another layer. The other choices are incorrect. *Review "The OSI Reference Model."*

2 **A.** Data Link. The Data Link Layer is the only layer of the OSI Model that defines sublayers (the Logical Link Control and Media Access Control sublayers). *Review "Data Link Layer (Layer 2)."*

3 **A.** Data Link Layer, 802.3. LAN protocols are defined at the Data Link Layer. IEEE 802.5 defines the token-ring standard. *Review "Data Link Layer (Layer 2)."*

4 **C.** ISDN. ISDN is circuit-switched. Packet-switched network technologies include X.25, frame relay, SMDS, ATM, and VOIP. *Review "WAN technologies and protocols."*

5 **C.** Layer 3. Routing protocols are defined at Layer 3, the Networking Layer. *Review "Network Layer (Layer 3)."*

6 **C.** 192.167.4.1. 17.5.5.1 is a Class A address, 127.0.0.1 is an interface loopback address, and 224.0.0.1 is a multicast address (Class D). *Review "Internet Protocol (IP)."*

7 **D.** 224.0.0.0. The private IP address ranges are 10.0.0.0, 172.16.0.0 through 172.31.0.0, and 192.168.0.0. *Review "Internet Protocol (IP)."*

8 **A.** Address Resolution Protocol. The Address Resolution Protocol (ARP) is responsible for mapping IP addresses to MAC addresses. *Review "Address Resolution Protocol (ARP)."*

9 **D.** Layer 7. Secure Remote Procedure Call (S-RPC), Secure HyperText Transfer Protocol (S-HTTP), and Secure Multipurpose Internet Mail Extensions (S/MIME) are all defined at the Application Layer (Layer 7). *Review "Application Layer (Layer 7)."*

10 **C.** Authentication. The three fundamental aspects of the C-I-A triad for information security are confidentiality, integrity, and availability. *Review "The Goal of Information Security."*

Part II
General Security Concepts

The 5th Wave   By Rich Tennant

ROCKET SOFT
DESIGN AND CONSTRUCTION

The feeling is, we may not have all the Internet security we should.

In this part . . .

The first content domain, General Security Concepts, covers many topics that are familiar, at some level, to almost all computer users. Most users have dealt with passwords, have seen a virus alert, and believe that hacker=bad. These are the things that most users associate with "computer security."

But you want more! Because to be a security expert (and to earn the Security+ certification) you have to be more than just familiar with these topics — you have to know them like the back of your hand (incidentally, how well do you *really* know the back of your hand?).

This part covers many important topics, such as authentication, auditing, malicious code (viruses, worms, and other things that go bump in the night), social engineering, and methods of attack (Judo chop!).

Chapter 3

Access Control

. . . .

In This Chapter

▶ Identification and authentication, authorization, and accountability

▶ Discretionary access control (DAC) and mandatory access control (MAC)

▶ Passwords, PINs, one-time passwords, tokens, tickets, biometrics, and single sign-on (SSO)

. . . .

During medieval times, castles were built to provide safety and security. The castle was normally built in a strategic location with towering walls surrounded by a moat. Battlements were positioned along the top of the wall with bastions at the corners. A heavily fortified and guarded entrance, secured by a drawbridge, controlled castle entry and exit. These measures created a security perimeter, preventing hostile forces from freely roaming through the castle grounds and attacking its inhabitants. Breaching the perimeter and gaining entry to the castle was the key to victory for an attacking force. After getting inside, the castle defenses were relatively simple, and the attackers were free to burn and pillage. Hard and crunchy on the outside; chewy in the middle.

Similarly, computer security requires a strong perimeter and elaborate defenses. Unfortunately, a drawbridge doesn't suffice for access control in computer security, and we can't pour cauldrons of hot oil on hackers! Threats to computer security are much more sophisticated and prevalent than marauding bandits and the occasional fire-breathing dragons. Access control is still critical to securing a perimeter, but it's not limited to a single point of entry. Instead, security professionals must protect their systems from a plethora of threats, including Internet-based attacks, viruses and Trojan horses, insider attacks, covert channels, software bugs, and honest mistakes. Additionally, security professionals must ensure that the drawbridge operator (the firewall administrator) is properly trained on how and when to raise or lower the drawbridge (policies and procedures), and you must be sure that he or she is not sleeping on the job (monitor your logs).

And so you begin your quest for the Grail . . . uhhh, Security+ certification at the front door — access control.

Quick Assessment

1 Access control systems provide three essential services:
_____, _____, and _____.

2 Multifactor authentication is based on at least two of the following
three factors: _____, _____, and
_____.

3 _____ means that a user cannot deny an action because
his identity is positively associated with his actions on a system.

4 An access control policy in which the owner of the file or resource
determines who is permitted access is known as a _____.

5 _____ access control assigns group membership based
on organizational or functional roles.

6 In a MAC-based system, the level of trust required for access to a
system or resource is determined by an object's _____.

7 A single computer system that handles multiple classification levels
between subjects and objects is known as a _____.

8 An access control technique that uses a mathematical structure to
define greatest lower-bound and least upper-bound values for a pair of
elements is known as a _____.

9 Kerberos is a _____-based authentication system that
provides mutual authentication between a _____ and
_____.

10 Biometric authentication systems verify a person's identity using a
unique _____ or _____ characteristic.

Answers

1 Identification and authentication (I&A), authorization (or establishment), and accountability. *Check out "Access Control Concepts."*

2 Something you know, something you have, and something you are. *Review "Identification and authentication (I&A)."*

3 Nonrepudiation. *See "Accountability."*

4 Discretionary access control (DAC). *Take a look at "Discretionary access control."*

5 Role-based. *Review "Discretionary access control."*

6 Sensitivity label. *Read all about it in "Mandatory access control."*

7 Multilevel system. *Review "Mandatory access control."*

8 Lattice model. *See "Mandatory access control."*

9 Ticket, client, server. *Read "Tickets (Kerberos)."*

10 Physiological, behavioral. *Check out "Biometrics."*

Access Control Concepts

Access control is the ability to permit or deny the use of an *object* (a passive entity, such as a system or file) by a *subject* (an active entity, such as an individual or process).

Access control systems provide three essential services:

- ✔ **Identification and authentication (I&A):** These determine who can log on to a system.
- ✔ **Authorization:** This determines what an authorized user can do.
- ✔ **Accountability:** This identifies what a user did.

Identification and authentication (I&A)

Identification and authentication (I&A) is a two-step process that determines who can log on to a system.

- ✔ *Identification* is how a user tells a system who he or she is (for example, by using a username).
- ✔ The identification component of an access control system is normally a relatively simple mechanism based on either of these:
  - Username
  - User ID
- ✔ In the case of a system or process, identification is usually based on either
  - Computer name
  - Media Access Control (MAC) address
  - Internet Protocol (IP) address
  - Process ID (PID)
- ✔ The only requirements for identification are that the identification
  - Must uniquely identify the user.
  - Shouldn't identify that user's position or relative importance in an organization (such as labels like *president* or *CEO*).
  - Should avoid using common or shared user accounts, such as *root*, *admin*, and *sysadmin*.

    Such accounts provide no accountability and are juicy targets for hackers.

Polly wanna hacker?

The term *hacker* is often used to describe both hackers and crackers in general, much as the terms *he* and *she* are used to describe people in general. However, important differences exist between hackers and crackers (much as there are important differences between men and women). *Hackers* perform a vital role in the Internet and computing community by helping to debug source code, identify vulnerabilities, and improve software development — all of which serve the greater good. *Crackers,* on the other hand, include script kiddies (wannabes), cyberpunks, cyberterrorists, common criminals, and other vermin . . . all motivated by less-noble causes.

✔ *Authentication* is the process of verifying a user's claimed identity (for example, by comparing an entered password to the password stored on a system for a given username).

Authentication is based on at least one of these three factors:

- **Something you know,** such as a password or a personal identification number (PIN). This assumes that only the owner of the account knows the password or PIN needed to access the account.

 Unfortunately, passwords are often shared, stolen, or guessed.

- **Something you have,** such as a smart card or token. This assumes that only the owner of the account has the necessary smart card or token needed to unlock the account.

 Unfortunately, smart cards or tokens can be lost, stolen, borrowed, or duplicated.

- **Something you are,** such as fingerprint, voice, retina, or iris characteristics. This assumes that the finger or eyeball attached to your body is actually yours and uniquely identifies you.

 Unfortunately, fingers and eyes can be lost or. . . . Actually, the major drawback with this authentication mechanism is user acceptance — many people are uneasy about using these systems.

Identification is the act of claiming a specific identity. *Authentication* is the act of verifying that identity.

The most basic and common form of authentication is typically based on *something you know,* such as your password.

Multifactor authentication requires more than one authentication factor:

- ✔ *Two-factor authentication* requires two of the three preceding factors for authentication.
- ✔ *Three-factor authentication* is the most effective. It requires all three preceding factors for authentication.

Authorization

Authorization (or *establishment*) defines a user's rights and permissions on a system. After a user (or process) is authenticated, authorization determines what that user can do on the system. In the castle of network security, rights and permissions prevent a traitorous knave or a foolish jester from lowering the drawbridge for plunder.

Most modern operating systems define sets of permissions that are variations or extensions of three basic types of access:

- ✔ **Read (R):** The user can
  - Read file contents
  - List directory contents
- ✔ **Write (W):** The user can *change* the contents of a file or directory with these tasks:
  - Add
  - Create
  - Delete
  - Rename
- ✔ **Execute (X):** If the file is a program, the user can run the program.

These rights and permissions are implemented differently in systems based on *discretionary access control* (DAC) and *mandatory access control* (MAC). This chapter explains the differences.

Authorization determines what a user can do.

Accountability

Accountability uses such system components as audit trails (records) and logs to associate a user with his actions. Audit trails and logs are important for

- ✔ Detecting security violations
- ✔ Re-creating security incidents

The most complete logs are of no use if no one is reviewing them. As I discuss in Chapter 17, if no one is regularly reviewing your logs and they are not maintained in a secure and consistent manner, they may not be admissible as evidence.

Accountability determines what a user did.

Many systems can generate automated reports based on certain predefined criteria or thresholds, known as *clipping levels*. For example, a clipping level may be set to generate a report for the following:

- ✔ More than three failed logon attempts in a given period of time
- ✔ Any attempt to use a disabled user account

These reports help a system administrator or security administrator more-easily identify possible break-in attempts.

Nonrepudiation means that a user cannot deny an action because his identity is positively associated with his actions on a system.

Access Control Techniques

Access control techniques are generally categorized as either *discretionary* or *mandatory*. Understanding the differences between discretionary access control (DAC) and mandatory access control (MAC), as well as specific access control methods under each category, is critical for passing the Security+ exam.

Discretionary access control

Discretionary access control (DAC) is an access policy determined by the owner of a file (or other resource). The owner decides who is allowed access to the file and what privileges they have.

In DAC, the owner determines the access policy.

Two important concepts in DAC are

- **File and data ownership:** Every object in a system must have an owner. The access policy is determined by the owner of the resource (including files, directories, data, system resources, and devices). Theoretically, an object without an owner is left unprotected.

   Normally, the owner of a resource is the person who created the resource (such as a file or directory).

- **Access rights and permissions:** These are the controls that an owner can assign to individual users or groups for specific resources.

Discretionary access controls can be applied through the following techniques:

- *Access control lists* (ACLs) name the specific rights and permissions that are assigned to a subject for a given object.

   Access control lists provide a flexible method for applying discretionary access controls.

- *Role-based access control* assigns group membership based on organizational or functional roles. This strategy greatly simplifies the management of access rights and permissions:

  - Access rights and permissions for objects are assigned to any group or, in addition to, individuals.

  - Individuals may belong to one or many groups. Individuals can be designated to acquire *cumulative* permissions (every permission of *any* group they are in) or disqualified from any permission that isn't part of *every* group they are in.

  - A group could contain only one individual. For example, you could assign specific permissions to Intern and make each rotating intern the only member of the group.

Major disadvantages of discretionary access control techniques include the following:

- Lack of centralized administration

- Dependence on security-conscious resource owners

- Many popular operating systems defaulting to full access for "everyone" if the owner doesn't explicitly set permissions

- Difficult, if not impossible, auditing

Mandatory access control

Mandatory access control (MAC) is an access policy determined by the system, not the owner. MAC is used in *multilevel systems* that process highly sensitive data, such as classified government and military information. A *multilevel system* is a single computer system that handles multiple classification levels between subjects and objects.

Two important concepts in MAC are the following:

- ✔ **Sensitivity labels:** In a MAC-based system, all subjects and objects must have *labels* assigned to them.

  A subject's sensitivity label specifies its level of trust. An object's sensitivity label specifies the level of trust required for access.

  In order to access a given object, the subject must have a sensitivity level equal to or higher than the requested object. For example, a user (subject) with a Top Secret clearance (sensitivity label) is permitted access to a file (object) with a Secret classification level (sensitivity label) because her clearance level exceeds the minimum required for access.

- ✔ **Data import and export:** Controlling the import of information from other systems and export to other systems (including printers) is a critical function of MAC-based systems, which must ensure that sensitivity labels are properly maintained and implemented so that sensitive information is appropriately protected at all times.

In MAC, the system determines the access policy.

Two methods are commonly used for applying mandatory access control:

- ✔ **Rule-based access controls:** This type of control further defines specific conditions for access to a requested object.

  All MAC-based systems implement a simple form of rule-based access control to determine whether access should be granted or denied by matching

  - An object's sensitivity label
  - A subject's sensitivity label

- ✔ **Lattice-based access controls:** These can be used for complex access control decisions involving multiple objects and/or subjects. For example, lattice-based access controls can determine the minimum clearance level that a user requires to access a specific set of files.

  A *lattice model* is a mathematical structure that defines *greatest lower-bound* and *least upper-bound* values for a pair of elements, such as a subject and an object.

Major disadvantages of mandatory access control techniques include

- ✔ Lack of flexibility
- ✔ Difficulty in implementing and programming
- ✔ User frustration

Access Control Systems

Access control systems use such I&A techniques as the following:

- ✔ Usernames and passwords
- ✔ Personal Identification Numbers (PINs)
- ✔ One-time passwords
- ✔ Tokens
- ✔ Tickets
- ✔ Biometrics
- ✔ Single sign-on (SSO)
- ✔ Certificates
- ✔ Challenge Handshake Authentication Protocol (CHAP)

The following sections cover I&A techniques.

Usernames and passwords

"A password should be like a toothbrush. Use it every day; change it regularly; and DON'T share it with friends." — USENET

A username uniquely identifies a user on the network. *Passwords* are easily the most common authentication mechanism in use today. Although more-advanced and secure authentication technologies are available, including tokens and biometrics, these more-advanced authentication technologies are typically used as supplements to or in combination with — rather than as replacements for — traditional usernames and passwords. A *passphrase* is a variation on passwords that uses a sequence of characters or words instead of a single password. Although passphrases are generally more difficult to break than regular passwords, they're also inconvenient to enter and share the same problems associated with passwords.

Several general problems associated with passwords/passphrases include

- ✔ **Insecure:** Passwords/passphrases are generally insecure for several reasons, including

  - **Human nature:** In the case of user-generated passwords, users normally choose passwords that are easily remembered and consequently easily guessed (such as a spouse's name or birthday). Users may also be inclined to write down or share their passwords.

  - **Transmission and storage:** Many applications and protocols (such as file transfer protocol [FTP] and password authentication protocol [PAP]) transmit passwords in clear text. Passwords may also be stored in plaintext files or encrypted with a weak algorithm.

- ✔ **Easily broken:** Passwords/passphrases are susceptible to brute force and dictionary attacks (which I discuss in Chapter 4) by readily available programs, such as the following:

  - Crack

  - John the Ripper

  - l0phtcrack (pronounced *loft-crack*)

- ✔ **Inconvenient:** Entering passwords/passphrases can be tiresome for users who are easily agitated. In an attempt to bypass these controls, users may

  - Select an easily typed, weak password

  - Automate logons (*Remember my password* in a browser)

  - Neglect to lock workstations or log out

- ✔ **Refutable:** Transactions authenticated with only a password don't necessarily provide absolute proof of a user's identity. Authentication mechanisms must guarantee nonrepudiation, which is a critical component of accountability. (For more on nonrepudiation, see the section "Accountability," earlier in this chapter.)

Most access control systems have built-in control and management features that should be configured in accordance with your organization's security policy and best practices. Common settings include the following features:

- ✔ **Length:** The longer the better. A password is, in effect, an encryption key (see Chapter 12). Just as larger encryption keys (such as 128-bit or 256-bit) are better, so too are longer passwords. Systems should be configured to require a minimum password length of 6–8 characters. A minimum of 8 characters is typically the industry standard.

✔ **Complexity:** Strong passwords contain a mix of uppercase and lowercase letters, numbers, and special characters, such as # and $. Be aware that certain special characters may not be accepted by some systems or may perform special functions (for example, in terminal emulation software).

✔ **Aging:**

- Maximum password aging should be set to require passwords to be changed at regular intervals.

- Minimum password aging should also be set to prevent users from quickly circumventing password history controls.

✔ **History:** Password history settings allow a system to remember previously used passwords. This prevents users from circumventing maximum password aging by alternating between several familiar passwords when required to change their passwords.

✔ **Limited attempts:** This limits the number of unsuccessful log-on attempts.

✔ **Lockout duration:** When the limit on unsuccessful logon attempts (described in the preceding bullet) has been exceeded, the account is locked out. Lockout duration is often set in combination with other settings, such as password length and limited attempts, to make it mathematically infeasible for an attacker to crack the account. For example, an 8-character password set to lockout for 30 minutes after 3 bad attempts might theoretically take an attacker 243 years to crack. (And during that time, either the system would crash or the attacker would die, theoretically!) Another common setting for lockout duration is "forever," which requires an administrator to unlock the account.

✔ **Limited time periods:** This control restricts the time of day that a user can log in. For example, a user may only be able to log in during normal business hours. However, this control setting is becoming less common in the modern age of the global economy and the workaholic.

✔ **System messages:** System messages include the following:

- **Logon banner:** Welcome messages invite criminals to access your systems. This has been successfully argued in court! Remember: Never invite a vampire into your home or a hacker into your system. (Try to avoid all such bloodsuckers in general!) Disable any welcome message and replace it with a legal warning that requires the user to click OK to acknowledge.

- **Last username:** Many popular operating systems display the username of the last successful logon. This feature is a convenience for users (who only need to type in their password) and hackers (who only need to crack the password and not worry about matching it to a valid user account). Disable this feature.

- **Last successful logon:** After successfully logging on to the system, this message tells the user the last time that he logged on. If the system shows that the last successful logon for a user was Saturday morning at 2 a.m. and the user knows that couldn't possibly have been him because he has a life, he'll know that his account has been compromised and can report the incident accordingly.

You are probably familiar with many of the following widely available and well-known guidelines for creating more-secure passwords:

- ✔ Mix uppercase and lowercase characters.
- ✔ Replace letters with numbers (for example, replace o with 0).
- ✔ Combine two words by using a special character.
- ✔ Use the first letter from each word of a nonsense phrase.

The problem with these guidelines is that they're widely available and well known. One solution is a software tool that helps users evaluate the quality of their passwords as they create them. These tools are commonly known as *password/passphrase generators* or *password appraisers*.

Personal identification numbers (PINs)

A PIN in itself is a relatively weak authentication mechanism because only 10,000 possible combinations for a 4-digit numeric PIN are available. Therefore, some other safeguard is normally used in combination with a PIN.

For example, many ATMs confiscate your ATM card after three incorrect PIN attempts. A PIN used with a one-time token password and an account lockout policy is also very effective. This combination allows a user to attempt only one PIN/password combination per minute and then locks the account after three or five failed attempts as determined by the security policy.

One-time passwords

A *one-time password* is a password that is valid for one logon session only. A one-time password provides maximum security for access control.

A one-time password is considered a *dynamic password;* it is changed at a regular interval or event.

A *static password* is a password that is the same for each logon.

Two examples of one-time password implementations are the following:

- ✔ **Tokens:** Tokens are covered in the following section.
- ✔ **The S/Key protocol:** This protocol generates one-time passwords on client/server systems by using MD4 and MD5 algorithms to generate one-time passwords.

  I describe MD4 and MD5 algorithms in Chapter 12.

Tokens

Tokens are access control devices that either

- ✔ Store static passwords or digital certificates
- ✔ Generate dynamic passwords

A token can be a device, such as a:

- ✔ Key fob
- ✔ Smart card
- ✔ Magnetic card
- ✔ Keypad card

The three general types of tokens are

- ✔ **Static password tokens:** These store a static password or digital certificate.
- ✔ **Synchronous dynamic password tokens:** These continuously generate a new password or passcode at one of these intervals:
  - Fixed time interval (for example, every 60 seconds)
  - Event interval (for example, every time that a button on the token is pressed)

  Typically, the password or passcode is valid only
  - During a fixed time window (for example, two minutes)
  - For a single logon

  If logging on to more than one system, you must wait for the next password or passcode.
- ✔ **Asynchronous (or challenge-response) dynamic password tokens:** These generate a new password or passcode asynchronously by calculating the correct response to a system-generated random challenge string that's manually entered into the token by its owner.

Tokens provide two-factor authentication (*something you have* and *something you know*) by either

✔ Requiring user authentication to the token (for example, entering a PIN or scanning a thumbprint on the token)

✔ Requiring entry of a secret PIN with the token-generated password

Two examples of token-based authentication devices are

✔ Key fobs

✔ Smart cards

Tickets (Kerberos)

Perhaps the most popular ticket-based authentication protocol in use today is *Kerberos,* named for the fierce, three-headed dog that guards the gates of Hades in Greek mythology (not to be confused with Ker-beer-os, the fuzzy, six-headed "dog" sitting at the bar that keeps looking better and better!).

Kerberos provides mutual authentication of both clients and servers. Because tickets issued in a Kerberos system are valid for a limited period of time, time synchronization between systems is critical for proper operation. The following step-by-step discussion is a basic description of Kerberos operation:

1. **The Kerberos client prompts the subject (user) for the following:**

    • Identification (username)

    • Authentication (password)

2. **Using the authentication information (password), the Kerberos client temporarily generates and stores the subject's secret key by using a *one-way hash function* (see Chapter 12 for a discussion of hash functions) and then sends the subject's identification (username) to the Key Distribution Center (KDC).**

    The password/secret key *is not* sent to the KDC. (See Figure 3-1.)

3. **The KDC Authentication Service (AS) verifies that the subject (known as a *principal*) exists in the KDC database. The KDC Ticket Granting Service (TGS) then generates the following:**

    • A Client/TGS Session Key encrypted with the subject's secret key, which is known only to the TGS and the client (temporarily).

    • A Ticket Granting Ticket (TGT), comprising the subject's identification, the client network address, the valid period of the ticket, and the Client/TGS Session Key.

Client

KDC

Username:
Password:

Username

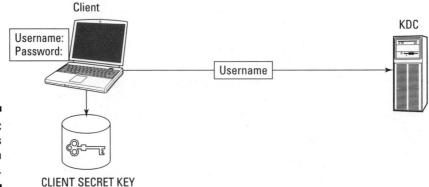

Figure 3-1:
Kerberos
logon
initiation.

CLIENT SECRET KEY

4. **The TGT is encrypted by using the secret key of the TGS server, which is known only to the TGS server.**

5. **The Client/TGS Session Key and TGT are then sent back to the client. (See Figure 3-2.)**

6. **The client decrypts the Client/TGS Session Key with the secret key that was generated with the subject's password, authenticates the subject (user), and then erases the stored secret key to avoid possible compromise.**

   The TGT, which was encrypted with the secret key of the TGS server, cannot be decrypted by the client. (See Figure 3-3.)

7. **When the subject requests access to a specific object (such as a server, also known as a *principal*), it sends these items to the TGS server:**

   • The TGT

   • The object identifier (such as a server name)

Client

KDC

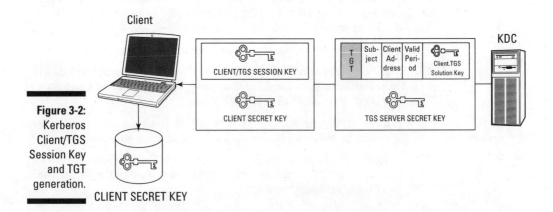

CLIENT/TGS SESSION KEY

CLIENT SECRET KEY

TGS SERVER SECRET KEY

Figure 3-2:
Kerberos
Client/TGS
Session Key
and TGT
generation.

CLIENT SECRET KEY

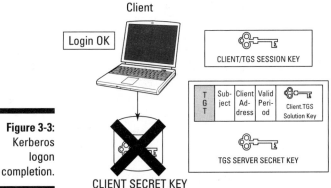

Figure 3-3:
Kerberos
logon
completion.

- An authenticator

   The *authenticator* is a separate message that contains the client ID
   and a timestamp. It is encrypted by using the Client/TGS Session
   Key. (See Figure 3-4.)

8. **The TGS server generates the following:**

   - A Client/Server Session Key, which is encrypted by using the
     Client/TGS Session Key

   - A Service Ticket comprising the subject's identification, the client
     network address, the valid period of the ticket, and the
     Client/Server Session Key

   The Service Ticket is encrypted by using the secret key of the
   requested object (server), which is known only to the TGS server
   and the object.

9. **The Client/Server Session Key and Service Ticket are then sent back
   to the client. (See Figure 3-5.)**

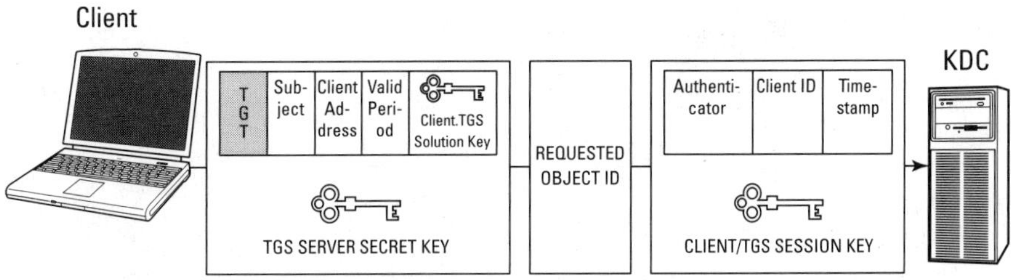

Figure 3-4:
Kerberos
requesting
services.

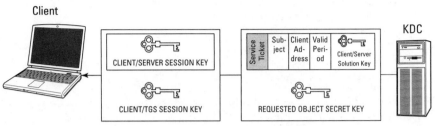

10. **The client decrypts the Client/Server Session Key by using the Client/Server TGS Key. (See Figure 3-6.)**

    The Service Ticket, which was encrypted with the secret key of the requested object, cannot be decrypted by the client.

    The client can now communicate directly with the requested object (server).

11. **The client sends these to the requested object (server):**

    • The Service Ticket

    • An authenticator

    The authenticator, comprising the subject's identification and a timestamp, is encrypted by using the Client/Server Session Key that was generated by the TGS.

12. **The object (server) decrypts the Service Ticket by using its secret key.**

    The Service Ticket contains the Client/Server Session Key, which allows the object (server) to then decrypt the authenticator.

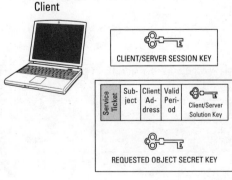

13. **Communication between the client and server is established if the subject identification and timestamp are valid according to these factors specified in the Service Ticket:**

    • Subject identification

    • Client network address

    • Valid period

14. **The Client/Server Session Key is then used for secure communications between the subject and object. (See Figure 3-7.)**

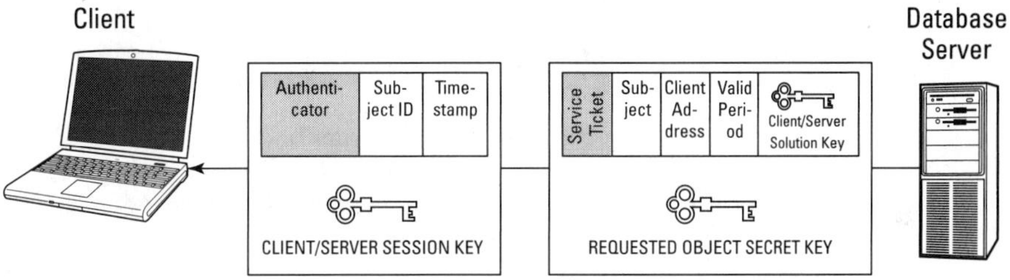

Figure 3-7: Kerberos client-server communications.

Biometrics

The only absolute method for positively identifying an individual is to base authentication on some unique personal *physiological* or *behavioral* characteristics, known as a biometric characteristic.

Physiological characteristics, including fingerprints, hand geometry, and facial features, such as retina and iris patterns, are used for biometric identification.

Behavioral biometrics are based on unique actions, such as voice measurement, signature, or keystroke pattern (intervals between keystrokes).

The necessary factors for an effective biometrics access control system include the following:

✔ **Accuracy:** This is the most important characteristic of any biometric system. The *uniqueness* of the body organ or characteristic being measured to guarantee positive identification is an important element of accuracy. In common biometric systems today, the only body parts that satisfy this requirement are these:

   • Fingers

   • Hands

   • Eyes

✔ **Speed and throughput:** This describes the length of time required to complete the entire authentication procedure. These events include

- Stepping up to the system

- Inputting a card or PIN (if required)

- Entering biometric data (such as inserting a finger or hand in a reader, pressing a sensor, aligning an eye with a camera or scanner, speaking a phrase, or signing a name)

- Processing the input data

- Opening and closing an access door (in the case of a physical access control system)

Another important aspect of speed and throughput is the initial enrollment time required to create a biometric file for a user account.

✔ **Data storage requirements:** This has become a less significant issue with the decreases in cost for data storage media. Biometric system input file sizes can be as small as 9 bytes or as large as 10,000 bytes, averaging from 256 to 1000 bytes.

✔ **Reliability:** The system must operate continuously and accurately without frequent maintenance outages.

✔ **Acceptability:** Certain privacy and ethical issues arise with the prospect of these systems being used to collect medical or other physiological data about employees. Other factors include intrusiveness of the data collection procedure and required physical contact with common system components, such as pressing an eye against a plastic cup or placing lips close to a microphone for voice recognition.

Common types of biometric systems include the following:

✔ **Finger scan systems:** These are the most common biometric systems in use today. Finger scan systems analyze the ridges, whorls, and minutiae of a fingerprint to create a digitized image that uniquely identifies the owner of the fingerprint.

✔ **Hand geometry systems:** Like finger scan systems, hand geometry systems are also nonintrusive and, therefore, generally more easily accepted than other biometric systems. Three-dimensional hand geometry data is acquired by a digital camera that simultaneously captures a vertical and a horizontal image of a subject's hand.

✔ **Retina pattern:** These systems record unique elements in the vascular pattern of the retina (the retina, located at the back of the eye, converts light signals to neural signals). Major concerns with this type of system are fears of eye damage from a *laser beam* (which is actually only a camera with a focused low-intensity light) directed at the eye and, more feasibly, privacy concerns.

Such health conditions as diabetes and heart disease are known to cause changes in the retinal pattern, which may be detected by these types of systems.

- **Iris pattern:** These systems are by far the most accurate on any type of biometric system. The *iris* is the colored portion of the eye surrounding the pupil. The iris is so unique that even the two eyes of a single individual have different patterns. The iris pattern is scanned by a camera directed at an aperture mirror from a distance of approximately three to ten inches.

- **Voice recognition:** These systems capture unique characteristics of a subject's voice and may also analyze *phonetic* or *linguistic* patterns. Most voice recognition systems are text dependent, requiring the subject to repeat a specific phrase. This functional requirement of voice recognition systems can be used to provide two-factor authentication:

  - *Something you know* (phrase)
  - *Something you are* (voice)

- **Signature dynamics:** These systems typically require the subject to sign his or her name on a signature tablet.

  Signatures commonly exhibit some slight changes because of different factors, and they can be forged.

In general, biometric access control systems are more expensive than other more common types, including passwords, tokens, and smart cards.

Single sign-on (SSO)

The concept of single sign-on (SSO) addresses a common problem for users and security administrators alike.

Users that require access to multiple systems or applications must often maintain numerous different passwords. This inevitably leads to shortcuts in creating and recalling passwords:

- Weak passwords with only slight variations often are used.
- Passwords are more likely to be written down.

This process also affects user productivity by requiring multiple logons and additional support, such as resetting passwords and unlocking accounts.

Additional disadvantages associated with multiple accounts include the following:

- ✔ More accounts mean multiple vulnerabilities. Every account that exists in a system, network, or application is a potential point of unauthorized access.
- ✔ A user with multiple accounts is more likely to use weak passwords or write them down.
- ✔ Someone has to create, maintain, support, and remove (or disable) all those accounts!

SSO is that great utopian solution that users and security administrators alike seek.

1. **A user presents a single set of log-on credentials, typically to an authentication server.**
2. **The authentication server transparently logs the user on to all other enterprise systems and applications for which that user is authorized.**

Of course, SSO is not without disadvantages, which include

- ✔ **No boundaries:** After you're authenticated, you've got the keys to the kingdom (sort of). Read that as *unrestricted access to all authorized resources!*
- ✔ **Labor intensive:** SSO is difficult to implement. But, hey! That's why you get paid (or should get paid) the big bucks!

Certificates

Digital certificates are increasingly being used for identification and authentication, particularly on Internet-based systems. Digital certificates may be issued by either of these:

- ✔ An organization maintaining its own certificate authority (CA) server
- ✔ A trusted third-party organization (such as VeriSign)

I discuss certificates in greater detail in Chapter 13.

Challenge Handshake Authentication Protocol (CHAP)

The Challenge Handshake Authentication Protocol (CHAP) is a remote access authentication protocol that provides mutual authentication between a client and server.

I discuss CHAP and other remote access authentication protocols in Chapter 5.

Prep Test

1 Access control systems provide the following three essential services, except:

A ○ Authentication
B ○ Authorization
C ○ Availability
D ○ Accountability

2 Authentication can be based on any combination of the following factors except:

A ○ Something you know
B ○ Something you have
C ○ Something you need
D ○ Something you are

3 Automated violation reports may be generated based on predefined criteria or thresholds known as:

A ○ Error rate
B ○ Clipping levels
C ○ BAC
D ○ Least upper-bound limit

4 *A user cannot deny an action* describes the concept of:

A ○ Authentication
B ○ Accountability
C ○ Nonrepudiation
D ○ Plausible deniability

5 Sensitivity labels are a fundamental component in which type of access control systems?

A ○ Mandatory access control
B ○ Discretionary access control
C ○ Access control lists
D ○ Role-based access control

6 All the following devices and protocols can be used to implement one-time passwords except:

A ○ Tokens
B ○ S/Keys
C ○ Smart cards
D ○ Kerberos

7 **Which of the following is not a general type of token?**

A ○ Static password

B ○ Synchronous dynamic password

C ○ Challenge-response dynamic password

D ○ Asymmetric password

8 **Kerberos authentication begins with the client generating a one-way hash function of the user's authentication information using a _____.**

A ○ Public key

B ○ Shared secret key

C ○ Asymmetric key

D ○ One-time password

9 **An access control system that allows a user to present a single set of logon credentials, which then transparently logs the user on to all other authorized systems describes:**

A ○ One-time passwords

B ○ Tokens

C ○ SSO

D ○ Tickets

10 **Which of the following is considered a significant disadvantage of biometric access control systems?**

A ○ Accuracy

B ○ Expense

C ○ Speed and throughput

D ○ Data storage requirements

Answers

1 **C.** Availability. Although access control systems may indirectly assure system availability, the three essential services are Authentication, Authorization, and Accountability. *Review "Access Control Concepts."*

2 **C.** Something you need. The three factors of authentication are *something you know*, *something you have*, and *something you are*. *Review "Identification and authentication (I&A)."*

3 **B.** Clipping levels. Answer choices A, C, and D are all bogus answers. *Review "Accountability."*

4 **C.** Nonrepudiation. Authentication and accountability are related to, but aren't the same as, nonrepudiation. Plausible deniability is a bogus answer. *Review "Accountability."*

5 **A.** Mandatory access control. The fundamental components in discretionary access controls are file (and data) ownership and access rights and permissions. Access control lists and role-based access control are types of discretionary access control systems. *Review "Mandatory access control (MAC)."*

6 **D.** Kerberos. Kerberos is a ticket-based authentication protocol. Although the tickets that are generated are unique for every logon, Kerberos relies on shared secrets that are static. Therefore, Kerberos isn't considered a one-time password protocol. *Review "Tokens" and "Tickets (Kerberos)."*

7 **D.** Asymmetric password. Static password, synchronous dynamic password, and challenge-response (or asynchronous) dynamic passwords are all general types of tokens. *Review "Tokens."*

8 **B.** Shared secret key. Kerberos authentication begins by creating a one-way hash of a username and password using a secret key that is shared by the client and the Key Distribution Center (KDC). *Review "Tickets (Kerberos)."*

9 **C.** SSO. SSO allows a user to present a single set of logon credentials, typically to an authentication server, which then transparently logs the user on to all other enterprise systems and applications for which that user is authorized. *Review "Single sign-on (SSO)."*

10 **B.** Expense. Biometric access control systems are generally more expensive than other more common types including passwords, tokens, and smart cards. *Review "Biometrics."*

Chapter 4

Attacks and Malicious Code

• •

In This Chapter

▶ Denial-of-service attacks

▶ Backdoors, packet sniffing, and man-in-the-middle attacks

▶ Replay attacks, weak keys, and session hijacking

▶ Social engineering

▶ Birthday attacks, brute force, and dictionary attacks

▶ Malicious code (viruses, worms, Trojan horses, and logic bombs)

• •

*I*n this chapter, I give you a look at some of the various methods of attack a hacker may use to gain unauthorized access to your systems and network. I also tell you about malicious code. Although most computer users are somewhat familiar with the threat of viruses, viruses are often misunderstood.

Quick Assessment

1   SYN floods, ICMP floods, UDP floods, Smurf, fraggle, and teardrop attacks are classified as what type of attacks?

2   In a _____ attack, TCP packets requesting a connection are sent to the target network with a spoofed source address.

3   A _____ attack is a variation of an ICMP flood attack.

4   In a _____ attack, the length and fragmentation offset fields of sequential IP packets are modified, causing the target system to crash.

5   A _____ is a small program installed on a computer by hackers that allows them to access a system undetected.

6   Replay attacks can be countered by incorporating a _____ in a session key.

7   _____ involves altering a TCP packet so that it appears to be coming from a known, trusted source.

8   A _____ is a small, self-replicating program that typically attaches itself to a legitimate system file and spreads throughout the system.

9   A _____ is similar to a virus in that it is self-replicating, but it does not necessarily require a host file to attach itself to.

10   Code Red and NIMDA are examples of _____ .

Answers

1   Denial-of-service attacks. *See "Denial-of-service and distributed denial-of-service attacks."*

2   SYN flood. *Review "Denial-of-service and distributed denial-of-service attacks."*

3   Smurf. *Review "Denial-of-service and distributed denial-of-service attacks."*

4   Teardrop. *See "Denial-of-service and distributed denial-of-service attacks."*

5   Root kit. *See "Backdoor."*

6   Time stamp. *See "Replay attack."*

7   IP spoofing. *See "Session hijacking (spoofing)."*

8   Virus. *See "Viruses."*

9   Worm. *See "Worms."*

10   Worms. *See "Worms."*

Types of Attacks

Attacks against computer systems come in many different forms and have different purposes. These attacks include denial-of-service, brute force, social engineering, and many others. The following discussion is a broad overview of the various types of attacks, which will familiarize you with these attacks. It is not all-inclusive, and it is certainly not a hacker's cookbook for mayhem. (Other books on this topic are available for those readers wanting to delve deeper into the dark side!)

Denial-of-service attacks and distributed denial-of-service attacks

Most attacks against networks today are denial-of-service (DoS) or distributed denial-of-service (DDoS) attacks in which the objective is to consume a network's bandwidth to make network services unavailable. DoS and DDoS attacks include SYN floods, ICMP floods, UDP floods, Smurf, Fraggle, and teardrop attacks.

SYN flood

In a *SYN flood attack,* TCP packets requesting a connection (SYN bit set) are sent to the target network with a spoofed source address. The target responds with a SYN-ACK packet, but the spoofed source never replies (assuming that the spoofed IP address is unreachable). *Half-open connections* are incomplete communication sessions awaiting completion of the TCP three-way handshake. These connections can quickly overwhelm a system's resources while waiting for the connections to time out. This causes the system to crash or otherwise become unusable.

SYN floods are countered on routers and firewalls by establishing proxies for half-open connections and limiting the bandwidth available to certain types of traffic. Other defenses include decreasing the maximum number of permitted TCP half-open connections and reducing the time-out period on networked systems.

ICMP flood

In an *ICMP flood attack,* large numbers of ICMP packets (usually Echo Request) are sent to the target network to consume available bandwidth and/or system resources. Because ICMP isn't required for normal network operations, the easiest defense is to drop ICMP packets at the router or filter them at the firewall.

UDP flood

In a *UDP flood attack,* large numbers of UDP packets are sent to the target network to consume available bandwidth and/or system resources. UDP floods can generally be countered by dropping unnecessary UDP packets at the router. However, if the attack is using a required UDP port (DNS port 53), other countermeasures need to be employed.

Smurf

A Smurf attack is a variation of the ICMP flood attack. (Read the earlier section "ICMP flood.") In a *Smurf attack,* ICMP Echo Request packets are sent to the broadcast address of a target network by using a spoofed IP address on the target network. The target, or *bounce site,* then transmits the ICMP Echo Request to all hosts on the network. Each host then responds with an Echo Reply packet, overwhelming the available bandwidth and/or system resources. Countermeasures against Smurf attacks include dropping ICMP packets at the router.

Fraggle

The *Fraggle attack* is a variant of the Smurf attack (see the previous section) that uses UDP Echo packets (UDP port 7) instead of ICMP packets. Cisco routers can be configured to disable the TCP and UDP services (known as *TCP and UDP small servers*) commonly used in Fraggle attacks. (Current Cisco IOS versions disable these services by default.)

Buffer overflow (teardrop attack)

Buffer (or stack) overflows exploit vulnerabilities in applications, protocols, and operating systems. Buffer overflow attacks constitute one of the most common and successful types of computer attacks today. Although often used in denial-of-service attacks, buffer overflows in certain systems or applications may enable an attacker to gain unauthorized access to a system or directory. A *teardrop attack* is a type of stack overflow attack that exploits vulnerabilities in the IP protocol. In a teardrop attack, the length and fragmentation offset fields of sequential IP packets are modified, causing the target system to become confused and crash.

Backdoor

A *backdoor program* allows an attacker to access a "secure" system. Backdoor programs are widely available on the Internet and include popular programs, such as SubSeven and BackOrifice. Other terms loosely associated with backdoor attacks include the following:

- ✔ **Root kit.** A *root kit* is a small program installed on a system by a hacker; it allows the hacker to access a system undetected. In order to install a root kit, a system must already have been compromised. However, root kits are easily overlooked when a compromised system is cleaned up, allowing the attacker to return by using the root kit as a backdoor.

- ✔ **Trap door.** A *trap door* is an undocumented function of a system that may perform an undesirable function (for example, allowing a normal user to log on with supervisor rights).

- ✔ **Maintenance hook.** A *maintenance hook* is a backdoor that allows legitimate access to a system or application for maintenance purposes. These may include certain procedures that enable a programmer to gain access to a system, password recovery routines, and maintenance or default accounts. Unfortunately, maintenance hooks are often well known and publicized among attackers.

Packet (or password) sniffing

In this method, an attacker uses a *sniffer* to capture network packets and analyze their contents, such as usernames/passwords and shared keys (analogous to tapping a line). A sniffer captures raw data being transmitted across a network medium. A typical network intrusion detection system incorporates a sniffer and an automated analysis of data based on rules or behavior patterns.

Man-in-the-middle attacks

The *man-in-the-middle attack* involves an attacker intercepting messages between two parties and forwarding a modified version of the original message. For example, an attacker may substitute his own public key during a public key exchange between two parties. The two parties believe that they're still communicating with each other and unknowingly encrypt messages by using the attacker's public key rather than the intended recipient's public key. The attacker can then decrypt secret messages between the two parties, modify their contents as desired, and send them on to the unwary recipient.

Replay attack

A *replay attack* occurs when a session key is intercepted and used against a later encrypted session between the same two parties. Replay attacks can be countered by incorporating a time stamp in the session key.

Weak keys

A weak encryption key can be cracked by using a variety of mathematically based cryptographic attacks including

- ✔ **Ciphertext Only Attack (COA).** The cryptanalyst obtains the ciphertext of several messages, all encrypted by using the same encryption algorithm but without the associated plaintext, and then attempts to decrypt the data by searching for repeating patterns and through statistical analysis.

  The term *cryptanalyst* is used in this section to describe an attacker attempting various cryptographic attacks. *Cryptanalysis* is the science of deciphering ciphertext without the cryptographic key. Cryptanalysts perform such analysis legitimately to test the strength or validity of a cryptographic algorithm. Although these methods can also be used by an attacker to crack an algorithm, you typically won't hear of any hackers bragging about their crafty use of an Adaptive Chosen Ciphertext Attack to break into a system!

- ✔ **Chosen Text Attack (CTA).** The cryptanalyst selects a sample of plaintext and obtains the corresponding ciphertext. Several types of Chosen Text Attacks exist, including Chosen Plaintext, Adaptive Chosen Plaintext, Chosen Ciphertext, and Adaptive Chosen Ciphertext.

  - **Chosen Plaintext Attack (CPA):** The cryptanalyst chooses plaintext to be encrypted, and the corresponding ciphertext is obtained.

  - **Adaptive Chosen Plaintext Attack (ACPA):** The cryptanalyst chooses plaintext to be encrypted; then, based on the resulting ciphertext, he chooses another sample to be encrypted.

  - **Chosen Ciphertext Attack (CCA):** The cryptanalyst chooses ciphertext to be decrypted, and the corresponding plaintext is obtained.

  - **Adaptive Chosen Ciphertext Attack (ACCA):** The cryptanalyst chooses ciphertext to be decrypted; then, based on the resulting ciphertext, he chooses another sample to be decrypted.

- ✔ **Known Plaintext Attack (KPA).** The cryptanalyst has obtained the ciphertext and corresponding plaintext of several past messages.

- ✔ **Meet-in-the-middle.** A *meet-in-the-middle attack* involves an attacker encrypting known plaintext with each possible key on one end, decrypting the corresponding ciphertext with each possible key, and then comparing the results *in the middle.*

You should also be aware that a password is nothing more than a weak key — extremely weak! We're talking about a couple of bits here! So if you think a 56-bit DES key is weak, passwords should make you nervous!

Session hijacking (spoofing)

This method is similar to a man-in-the-middle attack except that the attacker impersonates the intended recipient rather than modifying messages in transit. IP *spoofing* involves altering a TCP packet so that it appears to be coming from a known, trusted source, thus giving the attacker access to the network.

Social engineering

Social engineering is a little-known aspect of the human genome mapping project! Actually, *social engineering* is just a spiffy name for a low-tech attack method, yet one of the most effective and easily perpetrated forms of attack. Common techniques involve dumpster diving, shoulder surfing, raiding cubicles (passwords on monitors and under mouse pads), and plain ol' asking. This latter brazen technique can simply be the attacker (pretending to be a system administrator) calling a user and asking for the user's password or calling a help desk, pretending to be a user and asking to have their password changed.

The birthday attack

The *birthday attack* has absolutely nothing to do with social engineering (though at first glance it would seem the perfect lead-in: You say it's your birthday? Well, it's my birthday too — so what's your password?!). A birthday attack attempts to exploit the probability of two messages using the same hash function and producing the same message digest. It's based on a well-known statistical probability problem: The probability that 2 or more people in a room will have the same birthday (month and day, not necessarily year) is greater than 50 percent if there are 23 or more people in the room (about 50.7 percent). The probability of 2 people sharing a birthday if there are 70 people in the room is almost 100 percent (99.9 percent)! However, for 2 people in a room to share a *given* birthday, there must be 253 or more people in the room to have a statistical probability of greater than 50 percent.

Brute force and dictionary attacks

Brute force and dictionary attacks can be classified as password-guessing attacks. In a *brute force attack,* the attacker attempts every possible combination of letters, numbers, and characters to crack a password, passphrase, or PIN. A *dictionary attack* is essentially a more focused type of brute force attack in which a predefined word list is used. Such word lists or dictionaries, including foreign language and special-interest dictionaries, are widely available on the Internet for use in password-cracking utilities, such as l0phtcrack and John the Ripper.

Malicious Code

Malicious code is the general term used to refer to a very ugly side of computing with which most of us are, unfortunately, all too familiar: viruses, worms, Trojan horses, and logic bombs.

Viruses

A *computer virus* is a small, self-replicating program that typically attaches itself to a legitimate system file and spreads throughout the system. A virus is usually written to cause some destructive effect, such as modifying or erasing files. Early viruses included boot sector viruses and multipartite viruses, and they were often spread through shared floppy disks. Although viruses are less common today, the following practices regarding floppy disks are still prudent:

- ✔ **Avoid sharing floppy disks.**
- ✔ **Write-protect floppy disks.**
- ✔ **Do not boot your computer from a floppy disk.** A good antivirus program will detect the presence of a floppy disk in your computer when you attempt to shut down and warn you accordingly.

Today, macro viruses and e-mail viruses are far more common and more easily spread.

A *macro virus* uses a macro (commonly used in such applications as Microsoft Word and Excel) to spread. A *macro* is a small program that a user can create to automate a sequence of routine or repetitive steps (such as typing a repeated phrase or symbol). Many applications now provide some level of macro security, allowing a user to decide whether or not a macro should be enabled.

E-mail is so commonplace today that it provides an ideal medium for spreading viruses. Small programs are routinely sent as attachments in e-mail messages and may contain a virus. Many e-mail gateways are set up to block certain attachments with .exe, .scr, and .vbs extensions. A *virus hoax* is another form of e-mail virus — call it a *poor-man's virus.* These hoaxes typically use pseudotechnical language to describe a fake virus and may instruct a user to delete an important system file. See Chapter 6 for more information on hoaxes.

The best defense against viruses is to use an antivirus program and keep it up-to-date with the latest signatures.

Worms

Similar to a virus, a *worm* is designed to self-replicate and cause damage to systems or large networks. Unlike a virus, a worm does not necessarily require a host file to attach itself to. Worms are easily spread across the Internet via e-mail and chat programs. Worms have gained recent notoriety with such widespread epidemics as Code Red and NIMDA. Worms can be designed to destroy files, cause a denial-of-service, and/or exploit vulnerabilities in software allowing an attacker to plant logic bombs, root kits (described in the "Backdoor" section, earlier in this chapter), or other malicious code on a system.

Trojan horses

A Trojan horse is a variant of viruses and worms that typically does not replicate itself. A Trojan horse masquerades as a legitimate program (such as a joke, a game, or a screen saver), which may be innocently transmitted among friends via e-mail, for example. After Trojan horses (such as SubSeven or BackOrifice) are installed on a system, they enable an attacker to control a system and possibly launch attacks against other systems.

Logic bombs

A *logic bomb* is a malicious program designed to cause damage when triggered by some event, such as a specific date or execution of a certain program on a system. Logic bombs are typically not self-replicating and may be written as part of a virus or worm.

Prep Test

1 _____ are incomplete communication sessions awaiting completion of the TCP three-way handshake.

A ○ Half-open connections
B ○ Half-closed connections
C ○ Incomplete connections
D ○ Two-way connections

2 In a _____ attack, ICMP Echo Request packets are sent to the broadcast address of a target network by using a spoofed IP address on the target network. Each host then responds with an Echo Reply packet, which overwhelms the networks resources.

A ○ Teardrop
B ○ SYN flood
C ○ Smurf
D ○ Fraggle

3 The _____ attack is a variant of the Smurf attack that uses UDP Echo packets instead of ICMP packets.

A ○ Spoofing
B ○ Fraggle
C ○ Teardrop
D ○ Birthday

4 A _____ is an undocumented function of a system that may perform an undesirable function.

A ○ Trap door
B ○ Root kit
C ○ Maintenance hook
D ○ Feature set

5 A _____ attack involves an attacker intercepting messages between two parties and forwarding a modified version of the original message.

A ○ Replay
B ○ Smurf
C ○ Meet-in-the-middle
D ○ Man-in-the-middle

6 _____ involves altering a TCP packet so that it appears to be coming from a known, trusted source.

A ○ IP spoofing

B ○ social engineering

C ○ Birthday attack

D ○ Meet-in-the-middle

7 A _____ attack attempts to exploit the probability of two messages using the same hash function and producing the same message digest.

A ○ Birthday

B ○ Social engineering

C ○ Man-in-the-middle

D ○ Brute force

8 A dictionary attack is a type of _____ attack.

A ○ Denial-of-service

B ○ Distributed denial-of-service

C ○ Brute force

D ○ Social engineering

Answers

1 **A.** Half-open connections. Half-open connections can quickly overwhelm a system's resources, causing the system to crash. *Review "SYN flood."*

2 **C.** Smurf. A Smurf attack is a variation of the ICMP flood attack. *Review "Smurf."*

3 **B.** Fraggle. A fraggle attack uses UDP Echo packet (UDP port 7) to overwhelm a network, similar to a Smurf attack. *Review "Fraggle."*

4 **A.** Trap door. Maintenance hooks and root kits are other types of backdoors. A feature set is the Microsoft term for a bug (just kidding!). *Review "Backdoor."*

5 **D.** Man-in-the-middle. A replay attack occurs when a session key is intercepted and used against a later session between the same two parties. A Smurf attack is a type of denial-of-service attack. A meet-in-the-middle attack is a type of cryptographic attack. *Review "Man-in-the-middle attacks."*

6 **A.** IP spoofing. IP spoofing is used to hijack a session, giving an attacker access to a network. *Review "Session hijacking (spoofing)."*

7 **A.** Birthday. The birthday attack is based on the statistical probability that 2 or more people in a room will have the same birthday (greater than 50 percent for 23 or more people). *Review "The birthday attack."*

8 **C.** Brute force. A dictionary attack is a focused type of brute force attack in which a predefined word list is used. *Review "Brute force and dictionary attacks."*

Part III
Communication Security

The 5th Wave   By Rich Tennant

"Face it Vinnie— you're gonna have a hard time getting people to subscribe online with a credit card to a newsletter called 'Felons Interactive.'"

In this part . . .

The Communications Security domain includes remote access, e-mail security, Internet security, directory services and file transfer, and wireless security. These topics represent some of the greatest areas of exposure for network security.

Chapter 5

Remote Access

· ·

· ·

The problem of remote access presents many security challenges for systems and security administrators. Because you can almost never control the remote end of the connection, inherent vulnerabilities will always exist in remote access. However, several technologies and methods for making remote access more secure are available.

In this chapter, I tell you about traditional RAS (remote access services), the Point-to-Point Protocol (PPP), and basic security techniques, as well as about more advanced topics, such as RADIUS and TACACS. Next, I give you a look at virtual private networks (VPNs) and the protocols used to implement a VPN: PPTP, L2TP, L2F, and IPSec. Finally, I cover several applications that provide remote control access to servers including telnet, rlogin, and ssh.

Some of the discussions in this chapter are fairly detailed and technical (such as IPSec). You need to understand these protocols and concepts at this level for the Security+ exam.

Quick Assessment

1 The restricted address method for remote access security can be easily defeated by _____.

2 The callback method for remote access security can be easily defeated by _____.

3 The _____ is an authentication protocol used in PPP that authenticates a peer to a server and transmits passwords in clear text.

4 A _____ creates a secure tunnel over a public network, such as the Internet.

5 In IPSec operation, the _____ mode encrypts the data only.

6 In IPSec operation, the _____ mode encrypts the entire packet.

7 In IPSec, a _____ is a one-way connection between two communicating parties.

8 Three parameters that uniquely identify an SA in an IPSec session are _____, _____, and _____.

9 Key management in IPSec is provided by using what protocol?

10 Secure Shell (SSH) operates on what TCP port?

Answers

1   Spoofing. *See "Remote Access Vulnerabilities and Security Methods."*

2   Call forwarding. *Review "Remote Access Vulnerabilities and Security Methods."*

3   Password Authentication Protocol (PAP). *Review "RAS."*

4   Virtual private network (VPN). *See "Virtual Private Networks (VPNs)."*

5   Transport. *See "IPSec."*

6   Tunnel. *Take a look at "IPSec."*

7   Security Association (SA). *See "IPSec."*

8   Security Parameter Index (SPI), destination IP address, and Security Protocol ID. *Check out "IPSec."*

9   Internet Key Exchange (IKE). *See "IPSec."*

10   22. *Review "Remote Access Applications."*

Remote Access Vulnerabilities and Security Methods

Several basic security methods can be implemented to provide some security for remote access systems. Remote access security methods include the following:

- Restricted addresses
- Caller ID
- Callback

Restricted address

The *restricted address* method restricts access to the network based on allowed IP addresses, essentially performing rudimentary *node* authentication but not *user* authentication. This method can be defeated by IP address spoofing. See Chapter 4 for more on spoofing.

Caller ID

The *caller ID* method restricts access to the network based on allowed phone numbers, thus performing a more secure form of node authentication; phone numbers are more difficult to spoof than IP addresses. This method can be difficult to administer for road warriors who routinely travel to several cities.

Callback

The *callback* method restricts network access by requiring a remote user to first authenticate to the remote access service (RAS) server. The RAS server then disconnects and calls the user back at a preconfigured phone number. Like caller ID, this method can be difficult to administer for road warriors. Callback can be easily defeated by using call forwarding.

Remote Access Security Technologies

Remote access security technologies include the following:

- ✔ RAS
- ✔ RADIUS
- ✔ TACACS

These access control systems and protocols provide centralized authentication and centralized administration of remote users.

RAS

Remote access service (RAS) servers utilize the Point-to-Point Protocol (PPP) to encapsulate IP packets and establish dial-in connections over serial and ISDN links.

PPP incorporates three authentication protocols:

- ✔ **PAP:** The Password Authentication Protocol (PAP) uses a two-way handshake to authenticate a peer to a server when a link is initially established.

  PAP transmits passwords in clear text and provides no protection from replay or brute force attacks.

- ✔ **CHAP:** The Challenge Handshake Authentication Protocol (CHAP) uses a three-way handshake to authenticate both a peer and server when a link is initially established and, optionally, at regular intervals throughout the session. Both the peer and server must be preconfigured with a shared secret that is stored in plain text (see Chapter 12 for more on shared secret keys and symmetric cryptography). The peer uses the secret to calculate the response to a server challenge by using an MD5 one-way hash function (see Chapter 12 for more on hash functions).

  MS-CHAP, a Microsoft enhancement to CHAP, allows the shared secret to be stored in an encrypted form.

- ✔ **EAP:** The Extensible Authentication Protocol (EAP) adds flexibility to PPP authentication by implementing such authentication mechanisms as the following:

    - MD5-challenge
    - S/Key (see chapter 3 for more on S/Key and one-time passwords)
    - Generic token card
    - Digital certificates

  With an EAP implementation, the RAS server doesn't perform authentication for remote access. Instead, the RAS server coordinates communication between the remote user and an authentication server (using a protocol such as RADIUS). EAP is implemented in many wireless networks.

RADIUS

The Remote Authentication Dial-In User Service (RADIUS) protocol is an open-source, UDP-based client-server protocol. Defined in RFC 2058 and RFC 2059, RADIUS provides authentication and accountability. A user provides username/password information to a RADIUS client by using PAP or CHAP.

The RADIUS client encrypts the password and sends the username and encrypted password to the RADIUS server for authentication.

Passwords exchanged between the RADIUS client and RADIUS server are encrypted, but passwords exchanged between the PC client and the RADIUS client are not necessarily encrypted — if using PAP authentication, for example. However, if the PC client also is the RADIUS client, all password exchanges are encrypted regardless of the authentication protocol being used.

TACACS

The Terminal Access Controller Access Control System (TACACS) is a UDP-based access control protocol, which provides authentication, authorization, and accountability (AAA).

The original TACACS protocol has been significantly enhanced.

✔ TACACS+ (the most common implementation of TACACS).

   TACACS+ is TCP-based (port 49) and supports practically any authentication mechanism, such as

- PAP

- CHAP

- MS-CHAP

- EAP

- Token cards

- Kerberos

   The basic operation of TACACS+ is similar to RADIUS, including the caveat about encrypted passwords between client and server.

   The major advantages of TACACS+ are

- Support of many authentication mechanisms

- Granular control of authorization parameters

✔ XTACACS (no longer used)

Virtual Private Networks (VPNs)

A *virtual private network* (VPN) creates a secure tunnel over a public network, such as the Internet. A secure tunnel is created by either *encrypting* or *encapsulating* the data as it's transmitted across the VPN. The two ends of a VPN tunnel are commonly implemented by using one of the following methods:

- ✔ Client-to-VPN concentrator (or device)
- ✔ Client-to-firewall
- ✔ Firewall-to-firewall
- ✔ Router-to-router

Common VPN protocol standards include the following:

- ✔ Point-to-Point Tunneling Protocol (PPTP)
- ✔ Layer 2 Forwarding Protocol (L2F)
- ✔ Layer 2 Tunneling Protocol (L2TP)
- ✔ Internet Protocol Security (IPSec)

Point-to-Point Tunneling Protocol (PPTP)

The Point-to-Point Tunneling Protocol (PPTP) was developed by Microsoft to enable the Point-to-Point Protocol (PPP) to be tunneled through a public network. PPTP uses native PPP authentication and encryption services, such as these:

- ✔ PAP
- ✔ CHAP
- ✔ EAP

PPTP is commonly used for secure dial-up connections on Microsoft Windows 9*x* or NT/2000 clients. PPTP operates at the Data Link Layer of the OSI model and is designed for individual client-server connections.

Layer 2 Forwarding Protocol (L2F)

The Layer 2 Forwarding Protocol (L2F) was developed by Cisco and provides functionality similar to that of PPTP. As its name implies, L2F operates at the Data Link Layer of the OSI model and permits tunneling of such Layer 2 WAN protocols as these:

- ✔ HDLC (High-Level Data Link Control)
- ✔ SLIP (Serial Line Internet Protocol)

Layer 2 Tunneling Protocol (L2TP)

The Layer 2 Tunneling Protocol (L2TP) is an IETF standard that combines Microsoft (and others) PPTP and Cisco L2F protocols. Like PPTP and L2F, L2TP operates at the Data Link Layer of the OSI model to create secure VPN connections for individual client-server connections. The L2TP addresses these end-user requirements:

- ✔ **Transparency:** Requires no additional software
- ✔ **Robust authentication:** Supports
  - PPP authentication protocols
  - Remote Authentication Dial-In User Service (RADIUS)
  - Terminal Access Controller Access Control System (TACACS)
  - Smart cards
  - One-time passwords
- ✔ **Local addressing:** IP addresses assigned by the VPN entities, not the ISP
- ✔ **Authorization:** Authorization managed by the VPN server-side similar to direct dial-up connections
- ✔ **Accounting:** Accounting performed by both the ISP and user

IPSec

Internet Protocol Security (IPSec) is an IETF open standard for VPNs that operates at the Network Layer of the OSI model. It's the most popular and robust VPN protocol in use today. IPSec ensures confidentiality, integrity, and authenticity by using Layer 3 encryption and authentication to provide an end-to-end solution. IPSec operates in two modes:

- ✔ **Transport mode:** Only the data is encrypted.
- ✔ **Tunnel mode:** The entire packet is encrypted.

The two main protocols used in IPSec are

- ✔ **Authentication Header (AH):** Provides
  - Integrity
  - Authentication
  - Nonrepudiation

✔ **Encapsulating Security Payload (ESP):** Provides

- Confidentiality (encryption)
- Limited authentication

Each pair of hosts communicating in an IPSec session must establish a security association.

A *security association* (SA) is a one-way connection between two communicating parties; thus, two SAs are required for each pair of communicating hosts. Additionally, each SA only supports a single protocol (AH or ESP). Therefore, if both an AH and ESP are used between two communicating hosts, a total of four SAs is required. An SA has three parameters that uniquely identify it in an IPSec session:

✔ **Security Parameter Index (SPI):** The SPI is a 32-bit string used by the receiving station to differentiate between SAs terminating on that station. The SPI is located within the AH or ESP header.

✔ **Destination IP address:** The destination address could be the end station or an intermediate gateway or firewall but must be a unicast address (not a broadcast or multicast IP address).

✔ **Security Protocol ID:** The Security Protocol ID must be either an AH or ESP association.

Key management (see Chapter 12 for an explanation of key management functions) is provided in IPSec by using the Internet Key Exchange (IKE). IKE is actually a combination of three complementary protocols:

✔ Internet Security Association and Key Management Protocol (ISAKMP)

✔ Secure Key Exchange Mechanism (SKEME)

✔ Oakley Key Exchange Protocol

IKE operates in three modes:

✔ Main Mode

✔ Aggressive Mode

✔ Quick Mode

Remote Access Applications

Several commonly used remote access applications that enable administrators to remotely control servers, routers, or other devices on a TCP/IP-based network are available. These include Telnet, rlogin, and SSH.

Telnet

Telnet is a terminal emulation program that provides remote control access to servers (such as Web servers) across TCP/IP networks. Entering commands at the console on a remote client will execute commands on the server. By default, Telnet operates on TCP port 23. Many well-known vulnerabilities are in the Telnet protocol because Telnet uses a simple authentication mechanism, and both passwords and data are transmitted in plain text.

Remote login (rlogin)

Remote login (rlogin) is a terminal emulation program (similar to Telnet) originally used for Unix-based systems. It has now been ported to Windows platforms as well. By default, rlogin operates on TCP port 513. As with Telnet, many well-known vulnerabilities can be found in the rlogin protocol because it uses a simple authentication mechanism and transmits passwords and data in plain text.

Secure Shell (SSH)

SSH (Version 2) is used for secure remote access as one alternative to Telnet and rlogin. It can be used to provide

- ✔ Confidentiality
- ✔ Integrity
- ✔ Authentication

SSH establishes an encrypted tunnel between the SSH client and SSH server and can authenticate the client to the server. SSH typically operates on TCP port 22. SSH (Version 1) is widely used, but it has inherent vulnerabilities that are easily exploited.

Prep Test

1 _____ is a security method that restricts remote access to a network based on allowed phone numbers.

A ◯ Restricted address

B ◯ Caller ID

C ◯ Callback

D ◯ Call Forwarding

2 The _____ uses a three-way handshake to authenticate a peer and server in a remote access connection and requires both the peer and server to be preconfigured with a shared secret.

A ◯ Point-to-Point Protocol (PPP)

B ◯ Password Authentication Protocol (PAP)

C ◯ Challenge-Handshake Authentication Protocol (CHAP)

D ◯ Extensible Authentication Protocol (EAP)

3 _____ is a UDP-based client-server protocol that provides authentication and accountability.

A ◯ RADIUS

B ◯ TACACS+

C ◯ L2TP

D ◯ PAP

4 By default, TACACS+ uses what TCP port?

A ◯ 21

B ◯ 22

C ◯ 49

D ◯ 25

5 Common VPN protocol standards include all of the following except _____.

A ◯ PPP

B ◯ PPTP

C ◯ L2F

D ◯ L2TP

6 **L2F and L2TP operate at which layer of the OSI model?**

A ○ Data Link

B ○ Network

C ○ Transport

D ○ Session

7 **The two modes of IPSec operation are _____ and _____.**

A ○ Transport, Transfer

B ○ Transfer, Tunnel

C ○ Transfer, Session

D ○ Transport, Tunnel

8 **If both AH and ESP are used between two communicating hosts in an IPSec session, how many SAs are required?**

A ○ One

B ○ Two

C ○ Three

D ○ Four

9 **By default, Telnet uses which TCP port?**

A ○ 21

B ○ 22

C ○ 23

D ○ 25

10 **By default, SSH uses which TCP port?**

A ○ 21

B ○ 22

C ○ 49

D ○ 25

Answers

1 **B.** Caller ID. Restricted address restricts access based on allowed IP addresses. Callback authenticates a remote user and then disconnects and calls them back at a preconfigured number. Call forwarding is a technique for circumventing the callback security method. *Review "Remote Access Vulnerabilities and Security Methods."*

2 **C.** Challenge-Handshake Authentication Protocol (CHAP). PPP is the remote access protocol that is used to encapsulate IP packets and establish dial-in connections. PAP uses a two-way handshake to authenticate the peer only. EAP uses such authentication mechanisms as MD5, token cards, digital certificates, and RADIUS. *Review "Remote Access Security Technologies."*

3 **A.** RADIUS. RADIUS is an open-source, UDP-based client-server protocol that provides authentication and accountability. *Review "Remote Access Security Technologies."*

4 **C.** 49. 21 is FTP, 22 is SSH, and 25 is SMTP. *Review "Remote Access Security Technologies."*

5 **A.** PPP. PPP is the Point-to-Point Protocol used for remote access in dial-in environments. *Review "Virtual Private Networks (VPNs)."*

6 **A.** Data Link. The Layer 2 Forwarding Protocol (L2F) and Layer 2 Tunneling Protocol (L2TP) both operate at Layer 2 of the OSI model, which is the Data Link layer. *Review "Virtual Private Networks (VPNs)."*

7 **D.** Transport, Tunnel. In Transport mode, only the data is encrypted. In Tunnel mode, the entire packet is encrypted. *Review "Virtual Private Networks (VPNs)."*

8 **D.** Four. Each security association (SA) is a one-way connection and can support only one protocol. *Review "Virtual Private Networks (VPNs)."*

9 **C.** 23. 21 is FTP, 22 is SSH, and 25 is SMTP. *Review "Remote Access Applications."*

10 **B.** 22. 21 is FTP, 49 is TACACS+, and 25 is SMTP. *Review "Remote Access Applications.*

Remote Access

Chapter 6

E-Mail and Internet Security

. . . .

In This Chapter

▶ Describing various secure e-mail standards and applications

▶ Identifying spam and hoaxes

▶ Understanding Internet security protocols, such as SSL/TLS and S-HTTP

▶ Discuss risks associated with instant messaging

▶ Identifying vulnerabilities and risks associated with Java and ActiveX, JavaScript, cookies, and CGI

. . . .

*F*or many organizations, e-mail and Internet access are the lifeblood of the company and the sole reason for the existence of an IT department. In this chapter, I explore the different standards and applications available for secure e-mail and Internet use. I also give you a look at several vulnerabilities and nuisances, including virus hoaxes and spam.

Quick Assessment

1   List four examples of secure e-mail standards or applications.

2   _____ is a freely available, open source secure e-mail add-on application that uses the IDEA cipher for encryption.

3   Mail servers that forward any received e-mail message without attempting to verify the originator of the message are referred to as an _____.

4   _____ provides session-based encryption and authentication for secure communication between clients and servers on the Internet.

5   SSL 3.0 is now an IETF standard known as _____.

6   S-HTTP is a _____-oriented protocol that encapsulates data after security properties for a session have been successfully negotiated.

7   Java security is based on the concept of a _____.

8   Two types of applets are _____ and _____.

9   A _____ is a simple text file message, given to a Web browser by a Web server, that stores personal information about a user and then transmits it back to the Web server.

10 (True/False) Cookies can be used to spread viruses.

Answers

1 S/MIME, MOSS, PEM, PGP. *See "E-Mail Security."*

2 PGP. *Review "E-Mail Security."*

3 open mail relay. *Review "E-Mail Security."*

4 SSL. *See "Internet Security."*

5 TLS 1.0. *See "Internet Security."*

6 connectionless. *See "Internet Security."*

7 sandbox. *See "Internet Security."*

8 ActiveX and Java. *See "Internet Security."*

9 cookie. *See "Internet Security."*

10 False. *See "Internet Security."*

E-Mail Security

Several applications employing cryptographic techniques have been developed for e-mail communications in order to provide the following:

- ✔ Confidentiality
- ✔ Integrity
- ✔ Authentication
- ✔ Nonrepudiation
- ✔ Access control

Secure Multipurpose Internet Mail Extensions (S/MIME)

Secure Multipurpose Internet Mail Extensions (S/MIME) provides a secure method of sending e-mail and is incorporated into several popular browsers and e-mail applications. S/MIME provides confidentiality and authentication by using the RSA asymmetric key system, digital signatures, and X.509 digital certificates. S/MIME complies with the Public Key Cryptography Standard (PKCS) #7 format and has been proposed as a standard to the Internet Engineering Task Force (IETF) (see Chapter 12 for more about cryptography).

MIME Object Security Services (MOSS)

MIME Object Security Services (MOSS) provides confidentiality, integrity, identification and authentication, and nonrepudiation by using MD2 or MD5, RSA asymmetric keys, and DES. MOSS has not been widely implemented on the Internet. See Chapter 12 for more about cryptography.

Privacy Enhanced Mail (PEM)

Privacy Enhanced Mail (PEM) was proposed as a PKCS-compliant standard by the IETF but hasn't been widely implemented on the Internet. It provides confidentiality and authentication by using 3DES for encryption, MD2 or MD5 message digests, X.509 digital certificates, and the RSA asymmetric system for digital signatures and secure key distribution. See Chapter 12 for more about cryptography.

Pretty Good Privacy (PGP)

Pretty Good Privacy (PGP) is freely available, open source e-mail software program developed by Phil Zimmerman. PGP provides confidentiality and authentication by using the IDEA (International Data Encryption Algorithm) cipher for encryption and the RSA asymmetric system for digital signatures and secure key distribution. (See Chapter 12 for more about cryptography.) Instead of a central certificate authority (CA), PGP uses a trust model, which is ideally suited to smaller groups for validation of user identity.

PGP is a freeware e-mail security application that uses the IDEA algorithm (symmetric) for encryption and the RSA algorithm (asymmetric) for key distribution and digital signatures.

E-Mail Vulnerabilities

In this section, I tell you about two very common and, no doubt, very familiar e-mail vulnerabilities for any user of e-mail today: spam and hoaxes.

Spam

We're not talking about that delightful, gourmet meal found in a can here! No, this is a vexing problem that plagues the Internet and threatens its viability. *Spam* is unwanted, unsolicited e-mail — the electronic equivalent of junk mail, but much worse. At least in a pinch, you can use junk mail as a substitute for Kleenex tissues!

Spam wastes valuable and limited bandwidth and computing resources. It costs companies and individuals millions of dollars annually in lost productivity. Arbitrarily deleting or blocking spam may cause an important and legitimate e-mail message to be missed. A great majority of spam is pornographic or otherwise offensive in nature. Currently available antispamming products have only limited effectiveness in eradicating this problem. No laws forbid sending e-mail spam (although several have been proposed). Your options for combating spam are limited, but include these:

- **Delete:** If you receive a relatively low volume of spam e-mail on a daily basis, perhaps the easiest thing to do is delete it. Doing this is not really a solution and is probably not what your users want to hear, but this is the most common method for dealing with spam.

✔ **Filter:** Most e-mail applications and Internet e-mail services provide some filtering capability. Several commercial third-party products provide better filtering capabilities. Just be sure you configure the filtering options carefully to avoid filtering legitimate e-mail!

✔ **Report:** There are many reputable organizations, such as SpamCop (`www.spamcop.net`), that help you fight spammers (for a price). If you suspect fraud or criminal activity, then you should definitely report the suspect e-mail to local law enforcement officials. If reporting spam is your company's e-mail policy, you may want to consider setting up a server for spam storage. Rather than have your users delete spam, dump it to this server. You may use this information to report spammers and collect evidence (possibly even quantify damages should a law against spamming be passed).

✔ **Educate:** Educate your users about spam. Users should know to *never* reply or unsubscribe to a spammed e-mail. This verifies the e-mail address and makes the problem worse.

✔ **Don't relay!** Perhaps the most important thing for a company to do is ensure that it is not already (or does not become) a part of the problem. Mail servers that are set up as an *open mail relay* (many are by default) can be used to send spam to anyone on the Internet. An open mail relay does not attempt to verify the originator of an e-mail message and forwards anything it receives. Spammers can even make the e-mail appear to originate from your organization. At the very least, your domain may be blacklisted, thus preventing legitimate recipients from getting your legitimate e-mail messages. Worse still, your company may be held liable for failing to exercise due diligence in securing its systems.

Hoaxes

E-mail hoaxes typically take the form of chain letters. As with spam (see the preceding section), e-mail hoaxes waste valuable time and resources. One specific type of e-mail hoax is the virus hoax. A *virus hoax* is an e-mail message that describes a fake virus using pseudotechnical language. The threat that is described may appear quite legitimate and may be sent from someone you know. (The hoaxes usually instruct you to forward it to everyone in your address book.) But virus hoaxes are almost always (99.9 percent of the time would probably be accurate) false. The proliferation of virus hoaxes confuses users and may even damage systems. (Many hoaxes instruct unsuspecting users to delete important system files.) Your defense against hoaxes should include these:

✔ **Educate:** Educate your users about e-mail hoaxes (particularly virus hoaxes). Instruct them never to forward a hoax, even if it is received from someone they know. Ensure that they report hoaxes to a system or security administrator.

> ✔ **Verify:** If you are concerned about the legitimacy of a virus hoax, verify its existence (or nonexistence) at `www.symantec.com` or `www.mcafee.com`. Although these antivirus software giants may not necessarily have an immediate fix for a new virus in the wild, they provide you with reliable information about any new threats (real or fraudulent).

Internet Security

As with e-mail applications, several protocols and standards have been developed to provide security for Internet communications and transactions. These include SSL/TLS and S-HTTP, discussed next in this section. I also discuss vulnerabilities associated with two Internet applications: browsers and instant messaging.

Secure Sockets Layer (SSL)/Transport Layer Security (TLS)

The *Secure Sockets Layer* (SSL) protocol provides session-based encryption and authentication for secure communication between clients and servers on the Internet.

SSL operates at the Transport Layer, is independent of the application protocol, and provides server authentication with optional client authentication.

SSL uses the RSA asymmetric key system; IDEA, DES, and 3DES symmetric key systems; and the MD5 hash function. See Chapter 12 for more about cryptography. The current version is SSL 3.0. SSL 3.0 was standardized as TLS 1.0 and released in 1999.

Secure HyperText Transfer Protocol (S-HTTP)

Secure HyperText Transfer Protocol (S-HTTP) is an Internet protocol that provides a method for secure communications with a Web server. S-HTTP is a connectionless-oriented protocol that encapsulates data after security properties for the session have been successfully negotiated. It uses

✔ Symmetric encryption (for confidentiality)

✔ Message digests (for integrity)

✔ Public key encryption (for client-server authentication and nonrepudiation)

Rather than encrypting an entire session as in SSL, S-HTTP can be applied to individual Web documents. See Chapter 12 for more about cryptography.

Instant messaging

Instant messaging programs have become very popular on the Internet because of their ease of use and instantaneous communications capability. Examples include

- ✔ ICQ
- ✔ AIM
- ✔ MSN Messenger
- ✔ Yahoo! Messenger

Many vulnerabilities and security risks, such as the following, are associated with instant messaging programs:

- ✔ **Viruses and Trojan horses:** IM programs are quickly becoming a preferred medium for spreading malicious code.

- ✔ **Social engineering:** Many users are oblivious to the open nature of IM and very casually exchange personal, private, or sensitive information to unknown parties.

- ✔ **Shared files:** Many IM programs (and related programs) allow users to share their hard drives or transfer files.

- ✔ **Man-in-the-middle attacks:** Typically, no authentication or very weak authentication is used in IM programs. This makes them very susceptible to man-in-the-middle attacks.

  See Chapter 4 for more on attacks and malicious code.

- ✔ **Packet sniffing:** As with almost all TCP/IP traffic, IM sessions can easily be sniffed for valuable information and passwords.

Internet browsers

Internet browsers, such as Microsoft's Internet Explorer and Netscape Navigator, are the basic Web surfing tools with which we are all familiar. (Okay, there may be some Lynx holdouts or AOL-impaired users out there.) To enhance your Web surfing experience, many cool tools have been designed to deliver dynamic and interactive content beyond basic HTML. Of course, these features often come at a price — additional security risks. These tools and risks include

✔ **JavaScript:** JavaScript is a scripting language that was developed by Netscape to provide dynamic content for HTML Web pages. JavaScript has many known vulnerabilities that can, for example, reveal private information about a user or allow someone to read files on your local machine.

✔ **ActiveX and Java applets:** ActiveX and Java can make Web browsers do some pretty neat things — and some pretty nasty things. The security model for ActiveX is based on trust relationships. (You accept a digital certificate, and the applet is downloaded.) Java security is based on the concept of a *sandbox,* which restricts an applet to communicating only with the originating host and prevents the applet from directly accessing a PC's hard drive or other resources — theoretically.

✔ **Buffer Overflows:** Buffer overflows are perhaps the most common and easily perpetrated denial-of-service attacks today. Vulnerabilities in Web browsers (particularly Internet Explorer) can be exploited, causing a system to crash or, worse, giving an attacker unauthorized access to a system or directory. See Chapter 4 for more on buffer overflows.

✔ **Cookies:** A *cookie* is a simple text file message given to a Web browser by a Web server. The cookie stores personal information about the user and sends it back to the Web server the next time the user visits that Web site. This information might include name, address, date of birth, social security number, bank account information, credit card numbers, browsing history, demographic information, passwords — are you worried yet? Good. Although cookies cannot be used to spread viruses and cannot directly access your hard drive, I think that you'll agree — that's just too much important information being sent across the Internet in a plain text file.

✔ **CGI:** The Common Gateway Interface (CGI) is an Internet standard that provides dynamic content for Web sites. For example, by using CGI, a Web browser can be used to run a query on a server-side database. The security risk associated with this enhanced functionality is that you are allowing anyone on the Internet to execute a program on your server.

Prep Test

1 _____ is a proposed IETF standard for securely transmitting e-mail that uses the RSA asymmetric key system, digital signatures, and X.509 digital certificates.

A ○ MOSS
B ○ S/MIME
C ○ PGP
D ○ PEM

2 Which of these secure e-mail applications uses 3DES for encryption?

A ○ S/MIME
B ○ MOSS
C ○ PEM
D ○ PGP

3 PGP uses what algorithm for encryption?

A ○ IDEA
B ○ 3DES
C ○ DES
D ○ RSA

4 SSL operates at what layer of the OSI model?

A ○ Network
B ○ Transport
C ○ Session
D ○ Presentation

5 TLS 1.0 is the IETF standard of _____.

A ○ S-HTTP
B ○ SSH-2
C ○ SSL 2.0
D ○ SSL 3.0

6 _____ is a scripting language developed by Netscape to provide dynamic content for HTML Web pages.

A ○ JavaScript

B ○ Java

C ○ ActiveX

D ○ CGI

7 Java security is based on the concept of a _____.

A ○ backdoor

B ○ sandbox

C ○ trust relationship

D ○ sand lot

8 A _____ attack is a common denial-of-service attack used against Web browsers, causing them to crash or grant unauthorized access to files or other directories.

A ○ Spoofing

B ○ Social engineering

C ○ Man-in-the-middle

D ○ Buffer overflow

9 Simple text files that store information about a user and then transmit that information to a Web server are known as _____.

A ○ Java applets

B ○ ActiveX applets

C ○ Cookies

D ○ JavaScript

10 _____ is an Internet standard that can be used to allow Internet users to query a Web server database.

A ○ CGI

B ○ JavaScript

C ○ PGP

D ○ Cookies

Answers

1 **B**. S/MIME. The Secure Multipurpose Internet Mail Extensions (S/MIME) provides a secure method of sending e-mail and is incorporated in several browsers and e-mail applications. *Review "E-Mail Security."*

2 **C**. PEM. Privacy Enhanced Mail (PEM) provides confidentiality and authentication by using 3DES for encryption. *Review "E-Mail Security."*

3 **A**. IDEA. Pretty Good Privacy (PGP) uses the International Data Encryption Algorithm (IDEA) for encryption and the RSA algorithm for key distribution. *Review "E-Mail Security."*

4 **B**. Transport. The Secure Sockets Layer (SSL) protocol operates at the Transport Layer. *Review "Internet Security."*

5 **D**. SSL 3.0. SSL 3.0 was standardized by the IETF in TLS 1.0 and released in 1999 with only minor modifications. *Review "Internet Security."*

6 **A**. JavaScript. Because JavaScript is a scripting language, it cannot alter data on a hard drive, but it can be used to read files or other personal information on a local machine. *Review "Internet Security."*

7 **B**. Sandbox. A sandbox restricts a java applet to communicating only with the original host from which the applet was downloaded and prevents the applet from directly accessing a PC's hard drive or memory. *Review "Internet Security."*

8 **D**. Buffer overflow. Spoofing, social engineering, and man-in-the-middle attacks are not denial-of-service attacks. *Review "Internet Security."*

9 **C**. Cookies. Java and ActiveX are both *applets* (small programs), not simple text files. JavaScript is a scripting language that creates dynamic content on a Web page. *Review "Internet Security."*

10 **A**. CGI. The Common Gateway Interface (CGI) provides dynamic content for Web sites by allowing an Internet user to execute a program or query on the Web server. *Review "Internet Security."*

Chapter 7

File Transfer and Directory Services

*T*his chapter discusses some of the common file transfer protocols. Next, we'll explore common file systems to get an understanding of how files and directories are stored on disks. Finally, we'll have a look at two common and widely used directory services, DNS and LDAP.

Quick Assessment

1   S/FTP uses _____ to encrypt packets.

2   The file transfer program that lacks authentication is _____.

3   FAT stands for _____.

4   The file system feature where every disk write is recorded is known as _____.

5   Domain Name Service is a directory service that converts domain names into _____.

6   Active Directory is a commercial implementation of _____.

7   NFS is an example of a _____ file system.

8   The principal weakness in FTP is that userids, passwords, and transmitted data travel over the network _____.

9   Windows file sharing is an example of _____ file sharing.

10   _____ allows a file system to occupy more than one physical disk.

Answers

1   SSL. *Review "File Transfer — S/FTP."*

2   TFTP, or Trivial File Transfer Protocol. *See "File Transfer — TFTP."*

3   File Allocation Table. *See "File Systems."*

4   Transaction logging. *Review "File Systems."*

5   IP addresses. *Learn more in the section on "Directory Services."*

6   LDAP. *See "Directory Services."*

7   Virtual. *See "File Systems."*

8   Unencrypted. *Review "File Transfer."*

9   Peer-to-peer. *See "File Transfer."*

10   Disk spanning. *See "File Systems."*

File Transfer

The term *file transfer* refers to any of several tools and procedures that are used to copy or move files from one computer to another. File transfer is not a fleeting activity, but one of the activities that is central to Information Technology. In fact, networks were invented because people wanted to transfer files from one computer to another, without having to resort to slow media like magnetic tape, punch cards, or removable disk packs.

In this section, we'll discuss FTP in its various forms, TFTP, Windows file sharing, and vulnerabilities present in all of these protocols.

FTP

FTP, or File Transfer Protocol, is the original method used to transfer files over a network from one computer to another. FTP was so well designed that it is still in wide use more than twenty years since its inception.

FTP is a client-server tool. In order to use FTP to copy files from one computer to another, one of the computers must be running an FTP server program. Without it, the FTP client will be unable to function.

FTP was originally a command-line tool. When FTP was written, there were no GUI interfaces — no Windows (X or Microsoft). While the command-line FTP interface is still widely available and supported (you'll find it on the latest Windows and UNIX systems), it is also used "under the covers" in many GUI interfaces and functions. For instance, many Web site downloads use the FTP protocol. Many Web site authoring tools employ FTP in order to transfer newly created or modified Web pages to the Web server. The most commonly used FTP commands are discussed later in this section.

FTP server

FTP file transfers cannot take place unless an FTP server program is running. Typically an FTP server program is run on a server where it is expected that one or more persons will be uploading and/or downloading files to/from the server.

Other than some configuration settings (which are typically stored in a file), the FTP server requires no human interaction — it runs unattended. An FTP server program is usually started when the system is booted, and the FTP server program just sits there and waits for an FTP client to connect to it and request file uploads or downloads. Until then, the FTP server program just sits, and sits, and sits. . . .

FTP client

FTP clients are where all the action is. In the command-driven mode, a person starts an FTP session by running an FTP client program. The person would then request a session be opened to a particular system that has a running FTP server. Next, the person would type in commands that will initiate uploads or downloads of one or more files. Figure 7-1 shows the FTP client server architecture.

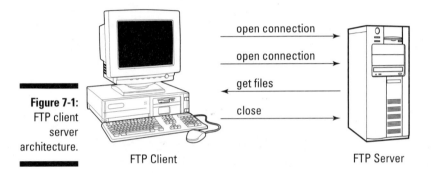

open connection

open connection

get files

close

Figure 7-1:
FTP client
server
architecture.

FTP Client   FTP Server

FTP access control

When initiating an FTP session to a server, you will be required to enter a userid and password before the session will be opened. If you do not have a userid and password on the server, you will not be able to open a session, unless the FTP server is configured for *Anonymous FTP* access, which is discussed later in this chapter.

FTP commands

For any readers new to the command line FTP program, our advice is this: Think DOS. Recall the simple tools such as *cd*, *dir*, *mkdir*, and *del*. These commands are used by FTP for basic navigation and file processing.

If you're not old enough to remember DOS, never mind.

- ✔ open *sitename*. This opens an FTP session between the client and the server *sitename*. You will be required to enter a userid and password.

- ✔ cd *directory*. This changes the current working directory to *directory*. If *directory* is blank, this displays the current working directory.

- ✔ dir *filespec*. This lists all files matching *filespec* located at the current directory.

- ✔ mkdir *directory*. This creates the directory *directory*, to be located in the current working directory.

- ✔ del *filespec*. This deletes the file(s) *filespec*.

✔ get *filespec*. This copies files *filespec* from the FTP server to the FTP client.

✔ mget *filespec*. This copies files *filespec* from the FTP server to the FTP client. Wildcard characters may be used.

✔ put *filespec*. This copies files *filespec* from the FTP client to the FTP server, to be located in the server's current working directory.

✔ mput *filespec*. This copies files *filespec* from the FTP client to the FTP server, to be located in the server's current working directory. Wildcard characters may be used.

✔ close. This terminates the FTP session between client and server. The FTP client program continues to run and awaits the next command.

✔ quit. This terminates the FTP session between client and server, and also terminates the FTP client program. Figure 7-2 is an example of the client window.

```
Ftp                                                          _ □ X
ftp> open ftp.geocities.com
Connected to ftp.geocities.com.
220-Welcome to the Yahoo! Web Hosting FTP server.
220-Need help? Get all details at:
220-http://help.yahoo.com/help/us/webhosting/gftp/
220-
220-No anonymous logins accepted.
220 Yahoo!
User (ftp.geocities.com:(none)): petergregory
331-Enter your Yahoo! member password
331
Password:
230-You are using 5.3% of your subscribed disk space
230 You have 23.666 MB of space available
ftp> _
```

Figure 7-2:
FTP client.

FTP access control

The userid and password does not just permit FTP to track who is permitted to access the FTP server, but are used to control which files and directories a user is permitted to create, view, alter, and remove. FTP lets the underlying operating system enforce file and directory access control as though the user were using a DOS or shell window right there on the server. If, for example, a given user is not permitted to create a directory in a given location, then FTP will likewise prohibit the operation.

Anonymous FTP

One of the disadvantages of FTP is the requirement for each user to have a userid and password on the server. While this may be reasonable in an organization, using FTP for public use is infeasible because every user must have a userid and password.

For this reason, anonymous FTP was created. Anonymous FTP permits someone without a userid and password to be able to connect to an FTP server and initiate a file transfer session. In the place of a userid, the word "ftp" or "anonymous" is entered, and instead of a password, the user enters his or her e-mail address.

Anonymous FTP is used to permit unauthenticated users to connect to the server.

Anonymous FTP enjoyed wide popularity in FTP "sites" (predating the World Wide Web, although FTP sites are still in use today) where anyone on the Internet could download or upload files.

An FTP server must be specifically configured to use anonymous access; it generally will not come this way "out of the box". Further, FTP servers are not configured to do userid/password or anonymous access., A regular FTP server, admitting users based on userid and password, can be configured to permit access by anonymous users.

Recall that regular FTP uses the directory, and file permissions associated with the userid and password are used to initiate the session. Likewise, anonymous FTP restricts anonymous users to a particular directory or directories, and can be configured to permit only uploads or only downloads, depending upon the server's needs. Figure 7-3 shows an FTP session.

```
 Ftp                                                          _ □ ×
ftp> open garbo.uwasa.fi
Connected to garbo.uwasa.fi.
220->
220->        @@@@                      @@@
220->       @@ @@                      @@
220->       @@        @@@@     @@ @@@   @@         @@@@
220->       @@           @@    @@@ @@   @@@@@     @@ @@
220->       @@ @@@     @@@@@    @@  @@   @@ @@     @@ @@
220->       @@  @@    @@  @@    @@  @@   @@  @@    @@ @@
220->        @@@@@     @@@ @    @@ @@@   @@  @@     @@@@
220->
220-> Welcome to Garbo ftp archives at the University of Vaasa, Finland!
220->
220-> Login as 'anonymous' and give your email address as the password.
220-> Also the first part (like joe@) will do (but use yours, *NOT* joe@).
220->
220-> If you have problems please see http://www.uwasa.fi/~ts/garbo.html#faq
220-
220-> You can log to Garbo also by http://garbo.uwasa.fi/
220-
220 garbo.uwasa.fi FTP server (Version wu-2.6.1(1) Fri Nov 30 11:46:11 EET 2001>
 ready.
User (garbo.uwasa.fi:(none>):
```

Figure 7-3:
Anonymous
FTP session.

S/FTP

FTP was written in a kindler, gentler time when system administrators could feel safe with their doors unlocked. But gangs have moved into the Internet neighborhood, and the vulnerabilities associated with FTP are no longer acceptable for many uses. Secure FTP eliminates these vulnerabilities through some changes that make it more secure than FTP.

Secure FTP, written as S/FTP or SFTP, was developed in order to address some of FTP's security deficiencies (for a complete description see "Vulnerabilities," at the end of this section). S/FTP uses SSL (Secure Socket Layer) technology to encrypt the entire file transfer session, which prevents anyone with a network sniffer from being able to capture the userid/password pair or the transferred files.

S/FTP uses SSL to encrypt and protect all data in transit.

S/FTP is not presently packaged with Windows or Unix systems, but it is easily added on. Of course, it will only be really effective when the FTP server also supports the S/FTP protocol. Otherwise, the S/FTP client will revert back to plain FTP. Figure 7-4 shows an S/FTP session.

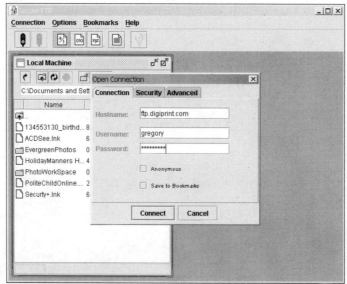

Figure 7-4:
S/FTP
session.

TFTP

Depending on whom you talk to and where you look, TFTP stands for Trivial File Transfer Protocol or Trivial File Transfer Program. It is so-called because the protocol is similar to, but simpler than, FTP. The primary difference between TFTP and FTP is that TFTP uses no authentication.

TFTP was also written in the Internet's very early days when you could walk around at night and leave your doors unlocked, open, and maybe even off their hinges. (Today, many people think that a system administrator running TFTP might be off his or her hinge.)

Thankfully, TFTP is not included in Windows systems, although most Unix systems still include it (although disabled by default).

Windows file sharing

Unlike FTP and TFTP, which are client-server tools, Windows file sharing is a peer-to-peer tool. Any Windows system can act like a file server and make any portion of its file system available to any other system on the network. Any person on the network can "browse" the network (by exploring Network Neighborhood and drilling down everything that can be found) looking for "shares" (directories or printers that are shared — made available — for others to find and use). Figure 7-5 shows an example of peer-to-peer Windows file sharing.

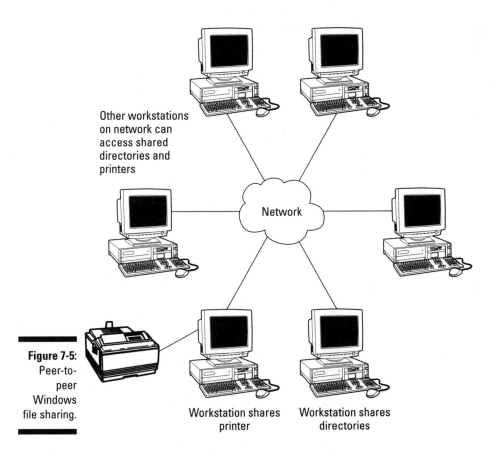

Other workstations on network can access shared directories and printers

Network

Figure 7-5:
Peer-to-peer Windows file sharing.

Workstation shares printer

Workstation shares directories

Sharing directories and printers

Sharing files and printers on a Windows system is easy; in Windows Explorer, just right-click on a directory or printer and click *Sharing*. Select the appropriate values from the *Properties, Sharing* dialog box, as shown in Figure 7-6. If sharing is turned on, then soon other users on the network will be able to see and access the share.

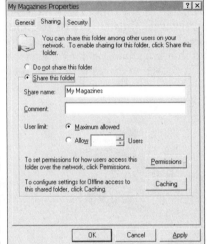

Figure 7-6:
Sharing
directories
and printers.

Accessing shared directories and printers

Finding, viewing, and accessing directories and printers that other systems have shared is even easier than sharing them. In Windows, the Windows Explorer tool is used to locate and access shared directories and printers.

To begin, double-click *Network Neighborhood*. (It may be called *My Network Places* or something else, depending upon the version of Windows you are using and whether you or someone else has changed the name of the icon.)

Inside Network Neighborhood, you will probably see an *Entire Network* icon, and perhaps one or more *Domains* (groups of computers), computers, or even shares you have recently or frequently used. Like someone who is a clumsy typist, you might have to hunt and peck to find what you are looking for, double-clicking an icon here, expanding another one there, until you tire of looking or find something interesting. Figure 7-7 shows an example.

Be very careful when exploring the network: If you accidentally delete someone else's computer or even the entire network, you could set the organization back days or weeks until the network administrators can restore everything (that is, if they ever backed it up in the first place).

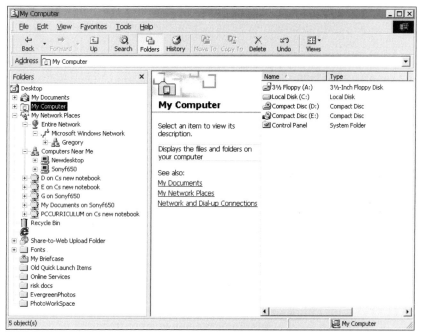

Figure 7-7:
Accessing
shared
directories
and printers.

If you routinely need to access another system's directory, you can create a shortcut to that directory on your system, or you can map it to a drive letter. This will give you a convenient way to access the other system's directory without having to browse for it every time you need it.

Much ado about peer-to-peer file sharing

Many a CIO and IT Manager are up in arms about Windows peer-to-peer file sharing, as though it were a plague about to descend upon them and gobble up all of their free disk space.

The concerns that IT Management have about peer-to-peer file sharing are actually rooted in common sense. IT Managers are afraid that ordinary computers will share files or directories that many other employees become dependent upon. If the employee(s) sharing the directories has a problem with his or her computer, then suddenly the other employees can be up a creek.

IT Managers really want only their production file servers to share directories, and here is why: The IT department can build file servers that are far more reliable, sophisticated, and robust than notebooks or desktop workstations. By using advanced technology, such as RAID (Redundant Array of Independent Disks) and SAN (Storage Area Network), the IT department can virtually guarantee that all shared files will always be there, and that they will be backed up regularly (once per day or perhaps even more often). There is no way that an IT department can guarantee this kind of availability from desktop or notebook systems.

If you routinely need to use another system's shared printer, you can likewise set up printing on your system by right-clicking the shared printer and adding it to your own system.

Vulnerabilities

Most forms of over-the-network file transfer have serious security vulnerabilities that you should be aware of prior to use. We'll discuss some of the more common vulnerabilities here.

FTP

FTP requires a userid and password in order to set up the session. The userid and password that the user types in is sent over the network "in the clear," meaning that it is not encrypted. Anyone with a network sniffer can detect and record that userid and password and possibly use it later to break in to the FTP server.

In addition to the userid and password being sent over the network in the clear, the entire contents of all transferred files is likewise sent in the clear. While this may be inconsequential if you are transferring patches from one system to another over the corporate LAN, this is a serious matter if you are transferring a customer file containing credit card numbers over the Internet.

Secure FTP addresses both of these vulnerabilities by encrypting the entire session using SSL.

Anonymous FTP

In addition to the vulnerabilities described earlier about FTP, Anonymous FTP has a serious deficiency: there is no way to tell who is connecting to the FTP server. All anonymous users type in the same userid: **ftp** (or **anonymous**), and in the password field they type in their e-mail address. The problem with this is that the e-mail address is not verified — and even if it could be, there is still no way to know whether the person who typed in the e-mail address is actually the person associated with it.

The origin of "sneakernet"

The term "sneakernet" has its roots in the need to transfer files from one computer to another when faster and more convenient means, such as networks or null modem cables, were unavailable.

Picture it: You copy files to a diskette, remove the diskette, walk across the room or down the hall (wearing your sneakers), insert the diskette in the destination computer, and copy the file(s) from the diskette to the destination computer.

TFTP

If you think that FTP is unsecure, TFTP is far worse. TFTP has no provision for authentication: If you know that a system is running a TFTP server, then you can connect to it by using TFTP and download whatever files are available. And like FTP, everything is transferred over the network in the clear.

TFTP uses no form of authentication.

Windows file sharing

Windows file sharing presents primarily procedural vulnerabilities. Because Windows systems are in the hands of users who probably have no formal system administration training or experience, frequently directories can be shared with no access control whatsoever. It is easiest to set up a share that requires no userid and password — anyone on the network who can explore the network and find the shares can read — and perhaps even write — any shared files.

File Systems

A file system is the system that the computer operating system and application programs use to access files on the computer. Disks are comprised of tracks, cylinders, clusters, and sectors, but we humans like to think of disks as hierarchical collections of files and directories. The file system provides the translation from bits and bytes to files and directories.

It is difficult to put one's finger on a file system — and not because a system's hard disk is sealed — but because a file system is somewhat intangible. A file system is an architecture — a method — of writing to and reading from a hard drive, floppy drive, or CD-ROM. Figure 7-8 is an example.

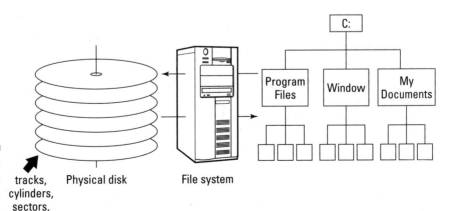

Figure 7-8: File systems make sense of disks.

tracks, cylinders, sectors, clusters

Physical disk

File system

One easy way to describe various file systems is by their characteristics and by the kinds of media they are used on. In this chapter, we'll describe some of the more commonly used file systems: FAT, FAT32, NTFS, ISO 9660, and NFS.

FAT and FAT32

FAT, which stands for File Allocation Table, is the original DOS and Windows file system. Over the years, newer versions of FAT, called FAT12, FAT16, and VFAT, were developed, with each version improving performance and reliability.

The FAT32 file system, first available in Windows 95, OSR2, and Windows 98, contained significant improvements in performance and efficiency. FAT32 supports disks up to 2 Terabytes in size.

The FAT and FAT32 file systems have no security features. Files and directories have no concept of ownership or permissions, aside from *read-only* and whether they are *hidden* or not. While adequate for a personal computer, FAT and FAT32 would never do in a production-computing environment where even the most rudimentary security procedures are in place.

NTFS

Short for NT File System, NTFS contains a number of significant advances that gave Windows NT systems a shot at real production computing.

The NTFS file system performs transaction journaling, a feature that increases the reliability of the file system.

NTFS supports the notion of assigning an *owner* to a file or directory, as well as *permissions* specifying what the owner — and others — are permitted to do with the file or directory (read, write, delete, and so on).

NTFS also supports transaction logging, which is to say that every change made to any file or directory is independently logged to another part of the file system. This feature helps a system administrator recover a damaged file system.

Finally, NTFS added *disk spanning*, which permits a single NTFS file system to occupy more than one physical disk.

NFS

NFS, or Network File System, is one of several types of *virtual file systems*. While NFS is primarily used by Unix systems, there have been NFS clients available for DOS and Windows systems for many years.

NFS is a client-server mechanism that provides for the *appearance* of a server's file system on a client system. By this, we mean that all application programs and utilities on an NFS client, when accessing files and directories over the network from the NFS server, actually believe that those files and directories are physically present on the client system. The fact that those files and directories actually exist on another system (the NFS server) is hidden from applications and tools.

NFS supports the notion of file ownership and access permissions, although mapping NFS access permissions to a Windows system is not trivial, because older versions of Windows lack enforceable and reliable user authentication.

NFS is not really much different from peer-to-peer file sharing; functionally they are equivalent.

Directory Services

As networks and the number of computers attached to them grows, it becomes painfully evident to those administering the network that some sort of centralized directory of people, computers, and other resources is needed.

Imagine for a moment a telephone system in a very small town. It is enough for each resident to have a sheet of paper containing the phone numbers of the other people they frequently call. But as the town and the number of telephone subscribers grows, it becomes increasingly difficult for each resident to keep track of everyone else's phone numbers.

The telephone directory solved this problem. The telephone book was *the* directory that everyone used to look up telephone numbers of other residents, and businesses too.

And so it is with computers, networks, e-mail, and music piracy. A central directory makes it easy for people (and applications) to find the other people and resources they need.

Domain name service (DNS)

DNS is the Internet-wide directory service that permits people to find computers — and computers to find each other — without having to work directly with their IP addresses. Let's look at some background information first.

Computers like to communicate over networks using their IP addresses (an example IP address is 192.168.16.31), but with the explosion of client-server computing such as the World Wide Web on the Internet, IP addresses just won't do for humans. Are you more likely to remember 65.54.248.222 or www.microsoft.com?

DNS is a network service that can look up a system name and return an IP address.

DNS structure

DNS has a hierarchical structure not unlike file systems. (We'll end the similarities here.) At the top of the hierarchy is dot (the "." character), usually called "root." The layer below root is the collection of "top level domains" such as .com, .net, .edu, .mil, .gov, .info, and so forth, as shown in Figure 7-9. This topmost level of DNS domains is maintained by a core group of organizations.

The next layer of domains consists of the individual domains owned by corporations, governments, educational institutions, and so forth.

Each layer in the DNS hierarchy has a set of DNS servers. Each server has a special software application called BIND (short for Berkeley Internet Name Daemon — yes there's interesting history behind the name, but for Security+ you don't need to know). If you're curious, look up BIND using your favorite search engine.

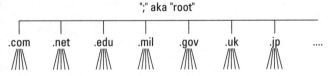

Figure 7-9:
DNS
hierarchy.

DNS lookups

Whether you know it or not, you use DNS every time you send e-mail or use your Web browser. Here are a couple of examples.

Web browsing use of DNS

You want to browse to www.comptia.org.

1. You type **www.comptia.org** into your Web browser.

2. Your browser creates a DNS lookup query asking, in effect, "at which IP address can I find the server named www.comptia.org?" and sends that query to the DNS server whose IP address can be found in the PC's network configuration.

3. That DNS server receives the query from the PC. If someone else recently asked the DNS server where www.comptia.org is, it may have the query and answer cached, in which case it can send the cached

answer directly back to the PC, and the DNS query is complete. If that DNS server does not have the answer cached, then the DNS server must get the answer itself.

4. The DNS server creates a query and sends it to one of the root DNS servers, asking, "Who is the .org DNS server?" The root server will return an answer. Chances are the DNS server has this information cached, so that it will probably not have to actually make this query.

5. The DNS server asks the .com DNS server which DNS server is responsible for the comptia.org domain and receives an answer.

6. The DNS server then asks the comptia.org DNS server for the IP address for the system named www.comptia.org. The comptia.org DNS server will return the result.

7. The DNS server will return the result back to the originating PC.

8. The PC's Web browser will now open an HTTP session directly to the CompTIA Web server using its IP address. The CompTIA Web server will return HTML content that will be displayed on your browser.

All of this will take place within just a few seconds. Figure 7-10 illustrates this query graphically.

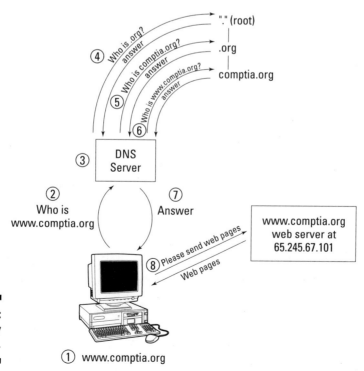

Figure 7-10:
DNS query
details.

Sending e-mail use of DNS

You want to send mail to your friend; his e-mail address is `gofish@yahoo.com`.

1. Your mail message is forwarded to an SMTP (Simple Mail Transfer Protocol — read more about SMTP in Chapter 6) server.

2. The SMTP server examines the destination address — in particular the portion to the right of the "@" sign. In this case, `yahoo.com`.

3. The SMTP server creates a DNS lookup query. Unlike the previous Web client example, in this case the SMTP server needs to know the name of the "mail exchanger" for `yahoo.com`. A mail exchange is a name that means the name of the destination SMTP server for `yahoo.com`.

4. The SMTP server sends the DNS query to a DNS server and receives the answer, `smtp.mail.yahoo.com`. Now the SMTP server knows the name of the system that it needs to send the message to, but it still needs to know its IP address.

5. The SMTP server creates a new query, this time asking for the IP address of `smtp.mail.yahoo.com`. It sends the query to the DNS server and receives a response.

Like in the first example, it is likely that the SMTP server will have to make several queries in order to arrive at the final answer to the query, what is the name of the mail exchanger for `yahoo.com`. Those intermediate steps have been omitted from this second example.

6. Finally, the SMTP server has the IP address for `smtp.mail.yahoo.com`. It can open an SMTP session with that server and send the mail message to it.

LDAP

LDAP, or Lightweight Directory Access Protocol, is a directory service that, on the surface, is not much different from Domain Name Service (DNS). However, LDAP is used primarily as a directory for *people* and secondarily for resources — whereas DNS is used only for resources.

LDAP is used to store information about individuals in an organization.

LDAP structure

LDAP traces its origins in X.400, a feature-rich and complex directory access protocol that did not see much commercial use. X.400 was too large and cumbersome, and it came ten years too soon. LDAP, a simpler version of X.400, is easier to manage, and it arrived on the scene just in time.

Also like DNS, LDAP has a hierarchical structure, with a "root" at the top of the hierarchy. Next in the hierarchy are the world's countries, and below that, organizations, then organizational units, which can be departments or locations.

At the "bottom" of the LDAP hierarchy are the records about people. Within each people record, there are many fields, such as the person's surname (last name), given name (first name), contact information (address, phone numbers, e-mail address, and so on), and organization information (title, supervisor's name, department name, and so on). People records can also contain security information such as a password (encrypted of course!), digital certificate, and authorization information (details on which applications — and functions within them — that a person is permitted to access or perform).

LDAP uses: Computer and application authentication

Larger organizations are likely to have hundreds, or even thousands, of servers and applications, built upon a variety of computing platforms and operating systems. The function called User Account Management — the task of managing user accounts on all of these systems — can be very challenging in larger organizations. It can be next-to-impossible to accurately know which employees have access to which applications and information when each platform and application has its own authentication database.

LDAP is the best bet for handling the complex problem of user account management. With each passing year, more and more computing platforms, operating systems, and major applications are supporting LDAP as the method for authenticating users logging in to e-mail, applications, and file servers.

If you are not yet convinced, or if the lights just have not yet come on, just compare environments with and without LDAP in the following list.

Scenario	With LDAP	Without LDAP
New Employee	Add one new record to LDAP.	Add records into all computers and applications.
Employee Name Change	Change name in LDAP.	Change name in every computer and application.
Employee Changes Positions Within the Organization	Change access permissions in LDAP.	Change access permissions on all computers and applications.

(continued)

Scenario	With LDAP	Without LDAP
Terminated Employee	Remove one record from LDAP.	Remove records from all computers and applications.
Determine access privileges for an employee	Examine LDAP record.	Examine access records in all computers and applications.
Send e-mail to employee	Look up employee's e-mail address in LDAP.	Look up employee's e-mail address in a dedicated database.

LDAP uses: Employee directories

LDAP is also very effective as a "white pages" resource. Larger organizations can find it difficult and expensive to create yet another application that functions as the employee database for looking up employees to find their phone number, location, or e-mail address. The organization that implements LDAP for server and application authentication can also use the very same LDAP database for white pages.

Commercial uses of LDAP

LDAP is finding its way into commercial products sold by Oracle, IBM, Sun, Microsoft, Novell, and many others. Perhaps the best-known implementations of LDAP are Microsoft's AD (Active Directory) and Novell's NDS (Novell Directory Service), both of which are standard LDAP with some proprietary extensions.

Prep Test

1 Which file transfer protocol lacks any authentication?

A ○ FTP
B ○ TFTP
C ○ SFTP
D ○ AFTP

2 Which of the following file transfer methods is NOT client-server?

A ○ FTP
B ○ S/FTP
C ○ TFTP
D ○ Windows file sharing

3 Which of the following file system types is NOT physical?

A ○ NTFS
B ○ FAT16
C ○ FAT12
D ○ NFS

4 Only the _____ file system supports access permissions.

A ○ FAT12
B ○ NTFS
C ○ VFAT
D ○ LDAP

5 What is the role of DNS in the process of a Web client communication to a Web server?

A ○ DNS plays no role in Web communication.
B ○ DNS finds the shortest path to the Web server.
C ○ DNS looks up host name and returns IP address.
D ○ DNS looks up IP address and returns host name.

6 NFS is known as a _____.

A ○ Real file system
B ○ Virtual file system
C ○ Physical file system
D ○ Passive file system

7 **Microsoft Active Directory is a commercial instance of** _____.

A ○ DNS

B ○ SMTP

C ○ X.500

D ○ LDAP

8 **One of the major vulnerabilities of FTP is** _____.

A ○ Userid and password are sent in the clear.

B ○ Data is sent in the clear.

C ○ Userid, password, and data are sent in the clear.

D ○ E-mail addresses are unverifiable.

9 **Secure FTP uses which protocol?**

A ○ LDAP

B ○ SSL

C ○ PGP

D ○ TFTP

Answers

1 **B.** TFTP. Trivial File Transfer Protocol has no authentication provisions at all. *Review "File Transfer."*

2 **D.** Windows file sharing. Windows file sharing is peer-to-peer, while FTP, S/FTP, and TFTP are all client-server based. Review *"File Transfer."*

3 **D.** NFS. NFS is a virtual file system type. *Review "File Systems."*

4 **B.** NTFS. Prior to NTFS, Windows file systems did not have any user access security features. *Review "File Systems."*

5 **C.** DNS looks up host name and returns IP address. DNS is used to translate a known host name into an IP address to which a Web client can initiate communications. *Review "Directory Services."*

6 **B.** Virtual file system. An NFS-based file system is not present on the client computer, but instead it resides on a server. *Review "File Systems."*

7 **D.** LDAP. Microsoft's Active Directory has, at its heart, an LDAP database. *Review "Directory Services."*

8 **C.** Userid, password, and data are sent in the clear. FTP does not encrypt any transmitted data. The userid and password, as well as all transferred data, are sent over networks in the clear. *Review "File Transfer."*

9 **B.** SSL. Secure FTP transports all data over the network using SSL. *Review "File Transfer."*

Chapter 8

Wireless LANs

● ●

In This Chapter

▶ Defining the WAP and WTLS protocols

▶ Identifying the 802.11a, 802.11b, and 802.11g standards

▶ Designing Ad-hoc and infrastructure networks

▶ Understanding Wired Equivalent Privacy (WEP) and its weaknesses

● ●

*A*hhh, the freedom of wireless! After you've experienced it, you'll never look back! The explosive growth of wireless networks rivals that of the Internet several years ago. But in the rush to deploy wireless networks, organizations are introducing enormous vulnerabilities into their networks, vulnerabilities that they have previously not seen. Many vendors of various wireless products have been all too willing to play to this market, making default installations of their products as simple as possible (and thus wide open to attack). Indeed, the various security standards associated with the wireless revolution even have inherent flaws that must be addressed to ensure that our information and information systems are secure.

Quick Assessment

1   _____ is the security layer in WAP, providing confidentiality, integrity, and authentication.

2   WTLS is based on _____ .

3   _____ is the protocol standard for wireless LANs at data rates up to 11 Mbps.

4   _____ and _____ are the protocol standards for wireless LANs at data rates up to 54 Mbps.

5   The two wireless network configurations defined in the 802.11 standard are _____ and _____ .

6   The SSID is a _____-character identifier that uniquely identifies a WLAN.

7   WEP operates at which two layers of the OSI model?

8   WEP uses what encryption algorithm?

9   EAP is an authentication protocol that is an extension of what protocol?

10 _____ uses EAP to provide authentication and key management.

Answers

1   WTLS. *See "WAP and WTLS."*

2   TLS v1.0. *Review "WAP and WTLS."*

3   802.11b. *Review "802.11x."*

4   802.11a and 802.11g. *See "802.11x."*

5   Ad-hoc and infrastructure. *See "802.11x."*

6   32. *See "SSID."*

7   Physical and Data Link. *See "Wired Equivalent Privacy (WEP)."*

8   RC4. *See "Wired Equivalent Privacy (WEP)."*

9   PPP. *See "Extensible Authentication Protocol (EAP)."*

10   802.1x. *See "Extensible Authentication Protocol (EAP)."*

WAP and WTLS

The Wireless Application Protocol (WAP) was developed to provide specifications for applications that are used over wireless network devices, such as mobile phones, pagers, and PDAs. WAP is supported by all modern operating systems and is optimized for the Wireless Markup Language (WML), although it is capable of supporting HTML as well.

Wireless Transport Layer Security (WTLS) provides confidentiality, integrity, and authentication for WAP-enabled devices. WTLS requires that both the client and server be authenticated with each other, and the entire session is encrypted. WTLS is based on TLS v1.0 (Transport Layer Security) but with several modifications needed to support a wireless environment. See Chapter 6 for more on SSL/TLS (Secure Sockets Layer/Transport Layer Security).

802.11x

The IEEE 802 standards define a group of networking standards. (See Chapter 2 for more on the IEEE 802 standards.) Wireless LAN technology is defined in 802.11. The current 802.11 specifications include

- **802.11:** Applies to wireless at data rates of 1 or 2 Mbps.

- **802.11a:** Applies to wireless LANs at data rates up to 54 Mbps.

- **802.11b (or):** Applies to wireless LANS at data rates up to 11 Mbps. Currently the most widely implemented wireless standard.

- **802.11g:** Wireless LANs at data rates up to 54 Mbps. Still in development, but it is potentially easier to upgrade from 802.11b to 802.11g than from 802.11b to 802.11a because it operates in the same frequency range as 802.11b (2.4Ghz for 802.11b versus 5Ghz for 802.11a).

The 802.11 standard also proposes two different network configurations:

- **Ad-hoc.** Wireless clients communicate with each other directly; there is no fixed access point (AP) or gateway, as shown in Figure 8-1.

- **Infrastructure.** Wireless clients communicate with an access point that functions as a bridge between the wireless client and the wireless (or wired) network, as shown in Figure 8-2.

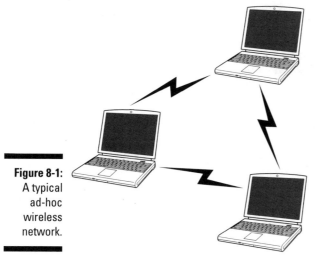

Figure 8-1:
A typical
ad-hoc
wireless
network.

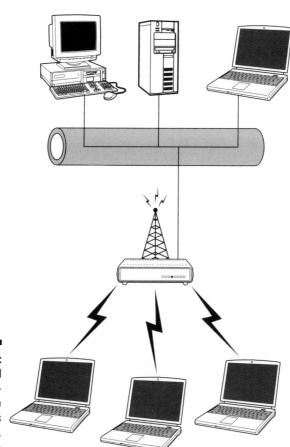

Figure 8-2:
A typical
Infrastruc-
ture
wireless
network.

SSID

The Service Set Identifier (SSID) is a 32-character identifier that uniquely identifies a WLAN. (The SSID can be thought of as a network name.) The SSID allows a wireless client to distinguish between different WLANs. In order to connect to a specific WLAN, the wireless client must use the same SSID that the WLAN uses. The SSID is sometimes treated as a password, and sadly, this is as far as many organizations go in securing their wireless networks. However, the SSID is transmitted in plain text and is broadcast by default on many access points. Therefore, matching the SSID is simply a matter of selecting the one you want from the list of available options! As a basic security setting, the broadcast mode can be disabled on a WAP, which prevents the SSID from being openly advertised.

Wired Equivalent Privacy (WEP)

Wired Equivalent Privacy (WEP) is a security protocol that, as its name implies, is supposed to provide the same level of security as is found on a wired LAN. Because a wired LAN can be somewhat protected by physical structures and limited access to the cable media, it is inherently more secure than a wireless LAN, which uses radio waves as the transmission medium. Although radio waves are range limited, they are capable of penetrating walls, and thus can be accessed by attackers outside the physical security perimeter of an organization using techniques commonly referred to as *war driving* and *parking lot attacks*. This involves roaming around with a small powered antenna looking for SSIDs that your wireless card detects. In many cases, attackers can then simply select an SSID and begin surfing an unsecured network!

The WEP protocol implementation itself is flawed; this flaw has been the major source of WLAN security's woes. WEP depends on a shared key between the client device and the access point. As a matter of practicality, most organizations use a single shared key for all client devices and access points. Shared keys are typically implemented without any key management functions necessary to ensure that a key remains secure and is not compromised.

WEP operates at the Physical and Data Link Layers of the OSI model (see Chapter 2 for more on the OSI model), thus WEP can only provide link encryption of data that is transmitted between wireless devices, such as a client PC and an access point (AP). This situation makes the data susceptible to vulnerabilities in link encryption, such as compromise of systems between end devices (in particular, at the AP when going from the wireless to wired network or vice versa).

WEP uses the RC4 encryption algorithm (see Chapter 13), a CRC-32 integrity check field, and a 24-bit Initialization Vector (IV). RC4 is a stream cipher (see Chapter 13), which is susceptible to statistical analysis attacks. The more often a given key is used, the more likely it is to be compromised. I have already mentioned the lack of key management functions in WEP, which plays right into the hands of this type of attack. The CRC-32 integrity check is a basic check sum that is commonly used in data communications and is also subject to compromise and modification, making the integrity of the data suspect. Finally, the 24-bit IV is comprised of a relatively small key space and is transmitted in plain text. Therefore, it is inevitable that the IV will be reused in a relatively short period of time (a matter of hours), making the WEP key further susceptible to statistical attack.

Extensible Authentication Protocol (EAP)

The Extensible Authentication Protocol (EAP) is an extension to the Point-to-Point Protocol (PPP) defined in RFC 2284. *EAP* is a flexible authentication protocol that supports various authentication methods, including MD5-challenge, S/Key (see Chapter 3), token cards, smart cards, digital certificates, Kerberos, and one-time passwords. In a wireless LAN using EAP, a user authenticates to an authentication server (such as RADIUS) via an AP before being granted access to the network.

802.1x is (yet) another IEEE standard (not to be confused with 802.11x) that utilizes EAP for authentication and key management. 802.1x can be implemented to generate encryption and authentication keys periodically to improve security on the wireless network.

Site Surveys

As with any major network installation, careful planning is critical to success. Special considerations for installing a wireless network include the following:

- **Throughput requirements:** What type of applications will users be accessing across the wireless network? Will 11 Mbps be sufficient, or will a higher rate be necessary? Also, remember your actual throughput will probably be somewhat less than the standard (that's *up to* 11 Mbps).
- **Coverage:** Where is coverage required?

✔ **Mobility:** Do users need continuous coverage as they roam?

✔ **Environmental considerations:** What factors may affect signal quality and range? What is the office layout (open: cubicles, or closed: offices)?

✔ **Security:** What security mechanisms will be implemented and how? What effect will such mechanisms have on performance? Are the security mechanisms adequate?

Finally, as part of your site survey, you should do actual performance measurements of the wireless network. You should measure actual area coverage, data throughput, and signal quality, determine optimum locations and numbers of access points (APs), and assess actual performance of applications on the wireless network.

Prep Test

1 WTLS provides all of the following for WAP-enabled devices, except:

A ○ Confidentiality

B ○ Integrity

C ○ Authentication

D ○ Availability

2 The 802.11b standard applies to wireless LAN's at data rates up to _____.

A ○ 1 or 2 Mbps

B ○ 11 Mbps

C ○ 54 Mbps

D ○ 100 Mbps

3 Wireless clients communicating directly, without an access point (AP), describes what type of 802.11 network configuration?

A ○ Ethernet

B ○ Peer-to-peer

C ○ Ad-hoc

D ○ Infrastructure

4 The SSID serves what purpose in a wireless network?

A ○ Authentication password

B ○ Network name

C ○ MAC address

D ○ IP address

5 The _____ is a 32-character identifier that uniquely identifies a WLAN.

A ○ MAC address

B ○ WEP

C ○ WTLS

D ○ SSID

6 WEP uses the _____ encryption algorithm to perform _____ encryption on wireless networks.

A ○ RC4; link

B ○ RC4; end-to-end

C ○ 3DES; link

D ○ 3DES; end-to-end

7 WEP operates at what two layers of the OSI model?

A ○ Layer 3, Layer 4

B ○ Layer 4, Layer 5

C ○ Layer 2, Layer 3

D ○ Layer 1, Layer 2

8 The Initialization Vector (IV) in WEP is a _____-bit, _____ value.

A ○ 24-bit, plain text

B ○ 32-bit, plain text

C ○ 24-bit, cipher text

D ○ 32-bit, cipher text

9 In a wireless LAN using EAP, a user authenticates to a(n) _____ via an Access Point.

A ○ SSID

B ○ Client device

C ○ Access point

D ○ Authentication server

10 _____ is an authentication and key management standard that utilizes EAP.

A ○ 802.1x

B ○ 802.11x

C ○ PPP

D ○ RADIUS

Answers

1 **D.** Availability. WTLS does not ensure availability. *Review "WAP and WTLS."*

2 **B.** 11 Mbps. 802.11b applies to wireless LANs at data rates up to 11 Mbps. *Review "802.11x."*

3 **C.** Ad-hoc. An infrastructure network uses an AP. The other choices are not valid 802.11 network configurations. *Review "802.11x."*

4 **B.** Network name. Although it is sometimes used as a simple password, the SSID is nothing more than a network name that uniquely identifies the wireless network. *Review "SSID."*

5 **D.** SSID. The SSID (or network name) uniquely identifies a wireless network. *Review "SSID."*

6 **A.** RC4; link. WEP uses the RC4 encryption algorithm to perform link encryption on wireless networks. *Review "Wired Equivalent Privacy (WEP)."*

7 **D.** Layer 1, Layer 2. WEP operates at the Physical and Data Link Layers of the OSI Model. *Review "Wired Equivalent Privacy (WEP)."*

8 **A.** 24-bit, plain text. The IV is a 24-bit, plaintext value. *Review "Wired Equivalent Privacy (WEP)."*

9 **D.** Authentication server. In a wireless LAN using EAP, a user authenticates to an authentication server, such as RADIUS. *Review "Extensible Authentication Protocol (EAP)."*

10 **A.** 802.1x. 802.1x is an IEEE standard for authentication and key management. *Review "Extensible Authentication Protocol (EAP)."*

Part IV

Infrastructure Security

In this part . . .

The Infrastructure Security domain includes devices and media, security topologies, and security baselines.

Chapter 9

Devices and Media

• •

In This Chapter

▶ Describe different types and characteristics of common security devices (firewalls, IDS, and VPNs)

▶ Identify common networking devices (routers, switches, PBXs, and cables)

▶ Discuss various end devices (workstations, servers, mobile devices, and removable media)

• •

*T*his chapter is all about hardware (mostly)! However, this chapter is not a hardware dictionary. It's more like an executive summary!

CompTIA recommends two years of networking experience and either A+ or Network+ certification prior to attempting the Security+ exam. The devices and media discussed in this chapter should be nothing more than a quick review or overview for you. You're not likely to see any detailed hardware questions or complex routing scenarios on the Security+ exam, so you definitely won't find any such discussions in this chapter!

Quick Assessment

Networking
Devices and
Media

1 A device that connects dissimilar networks and operates at Layer 3 of the OSI model is known as a _____.

Security
Devices

2 A device that creates a secure tunnel over a public network is known as a _____.

Networking
Devices and
Media

3 A switch can be used to implement a _____, which logically segregates a network and limits broadcast domains.

Wireless
networking

4 _____ are radio transceivers that provide the wireless connection to a wired network.

Cable
media

5 Two types of coaxial network cable are _____ and _____.

Security
Devices

6 A device that controls traffic flow between a trusted network and an untrusted network is commonly known as a _____.

7 _____ provide real-time monitoring and analysis of network activity and data for potential vulnerabilities and attacks.

Cable
media

8 The glass insulator inside a fiber optic cable is commonly known as _____.

9 Twisted pair cabling is limited to a maximum length of _____ meters.

10 Gigabit Ethernet operates on what category of twisted-pair cabling?

Answers

1   Router. *Review "Networking Devices and Media."*

2   Virtual Private Network (VPN). *See "Security Devices."*

3   Virtual LAN (VLAN). *See "Networking Devices and Media."*

4   Wireless Access Points (WAPs). *See "Wireless networking."*

5   Thinnet (RG-58) and Thicknet (RG-8 and RG-11). *See "Cable media."*

6   Firewall. *See "Security Devices."*

7   Intrusion Detection Systems (IDS). *See "Security Devices."*

8   Cladding. *See "Cable media."*

9   100. *Review "Cable media."*

10   CAT-6. *Review "Cable media."*

Security Devices

In this section, I discuss security devices typically found on a secure network perimeter, including

- Firewalls
- Intrusion detection systems (IDS)
- Virtual private networks (VPN)

Firewalls

A *firewall* controls traffic flow between the following:

- A trusted network (such as a corporate LAN)
- An untrusted or public network (such as the Internet)

A firewall can use *hardware, software,* or a combination of both.

Common commercial firewall products include the following:

- Checkpoint FW-1
- Cisco PIX
- Raptor Eagle
- SonicWall

See Chapter 11 for a complete discussion of firewalls.

Intrusion detection systems (IDSs)

Intrusion detection systems (IDSs) provide real-time monitoring and analysis of network activity and data for potential vulnerabilities and attacks. Popular IDS vendors and products include these:

- Internet Security Systems (ISS) products
  - Internet Scanner
  - System Scanner
  - RealSecure

✔ Cisco CSIDS (Cisco Secure Intrusion Detection System, formerly NetRanger)

✔ Snort (freeware IDS for Linux- and Windows-based systems)

I'll discuss IDS in depth in Chapter 11.

Virtual private networks (VPNs)

A *virtual private network* (VPN) creates a secure tunnel over a public network, such as the Internet. A secure tunnel is created by either encrypting or encapsulating the data as it's transmitted across the VPN. The two ends of a VPN tunnel are commonly implemented using one of these methods:

✔ Client-to-VPN concentrator (or device)

✔ Client-to-firewall

✔ Firewall-to-firewall

✔ Router-to-router

Common VPN protocol standards include the following:

✔ Point-to-Point Tunneling Protocol (PPTP)

✔ Layer 2 Forwarding Protocol (L2F)

✔ Layer 2 Tunneling Protocol (L2TP)

✔ Internet Protocol Security (IPSec)

See Chapter 5 for a complete description of VPN protocols.

Networking Devices and Media

Now I turn my attention to the devices that bring your network together and give your users access to the rest of the world (or access from the rest of the world!): routers, switches, RAS, network cables, and more!

Routers

Routers are intelligent devices that link dissimilar networks and forward data packets based on logical or physical addresses to the destination network only (or along the network path). Routers consist of both hardware and software components.

Routing algorithms (such as RIP, OSPF, and BGP) determine the best path to a destination based on such variables as

- ✔ Bandwidth
- ✔ Cost
- ✔ Delay
- ✔ Distance

Routers operate at Layer 3 of the OSI model.

See Chapter 2 for a quick review of the OSI Model.

Switches

A *switch* is essentially an intelligent hub that uses MAC addresses to route traffic. Unlike a hub, a switch transmits data only to the port connected to the destination MAC address. This creates separate collision domains (network segments) and effectively increases the data transmission rates available on the individual network segments. Additionally, a switch can be used to implement Virtual LANs (VLANs) to logically segregate a network and limit broadcast domains. (See Chapter 11 for more on VLANs.) Switches are traditionally considered to be Layer 2 (or Data Link Layer) devices, although newer technologies enable switches to function at the upper layers of the OSI model (Layer 3 and above).

Telecommunications and PBX equipment

Telecommunications and PBX equipment (such as phone switches) are potentially a major source of abuse.

PBX fraud and abuse is one of the most overlooked and costly aspects of a corporate telecommunications infrastructure. Many employees don't think twice about using a company telephone system for extended personal use, including long-distance calls. Perhaps the simplest and most effective countermeasure against internal abuses is to publish and enforce a corporate telephone use policy. Regular auditing of telephone records is also effective for deterring and detecting telephone abuses.

Another major security concern with the phone system involves the casual nature of phone conversations. Telephones are so commonplace that many people openly discuss sensitive information without regard to who else may overhear the conversation, including

✔ Others in the general vicinity

✔ Others on the receiving end of the phone call

✔ Anyone that may be intercepting or tapping the line between the two parties

In the early days of hacking, phone systems were the target for wily hackers attempting to make long-distance calls for free. (Actually, someone else always pays, and therein lies the crime.) Today, voice mail systems are a favorite target for phrackers or phone phreaks (I'm not making this frickin' frackin' stuff up!) that look for unused mailboxes in a corporate phone system. For example, a company may purchase a 500-user voice mail system, but only 430 mailboxes are actually set up and in use, leaving 70 unused mailboxes for a shady young entrepreneur's use! Be sure your unused mailboxes are locked down.

Modems and RAS

Modems and remote access service (RAS) servers provide systems and network access for remote users and telecommuters. Of course, remote access presents many unique security challenges as well, the subject of much discussion in Chapter 5!

Wireless networking

Wireless networking devices can be used as

✔ Mobility aids for portable computers and devices

✔ An alternative to traditional LAN cabling

Wireless Access Points (WAPs) are radio transceivers that provide the wireless connection to the wired network.

See Chapter 9 for a complete discussion of wireless technologies and associated security issues.

Cable media

Cables carry the electrical or light signals, which represent data, between devices on a network. The three basic cable types used in networks are

- ✔ Coaxial
- ✔ Twisted pair
- ✔ Fiber optic

Coaxial cable

Coaxial (coax) cable was very common in the early days of LANs and is rebounding (sort of) with the emergence of broadband networks. Coax cable consists of a solid copper-wire core surrounded by

- ✔ Plastic or Teflon insulator
- ✔ Braided-metal shielding
- ✔ A metal foil wrap (in some cases)
- ✔ Plastic outer sheath

This construction makes the cable very durable and resistant to Electromagnetic Interference (EMI) and Radio Frequency Interference (RFI) signals.

Coax cable comes in two flavors:

- ✔ **Thick:** Also known as *RG8* or *RG11* or *thicknet*. Thicknet cable uses a screw-type connector, known as an *Attachment Unit Interface (AUI)*.
- ✔ **Thin:** Also known as *RG58* or *thinnet*. Thinnet cable is typically connected to network devices by using a bayonet-type connector, known as a *BNC connector*.

Twisted pair cable

Twisted pair cable is the most popular LAN cable in use today because it's

- ✔ Lightweight
- ✔ Flexible
- ✔ Inexpensive
- ✔ Easy to install

One easily recognized example of twisted pair cable is common telephone wire. Twisted pair cable consists of copper wire pairs that are twisted together to improve the transmission quality of the cable. Currently, six classes of twisted pair cable are defined (see Table 9-1). However, only CAT-3, CAT-5, and CAT-6 cable are typically used for networking.

Table 9-1	Twisted Pair Cable Classes	
Class	*Use*	*Example*
1	Voice only	Telephone
2	Data (up to 4 Mbps)	Token-ring at 4 Mbps
3	Data (up to 10 Mbps)	Ethernet
4	Data (up to 20 Mbps)	Token-ring at 16 Mbps
5	Data (up to 100 Mbps)	Fast Ethernet
6	Data (up to 1000 Mbps)	Gigabit Ethernet

Twisted pair cable falls into two categories:

✔ **Unshielded (UTP):** UTP cable is common because it's easier to use and less expensive than shielded cable.

✔ **Shielded (STP):** STP cable is used when RFI or EMI is a major concern.

Fiber-optic cable

Fiber-optic cable is typically used in backbone networks and high-availability fiber distributed date interface (FDDI) networks. Fiber-optic cable carries data as light signals, not electrical signals. It is the most expensive and reliable type of network cabling.

Fiber-optic cable consists of

✔ Glass core or bundle

✔ Glass insulator (commonly known as *cladding*)

✔ Kevlar fiber strands (for strength)

✔ Polyvinyl chloride (PVC) or Teflon outer sheath

Advantages of fiber-optic cable include the following:

✔ Higher speeds

✔ Longer distances

✔ Resistance to interception and interference

Table 9-2 compares characteristics of these cable types.

Table 9-2	Cable Types and Characteristics	
Cable Type	*Ethernet Designation*	*Maximum Length*
RG58 (Thinnet)	10Base2	185 meters
RG8/11 (Thicknet)	10Base5	500 meters
UTP	10/100/1000BaseT	100 meters
STP	10/100/1000BaseT	100 meters
Fiber-optic	100BaseF	2000 meters

Network monitoring and diagnostics

Network monitoring and diagnostic tools include hardware devices and software applications. These tools are important for achieving the following:

✔ Confirming that your network is healthy

✔ Establishing baselines for monitoring network performance

Chapter 12 covers all aspects of network performance.

End Devices

And now, as I near the end of the chapter, I take a look at end devices! End devices consist of servers, user workstations, all sorts of gadgets, and various removable media.

Workstations and servers

User workstations present many security challenges. Workstations should be located in secure areas appropriate for the sensitivity of information being processed. Other physical security concerns for user workstations include ensuring some form of protection against power surges or other electrical anomalies. Minimally, workstations should be plugged into a surge protector. Ideally, a workstation should be connected to a small UPS (Uninterruptible Power Supply). User data should always be saved to a centralized server, not the local workstation. This helps to ensure that the data is backed up and available to other authorized users.

Servers present their own unique set of security challenges. Typically, account databases located on an authentication server are the first target of an attack.

After access is gained, file servers and database servers can be targeted. Servers often are physically located in a centralized server farm, usually within specialized facilities that provide physical security and environmental controls.

Mobile devices

Mobile devices, including PDAs, cellular phones, and other neat gadgets are often taken for granted. PDAs are commonly used to store valuable information such as:

- Passwords
- Personal data
- Private contact information

Effective security administrators must

- Address mobile devices in a comprehensive security policy
- Notify users of these security issues

Removable media

Removable storage media includes the following:

- Backup tapes
- CD-R and CD-RW discs
- DVD-R and DVD-RW discs
- Hard drives
- Floppy disks
- Flashcards
- Smartcards

Physical security is the main security consideration for most of these media types. Many of these storage mediums have a very high capacity for data storage (especially the new DVD-R and DVD-RWs). This fact makes it fairly easy for sensitive data to be copied and removed from the premises.

Backup tapes, in particular, should be maintained in a secure storage facility (preferably offsite). Too often, a tape full of critical server data is left casually on top of the tape drive or beside the server.

CD-R and CD-RW media may be used to copy large amounts of sensitive data by an employee engaged in corporate espionage or anticipating a pending termination. These storage media are also often used for software or music piracy.

Although floppy disks have a comparatively limited capacity, they are still very common to almost every computing environment. Computer viruses are another security risk associated with floppy disks. Although less common today than e-mail viruses and Internet worms, boot sector viruses can still be spread via floppy disks.

Removable hard drives have become far more commonplace in servers. Although doing so is unlikely, someone could remove a hot swappable hard drive from a server. Flashcards provide additional hard drive storage for laptop computers. A far more likely scenario, flashcards can easily *walk off.*

Smart cards are increasingly being used for such purposes as

- **Access control:** Although simply stealing a smart card won't necessarily give an intruder access to a system, it provides a necessary component for access.

- **Storing personal information:** Financial data or medical records, for example.

Prep Test

1 A device that provides real-time monitoring and analysis of network activity and data for potential vulnerabilities and attacks is known as a
_____.

A ○ Firewall

B ○ Router

C ○ Network sniffer

D ○ Intrusion detection system (IDS)

2 Common VPN protocol standards include all of these except:

A ○ IPSec

B ○ L2TP

C ○ PPTP

D ○ TFTP

3 Common VPN implementations include all of these except:

A ○ Client-to-router

B ○ Router-to-router

C ○ Client-to-firewall

D ○ Firewall-to-firewall

4 Which of these networking devices typically uses MAC addresses to route traffic?

A ○ Router

B ○ Switch

C ○ Hub

D ○ Multiplexer

5 Switches typically operate at what layer of the OSI Model?

A ○ Data Link

B ○ Network

C ○ Transport

D ○ Session

6 **CAT-4 twisted pair cabling is typically used for:**

A ○ Telephones

B ○ Ethernet

C ○ Token-ring

D ○ Fast Ethernet

7 **10Base2 is the Ethernet designation for which cable media type?**

A ○ UTP

B ○ STP

C ○ Thinnet

D ○ Thicknet

8 **Shielded Twisted Pair (STP) cabling is typically used in networking environments where _____ is a concern.**

A ○ Latency

B ○ Distance

C ○ Electromagnetic Interference (EMI)

D ○ Cost

9 **The maximum permitted length for a 10Base5 cable segment is   .**

A ○ 100 meters

B ○ 185 meters

C ○ 500 meters

D ○ 2000 meters

10 **Although less prevalent today, viruses spread via _____ media are still a viable threat.**

A ○ Backup tape

B ○ CD-ROM

C ○ Floppy disk

D ○ Paper

Answers

1 **D.** Intrusion detection system (IDS). Although a sniffer captures data similar to an IDS, it does not perform any analysis. *Review "Intrusion detection systems (IDS)."*

2 **D.** TFTP. TFTP is the Trivial File Transfer Protocol, a basic variation of the FTP protocol that provides limited file transfer capabilities. It has absolutely nothing to do with VPNs. *Review "Virtual private networks (VPNs)."*

3 **A.** Client-to-router. Router-to-router, client-to-firewall, and firewall-to-firewall are all valid VPN implementations. *Review "Virtual private networks (VPNs)."*

4 **B.** Switch. A router uses IP addresses to route traffic. Hubs and multiplexers do not route traffic. *Review "Switches."*

5 **A.** Data Link. Although some newer switches can operate at the upper layers, switches traditionally operate at Layer 2, the Data Link Layer. *Review "Switches."*

6 **C.** Token-ring. CAT-1 is used for telephones, CAT-3 for Ethernet, and CAT-5 for Fast Ethernet. *Review "Twisted pair cable."*

7 **C.** Thinnet. UTP and STP are both designated as 10/100/1000BaseT. Thicknet is designated as 10Base5. *Review "Cable media."*

8 **C.** Electromagnetic Interference (EMI). STP cabling is typically used in *noisy* environments where EMI and RFI may cause problems. *Review "Twisted pair cable."*

9 **C.** 500 meters. 10/100/1000BaseT is limited to 100 meters; 10Base2 is limited to 185 meters; 100BaseF is limited to 2000 meters. *Review "Cable media."*

10 **C.** Floppy disk. Internet worms and e-mail viruses are more common today, but boot sector viruses (and other types) can still be spread via floppy disks. *Review "Removable media."*

Chapter 10

Security Topologies

*T*his chapter covers some very exciting topics in security! I start with some basic definitions of LANs and WANs, just to make sure that we're speaking the same language. Then, I move onto firewalls, intrusion detection systems, and honeypots. Finally, I look at methods for deploying firewalls in security zones (or DMZs).

Quick Assessment

1 Three basic firewall types are _____, _____, and _____.

2 A packet filtering firewall references predefined rules configured in an _____ to determine whether a packet should be permitted or denied.

3 A _____ firewall permits or denies traffic based solely on the TCP, UDP, ICMP, and/or IP headers of individual packets.

4 An _____ IDS can be configured to automatically block suspected attacks in progress without any intervention required by an operator.

5 A _____ emulates a production system or network with the goal of luring attackers away from an organization's actual systems and data.

6 _____ is the illegal act of encouraging someone to commit a crime that the individual may have had no intention of committing.

7 _____ is the act of luring someone toward evidence after that individual has already committed a crime.

8 Four basic security zone designs include _____, _____, _____, and _____.

9 A _____ is a general term used to refer to proxies, gateways, firewalls, or any server that provides applications or services directly to an untrusted network.

10 A DMZ, or demilitarized zone, can be implemented using a _____ security zone architecture.

Answers

1 Packet filtering, circuit-level gateway, application-level gateway. *Review "Firewalls."*

2 Access Control List (ACL). *See "Firewalls."*

3 Packet filtering. *See "Firewalls."*

4 Active. *Review "Intrusion detection systems (IDS)."*

5 Honeypot. *Learn more in the section on "Honeypots."*

6 Entrapment. *See "Honeypots."*

7 Enticement. *See "Honeypots."*

8 Screening router, dual-homed gateway, screened host gateway, and screened-subnet. *Review "Security Zones."*

9 Bastion host. *See "Security Zones."*

10 Screened-subnet. *See "Security Zones."*

Data Network Types

Data networks are generally classified as *local area networks* (LANs) or *wide area networks* (WANs). In this section, I point out the differences between these two network types and give you some examples of each.

Local area network (LAN)

A *local area network* (LAN) is a data network that operates across a relatively small geographic area, such as a single building or floor.

A LAN connects workstations, servers, printers, and other devices so that network resources, such as files and e-mail, can be shared. Two variations of basic LANs are the following:

- ✔ **Campus area network (CAN):** This variation connects multiple buildings across a high-performance backbone.
- ✔ **Metropolitan area network (MAN):** A MAN is a LAN that extends across a large area, such as a small city.

Wide area network (WAN)

A *wide area network* (WAN) connects multiple LANs and other WANs by using telecommunications devices and facilities to form an internetwork.

A wide area network (WAN) is a data network that operates across a relatively large geographic area.

Examples of WANs include

- ✔ **Internet:** The Mother of all WANs, the *Internet* is the global network of public networks originally developed by the U.S. Department of Defense (DoD) Advanced Research Projects Agency (ARPA). Users and systems connect to the Internet via Internet Service Providers (ISPs).
- ✔ **Intranet:** An *intranet* can be thought of as a private Internet. An intranet typically uses Web-based technologies to disseminate company information that's available only to authorized users on the company network.
- ✔ **Extranet:** An *extranet* extends the basic concept of an intranet to include partners, vendors, or other related parties. For example, an automobile manufacturer may operate an extranet that connects networks belonging to parts manufacturers, distributors, and dealerships. Extranets are commonly operated across the Internet by using a Virtual Private Network (VPN) (see Chapter 5) or other secure connection.

Network Security Devices

Network security is implemented with such technologies as the following:

- Firewalls, which control traffic between two networks (such as a corporate network and the Internet)
- Intrusion detection systems (IDS), which detect (and can respond to) attempts by attackers to penetrate a network
- Honeypots, which collect information about attack methods

Firewalls

A *firewall* controls traffic flow between

- A trusted network (such as a corporate LAN)
- An untrusted or public network (such as the Internet)

A firewall can comprise hardware, software, or a combination of both hardware and software. Three basic types of firewalls are used:

- Packet filtering
- Circuit-level gateway
- Application-level gateway

Packet filtering

A *packet filtering* firewall (or *screening router*) is one of the most basic (and inexpensive) types of firewalls and is ideally suited for a low-risk environment. A packet filtering firewall permits or denies traffic based solely on an individual packet's headers for

- TCP (Transmission Control Protocol)
- UDP (User Datagram Protocol)
- ICMP (Internet Control Message Protocol)
- IP (Internet Protocol)

The packet filtering firewall examines

- Traffic direction (inbound or outbound)
- Source and destination IP addresses
- Source and destination TCP or UDP port numbers

This information is compared to predefined rules that have been configured in an Access Control List (ACL) to determine whether a packet should be permitted or denied. A packet filtering firewall usually operates at the Network or Transport Layer of the OSI model. Advantages of a packet filtering firewall include

- ✔ Inexpensive (can be implemented as a router ACL)
- ✔ Fast and flexible
- ✔ Transparent to users

Disadvantages of packet filtering firewalls are

- ✔ Access decisions are based only on address and port information.
- ✔ These firewalls provide no protection from IP or DNS address spoofing (see chapter 4).
- ✔ These firewalls don't support strong user authentication.
- ✔ Configuring and maintaining ACLs can be difficult.
- ✔ Logging information may be limited.

A more advanced variation of the packet filtering firewall is the *dynamic packet filtering firewall*. This type of firewall supports dynamic modification of the firewall rule base using ACLs that can be changed by the firewall on-the-fly using such techniques as context-based access control (CBAC) or reflexive ACLs.

Circuit-level gateway

A *circuit-level gateway* controls access by maintaining state information about established connections. When a permitted connection is established between two hosts, the gateway creates a *tunnel* (or virtual circuit) for the session, thus allowing packets to flow freely between the two hosts without the need for further inspection of individual packets. This type of firewall operates at the Session Layer of the OSI model.

Advantages of this type of firewall are

- ✔ Speed (After a connection is established, individual packets aren't analyzed.)
- ✔ Support for many protocols
- ✔ Easy maintenance

Disadvantages of this type of firewall include

- ✔ One factor is the dependence on trustworthiness of the communicating users or hosts. (After a connection is established, individual packets aren't analyzed.)

✔ Very limited logging information about individual data packets is available after the initial connection is established.

A *stateful inspection firewall* is a type of circuit-level gateway that captures data packets at the Network Layer and then queues and analyzes (examines state and context) these packets at the upper layers of the OSI model.

Application-level gateway

An application-level (or Application Layer) gateway operates at the Application Layer of the OSI model, processing data packets for specific IP applications. This type of firewall is generally considered the most secure and is commonly implemented as a proxy server. In a *proxy server*, no direct communication between two hosts is permitted. Instead, data packets are intercepted by the proxy server, which analyzes the packet's contents and (if permitted by the firewall rules) sends a copy of the original packet to the intended host.

Advantages of this type of firewall include the following:

✔ Data packets aren't transmitted directly to communicating hosts, thereby masking the internal network's design and preventing direct access to services on internal hosts.

✔ This type of firewall can be used to implement strong user authentication in applications.

Disadvantages of this type of firewall include

✔ It reduces network performance because every packet must be passed up to the Application Layer of the OSI model to be analyzed.

✔ It must be tailored to specific applications. (This type of firewall can be difficult to maintain or update for new or changing protocols.)

Intrusion detection systems (IDS)

Intrusion detection is defined as real-time monitoring and analysis of network activity and data for potential vulnerabilities and attacks in progress. One major limitation of current IDS technologies is the requirement to filter false alarms lest the operator (system or security administrator) be overwhelmed with data. Intrusion detection systems (IDS) are classified in such forms as the following:

✔ Active or passive

✔ Network-based or host-based

✔ Knowledge-based or behavior-based

Active and passive IDS

An *active IDS* is a system that's configured to block suspected attacks in progress automatically without any intervention required by an operator.

An active IDS has the advantage of providing real-time corrective action in response to an attack but has many disadvantages as well.

- ✔ An active system must be placed in-line along a network boundary; thus, the IDS system itself is susceptible to attack.

- ✔ If false alarms and legitimate traffic haven't been properly identified and filtered, authorized users and applications may be improperly denied access.

- ✔ The IDS system itself may be used to cause a *Denial of Service* (DoS) attack by intentionally flooding the system with alarms that cause it to block connections until no connections or bandwidth are available.

A *passive IDS* is a system that's configured to only monitor and analyze network traffic activity and alert an operator to potential vulnerabilities and attacks. It's not capable of performing any protective or corrective functions on its own. Passive IDS has a couple of advantages:

- ✔ Systems can be easily and rapidly deployed.
- ✔ Systems are not normally susceptible to attacks on themselves.

Network-based and host-based IDS

A *network-based IDS* is placed along a network segment or boundary and monitors all traffic on that segment. It usually consists of the following components:

- ✔ A network appliance (or sensor) with a Network Interface Card (NIC) operating in promiscuous mode (listens to all traffic on the network segment).
- ✔ A separate management interface.

A *host-based IDS* requires small programs (or *agents*) to be installed on individual systems to be monitored. The agents monitor the operating system and write data to log files and/or trigger alarms. A host-based IDS can only monitor individual host systems on which the agents are installed; it doesn't monitor the entire network.

Knowledge-based and behavior-based IDS

Knowledge-based IDS is more common than behavior-based IDS. A *knowledge-based* (or *signature-based*) *IDS* references a database of previous attack profiles and known system vulnerabilities to identify active intrusion attempts.

Advantages of knowledge-based systems include

- ✔ It has lower false alarm rates than behavior-based IDS.
- ✔ Alarms are more standardized and more easily understood than behavior-based IDS alarms.

Disadvantages of knowledge-based systems include

- ✔ The signature database must be continually updated and maintained.
- ✔ New, unique, or original attacks may not be detected or may be improperly classified.

A *behavior-based* (or *statistical anomaly-based*) *IDS* references an initial baseline of activity or a learned pattern of normal system activity to identify active intrusion attempts. Deviations from this baseline or pattern cause an alarm to be triggered. Advantages of behavior-based systems include the facts that they

- ✔ Dynamically adapt to new, unique, or original attacks
- ✔ Are less dependent on identifying specific operating system vulnerabilities

Disadvantages of behavior-based systems include

- ✔ Higher false alarm rates than knowledge-based IDS
- ✔ Usage patterns that may change often and may not be static enough to implement an effective behavior-based IDS

Honeypots

A *honeypot* is a security tool to help an organization either

- ✔ Mitigate risk to systems
- ✔ Learn about an attacker's methods

Designed to be compromised, a honeypot emulates a system or network with the goal of luring attackers away from an organization's actual systems and data. However, a honeypot does not actually protect any systems or data and should never be used as a protective security measure. By reviewing activity to and from a honeypot, an organization can learn a great deal about attack methods and potential vulnerabilities in the network.

When used for research as described previously, honeypots can be an extremely valuable security tool. However, honeypots have two significant legal issues that may preclude or limit the use of collected data as evidence.

If your organization decides to deploy a honeypot, these issues should be fully understood by senior management and clearly addressed in the organization's security policy as well as in your deployment strategy:

- *Entrapment* encourages someone to commit a crime that the individual may have had no intention of committing.

  Entrapment is *illegal.*

- *Enticement* lures someone toward evidence after that individual has committed a crime.

  Enticement is not necessarily illegal, but it does raise ethical arguments and may not be admissible in court.

Several commercial honeypots, including the following, are available:

- BackOfficer Friendly
- Mantrap
- Honeyd
- Specter

Security Zones

How a firewall is deployed is just as important a decision as what type of firewall (discussed in the preceding section) is deployed. Four basic techniques *(firewall architectures)* are used for implementing security zones using firewalls:

- Screening router
- Dual-homed gateway
- Screened host gateway
- Screened-subnet

Screening router

A *screening router* is the most basic type of firewall architecture:

- An external router is placed between the untrusted and trusted networks.
- A security policy is implemented by using ACLs.

Figure 10-1 illustrates the configuration of a screening router. Although a router functions as a choke point between a trusted and untrusted network, an attacker — after gaining access to a host on the trusted network — may potentially be able to compromise the entire network.

Figure 10-1:
A screening router architecture.

Untrusted Network

External Router

Trusted Network

Advantages of a screening router architecture include the following:

✔ It is completely transparent.

✔ It is relatively simple and inexpensive.

Disadvantages of the screening router architecture include the following:

✔ It is difficult to configure and maintain.

✔ It may have difficulty handling some traffic.

✔ It has limited or no logging available.

✔ It uses no user authentication.

✔ It is difficult to mask the internal network structure.

✔ It has a single point of failure.

✔ It doesn't truly implement a firewall choke-point strategy.

Using a screening router architecture is better than using nothing.

Dual-homed gateways

Another common firewall architecture is the dual-homed gateway. A *dual-homed gateway* (or *bastion host*) is a system with two network interfaces that sits between an untrusted and trusted network (see Figure 10-2). A *bastion host* is a general term often used to refer to proxies, gateways, firewalls, or any server that provides applications or services directly to an untrusted network. Because a bastion host is often the target of attackers, it is sometimes referred to as a *sacrificial lamb*. However, this term is misleading because a bastion host is typically a hardened system employing robust security mechanisms.

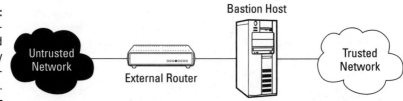

Figure 10-2:
A dual-homed gateway architecture.

A dual-homed gateway is often connected to the untrusted network via an external screening router. The dual-homed gateway functions as a proxy server for the trusted network and may be configured to require user authentication. A dual-homed gateway offers a more fail-safe operation than screening routers because, by default, data isn't normally forwarded across the two interfaces. Advantages of the dual-homed gateway architecture include

- ✔ It operates in a fail-safe mode.
- ✔ Internal network structure is masked.

Disadvantages of the dual-homed gateway architecture include

- ✔ It may inconvenience users.
- ✔ Proxies may not be available for some services.
- ✔ It may cause slower network performance.

Screened host gateways

A *screened host gateway* architecture employs an external screening router and an internal bastion host (see Figure 10-3). The screening router is configured so that the bastion host is the only host accessible from the untrusted network (such as the Internet). The bastion host provides any required Web services, such as HTTP and FTP, to the untrusted network as permitted by the security policy. Connections to the Internet from the trusted network are routed via an application proxy on the bastion host or directly through the screening router.

Advantages of the screened host gateway architecture include

- ✔ It provides distributed security between two devices.
- ✔ It has transparent outbound access.
- ✔ It has restricted inbound access.

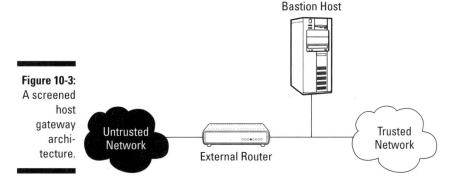

Disadvantages of the screened host gateway architecture include

✔ It's considered less secure than other firewall architectures because the screening router can bypass the bastion host for some trusted services.

✔ Masking the internal network structure is difficult.

✔ It can have multiple single points of failure (router or bastion host).

Screened-subnet (or DMZ)

The screened-subnet is perhaps the most secure of the basic firewall architectures. The screened-subnet employs three elements:

✔ External screening router

✔ Dual-homed (or multihomed) host

✔ Internal screening router

Figure 10-4 illustrates the screened-subnet architecture. This implements the
concept of a network DMZ (or demilitarized zone). Publicly available services
are placed on bastion hosts in the DMZ.

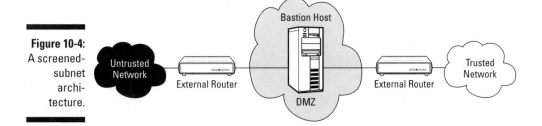

Advantages of the screened-subnet architecture include the following:

- ✔ It's transparent to end users.
- ✔ It's flexible.
- ✔ Internal network structure can be masked.
- ✔ It provides *defense in depth*, not relying on a single device to provide security for the entire network.

Disadvantages of a screened-subnet architecture include the following:

- ✔ It is more expensive than other firewall architectures.
- ✔ It is more difficult to configure and maintain than other types of firewall architectures.
- ✔ It can be more difficult to troubleshoot.

Prep Test

1 A data network that operates across a relatively large geographic area defines what type of network?

- **A** ○ LAN
- **B** ○ MAN
- **C** ○ CAN
- **D** ○ WAN

2 The three basic types of firewalls include all of these except:

- **A** ○ Packet filtering
- **B** ○ Circuit-level gateway
- **C** ○ Application-level gateway
- **D** ○ Screened-subnet

3 A circuit-level gateway operates at what layer of the OSI model?

- **A** ○ Application
- **B** ○ Network
- **C** ○ Transport
- **D** ○ Session

4 A stateful inspection firewall is an example of what type of firewall?

- **A** ○ Packet filtering
- **B** ○ Circuit-level gateway
- **C** ○ Application-level gateway
- **D** ○ None of the above

5 Which type of intrusion detection system requires agents that are installed on individual systems?

- **A** ○ Knowledge-based
- **B** ○ Network-based
- **C** ○ Host-based
- **D** ○ Signature-based

6 A type of intrusion detection system (IDS) that references a baseline of normal system activity to identify attacks is known as _____.

A ○ Knowledge-based

B ○ Behavior-based

C ○ Active

D ○ Passive

7 A legal consideration, associated with the use of honeypots, that is illegal is _____.

A ○ Enticement

B ○ Due diligence

C ○ Coercion

D ○ Entrapment

8 A network device that is often targeted by attackers and sometimes referred to as a *sacrificial lamb* is a _____.

A ○ Honeypot

B ○ Bastion host

C ○ Intrusion detection system (IDS)

D ○ Virtual private network (VPN)

9 Which of these firewall architectures employs an external and internal router as well as a bastion host?

A ○ Screening router

B ○ Screened-subnet

C ○ Screened-host gateway

D ○ Dual-homed gateway

10 Considered the most secure of the security zones, a _____ implements the concept of a network DMZ.

A ○ Dual-homed gateway

B ○ Screening router

C ○ Screened-host gateway

D ○ Screened-subnet

Answers

1 **D.** WAN. A LAN operates across a relatively small geographic area. A MAN and CAN are LAN variations. *Review "Data Network Types."*

2 **D.** Screened-subnet. Screened-subnet is a type of security zone. The other choices are incorrect. Review *"Firewalls."*

3 **D.** Session. A circuit-level gateway creates a tunnel for established sessions between two hosts. *Review "Firewalls."*

4 **B.** Circuit-level gateway. A stateful inspection firewall captures packets at the Network Layer and analyzes them at the upper layers of the OSI Model. *Review "Firewalls."*

5 **C.** Host-based. Host-based IDS requires small programs, called *agents,* to be installed and running on any systems to be monitored. *Review "Intrusion detection systems (IDS)."*

6 **B.** Behavior-based. Knowledge-based firewalls reference known signatures. Active and passive IDS refers to the method in which the IDS is deployed, not how it operates. *Review "Intrusion detection systems (IDS)."*

7 **D.** Entrapment. Although enticement is another important legal consideration and may be unethical, it is usually not illegal. Due diligence and coercion are legal issues not normally associated with honeypots. *Review "Honeypots."*

8 **B.** Bastion host. A bastion host is a general term often used to refer to proxies, gateways, firewalls, or some servers. The term *sacrificial lamb* is actually misleading because this device is typically a hardened system with robust security defenses. *Review "Security Zones."*

9 **B.** Screened-subnet. The screened-subnet employs an external screening router, a dual-homed (or multihomed) host, and a second internal screening router. *Review "Security Zones."*

10 **D.** Screened-subnet. A screened-subnet is also known as a DMZ (or demilitarized zone) and separates a trusted network from an untrusted network. *See "Security Zones."*

Chapter 11

Security Baselines

. . . .

In This Chapter

▶ Hardening Basics — the principles used to harden systems, devices, applications, and data

▶ OS/NOS Hardening — additional information you need to know in order to protect systems

▶ Network Hardening — specific information that applies to network devices

▶ Application Hardening — information specific to hardening common applications

▶ Database and Directory Service Hardening — more information that is specific to databases

. . . .

*T*his is where the rubber meets the road for many IT professionals: hardening systems and network devices. This is the bread and butter of information security — the first line of defense.

In this chapter, you learn the principles for hardening systems. Learn these well and you'll be able to apply your knowledge to everything with a power cord: servers, workstations, routers, firewalls, VPN devices, you name it.

After introducing the hardening principles, this chapter contains several sections that apply to computer systems, network devices, applications, and databases.

Quick Assessment

1   Unnecessary services should be _____ or _____.

2   Web servers are inherently complicated because they can access _____ and _____.

3   Shared volumes on file servers should be _____ from OS directories.

4   _____ should be used to prevent someone from consuming all disk space on a file server.

5   Security patches should be _____.

6   A DNS server should be configured to perform _____ between it and other known DNS servers.

7   E-mail servers should be configured to prevent _____, in order to prevent SPAMmers from using your e-mail server to originate SPAM.

8   _____ permits any public user on the Internet to upload or download files to or from an FTP server.

9   A _____ is a software fix issued by a software or hardware vendor.

10 Default _____ should be removed from all systems.

Answers

1 Disabled, removed. *Review "Hardening Basics."*

2 Databases, file systems. *See "Database and Directory Service Hardening."*

3 Kept separate. See *"Application Hardening — File/print servers."*

4 Quotas. *Review "Application Hardening — File/print servers."*

5 Installed immediately. *Learn more in the section on "Hardening Basics."*

6 Zone transfers. *See "Application Hardening — DNS servers."*

7 Relaying. *See "Application Hardening — E-mail servers."*

8 Anonymous FTP. *Review "Application Hardening — FTP servers."*

9 Patch. *See "OS/NOS Hardening — Updates."*

10 Passwords or accounts. *See "OS/NOS Hardening."*

Hardening Basics

Hardening refers to the process of making changes to a computer or network device in order to make it less vulnerable to intruders. This is important because the computers and networks that an organization uses are expected to continue functioning without interruption; the business information contained in or processed by them is expected to maintain its integrity.

For a number of reasons that are not germane to the topic of Security+ certification, systems do not come from their manufacturers in a completely hardened state. It is up to the organization that uses the systems to perform all hardening procedures that are appropriate for their environment.

The proper hardening of a system boils down to five principles:

- **Keep security patches and fixes current.** Virtually every hardware and software vendor, from time to time, releases security patches. It is essential that every organization using the product install the security patch as soon as possible in order to prevent security incidents.

- **Disable or remove unnecessary components.** If a software component on a system is unused, it is probably unnecessary. Every unnecessary component on a system must either be disabled or, better yet, removed altogether. When a software component is removed from a system, then any vulnerability discovered in that component cannot pose a risk to the system. If the flawed component is not running or is not present, then it cannot be used to break in to a system.

- **Disable default access configurations.** Systems and network devices may have default accounts and/or passwords that, if unchanged, provide easy access by an intruder. Guest accounts should be disabled or removed; default passwords must be changed; accounts with no passwords must be disabled or passwords assigned.

- **Tighten access controls.** Too often, access permissions to resources, such as programs or files, are too lax. In an effort to get a new service up and running, system administrators frequently change access controls to "wide open" and then, in their haste to complete the project, neglect to tighten down access. Later, the "wide open" access can be exploited by an intruder who can steal or damage information.

- **Turn on audit logging.** Many operating systems and applications, while they contain an event/access/audit logging feature, frequently are shipped with logging turned off or disabled. By using event logging, it may be possible to retrace some of the steps taken by an intruder.

These universal principles apply in just about every situation regarding computers and network devices. If system and network engineers are diligent and follow these principles, then the majority of potential security incidents will be prevented.

Security flaws and patches

Computers and network devices have at their core one or more software programs that control their operation. Being written, installed, and managed by imperfect humans, sometimes computers and network devices contain flaws that permit unexpected behavior. Once in a while, this unexpected behavior results in someone being able to control or alter the system. This is generally known as a security flaw.

Other malfunctions in software result in the system just not running as expected. While they may not take the form of security flaws, they may be irritating nonetheless.

The companies that make and support systems have people whose job it is to create software updates. Depending upon the reason for the creation of the update, it may take many forms:

- ✔ **Service Release.** Also known as a version upgrade or service pack (depending upon the vendor — they all seem to have their own unique names), service releases usually contain many fixes, and even feature enhancements or upgrades. Service releases are generally produced from once to three or four times per year.

- ✔ **Patch.** Also known as a hotfix, a patch is designed to change one specific problem. While the changes in a patch are usually included in a service release, generally a patch is produced because there is a heightened urgency. Typically, a vendor produces a patch because it believes that its customers should install it immediately instead of waiting for the next service release to address the issue.

Disable unnecessary services

As we mentioned earlier, an unused but running application or service can increase the risk to a system. Take, for example, the FTP service. FTP is reliable and adequate security when configured correctly.

Suppose, for instance, that a serious flaw was discovered in FTP. Say, if you provided a certain pattern in the password field, you would be able to control the system. This would jeopardize the integrity of the system. However, if FTP was not used on a given system, then it should be either disabled or removed. This would eliminate the threat caused by the FTP flaw, because if FTP is not running on the system, then it cannot be exploited in order to compromise the system.

Disable default access

In order to facilitate their initial configuration or use, many systems are shipped to the customer with a guest account and perhaps a default password on one or more administrative accounts. If these accounts are not changed or disabled, then an intruder who knows the factory default passwords or other access methods might be able to control a system.

It is imperative, then, to perform any or all of the following:

- ✔ Disable or remove guest accounts.
- ✔ Change any default passwords on accounts.
- ✔ Make sure that all accounts have passwords.

Accounts and passwords are a system's first line of defense, so it is important to not make it *too* easy for an intruder to compromise your system.

Tighten access controls

Access to everything related to computers and networks must be restricted to only those individuals who have a bona fide business reason to access them. We cannot make it any more plain than this, but we can provide some additional pointers related to this.

- ✔ Resist the temptation to change access permissions to "wide open" (permitting access to anyone and everyone).
- ✔ Adopt the principle of "denied unless explicitly permitted." In other words, the default access permission to a resource should be "denied." Then, explicitly permit access to specific groups or individuals as needed. This works better than "permitted unless explicitly denied," which permits new users to access an otherwise closed resource (unless the administrator is 100 percent diligent and always adds every new user to the "denied" list of every managed resource).
- ✔ Adopt the principle of "users only have the fewest privileges necessary for them to perform their job." This is known as the principle of "least privilege."

Turn on audit logging

Audit logging is a feature present in most OS's, databases, and larger applications where most (if not all) user and administrative transactions are independently recorded. This provides an audit trail that can be used to piece together routine or unusual events.

Audit logging, at a minimum, should contain the following items that describe a transaction or event:

- ✔ **Who** performed the transaction. This is generally the userid associated with the transaction.

- ✔ **When** the transaction was performed.

- ✔ **What** was contained in the transaction. Depending upon the nature of the transaction, this may contain "old" and "new" values or a description of the transaction.

- ✔ **Where** the transaction was performed. This will generally be a terminal ID or an IP address.

Defense in depth

Where possible provide a "defense in depth" philosophy when protecting computers and applications. This means that every means available should be employed; should one protection mechanism fail, at least one other will still be in place to continue protecting the system. Think of defense in depth like a castle surrounded by several moats (as in Figure 11-1), and also with locks on the main doors, armed soldiers, and moat monsters. If any one (or two) of these are taken away, the others are still offering some protection.

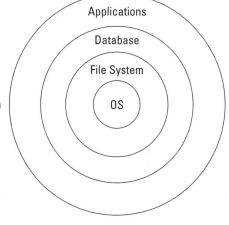

Protect All Layers
- patches
- remove unnecessary services
- no default access
- audit logging

Figure 11-1:
Protecting
all layers
using all
available
methods.

OS/NOS Hardening

Those of you with a few gray hairs remember not long ago when OS's were thought of as a grand toolbox and a lot of nifty features. But any more, the paradigm has changed as a result of many lessons learned. We put it to you plainly — we wanted a tear-out poster in the back of this book, but we had to settle for some bold print on this page:

- ✔ Disable (and actually remove if possible) all services and features that are unnecessary on a system.

- ✔ Install all security patches as soon as they are available.

- ✔ Disable or remove all guest accounts.

- ✔ Change all default passwords. Require that every account have a password.

- ✔ Turn on audit logging in order to capture routine as well as unusual system-level events.

- ✔ Manage access control from the perspective that "no one gets access except those who are explicitly granted access," as opposed to "everyone gets access except those who are explicitly denied access."

- ✔ Provide a "defense in depth."

These are the golden rules of OS security. If you faithfully live by these rules, chances are you will have a long and healthy career with few security-related nightmares.

Thankfully, the OS vendors are doing all of us a service by shipping their OSs far more "locked down" then just a few years ago. But because the vendors still have a ways to go, systems that you set up still need a good deal of scrutiny prior to being labeled "secure."

File system

Whether we are talking about a file system that is set up for sharing among hundreds or thousands of individuals or the file system containing all or part of the computer's operating system, access to the file system must follow the "denied unless specifically permitted" method.

Directories intended for sharing among users must be kept separate from application and operating system directories — ideally in entirely separate file systems. Problems which could occur were shared directories to share a file system with the operating system will all be prevented if they are made separate to begin with.

Updates

Microsoft, Sun, HP, IBM, and the rest of the OS vendors regularly publish information regarding updates to their operating systems and core utilities and tools. These updates are created in order to fix minor problems, correct deficiencies, and add minor features. These updates are changes to specific components in the operating system, generally replacing an individual file or a group of associated files.

When confronted with a situation that compels the vendor to create an update, the vendor has a number of choices to make: how important is it that the update be made available to its customers, and how soon should the update be made available to customers. The answer to these two questions will govern how the vendor goes about creating the update.

Types of updates

But first, we define some generic terms. Different OS vendors have different and varying terminology, and they produce updates in different ways, so not every vendor uses every form of update.

- ✔ **Hot fix.** This is an update that is produced in a hurry because of the seriousness of the problem that it addresses. A hot fix generally fixes one discrete portion of the operating system.

- ✔ **Patch.** This is a more ordinary update that has less urgency than a hot fix.

- ✔ **Service pack.** This is a larger, more-comprehensive update that will contain many fixes and updates. These are produced infrequently, perhaps once or twice each year.

- ✔ **Operating system release.** These are the granddaddy feature releases announced with fanfare as being all-new, but very often the reality is that the new OS release is mostly the old OS with a new coat of paint and a lot of old problems fixed.

To patch or not to patch

No one can deny the fact that patches, updates, and service packs seem to be released on an almost daily basis. Are *all* of these patches and updates supposed to be installed?

This is a contentious question without a simple answer, and here is why. Some software manufacturers recommend that all patches be installed, while others advise their customers to install patches only when they actually experience the symptoms that the patches are designed to resolve. And still other vendors do a combination of these two strategies: they advise customers to install all security patches, but not to install other patches unless they actually experience the related problem.

Which is right for you?

We have no silver bullets for you, except for this: consult with trained, experienced professionals within your organization and also with your software vendors. Find the strategy that is most appropriate for your organization.

In all cases, the vendors release these various kinds of updates so that their customers may update their systems as quickly as needed.

Applying updates

Different OS vendors have different general and specific recommendations about applying patches. And because not all organizations have equal needs, each organization needs to develop policies about updates that meet its needs.

These days, updates seem to fall into just two categories: security updates and all the rest. And general recommendations fall into one of these categories:

- Apply all security updates as soon as they are released. Apply any other updates only when the problems they address are actually encountered.

- Apply all security updates as soon as they are released. Apply any other updates if you feel that there is a likelihood that they will prevent a known problem.

- Apply all updates as soon as they are released.

Note that — in these examples anyhow — security patches are always to be applied as soon as possible. Any more the variability has more to do with whether non-security patches should be installed routinely or only if the specific problems that they address are encountered. But we digress. . . .

Test all updates

Even if your OS vendor recommends that all security updates be installed as soon as possible, it is highly recommended that all such updates be tested on test systems prior to the updates being applied to production systems. Every OS manufacturer will stress that updates — particularly security patches that are produced in a hurry in order to provide rapid protection to its customers and stave off negative public opinion — cannot reasonably be tested in every sort of environment and that unpredictable results may occur.

Keeping systems up-to-date

Nimda and Code Red were successful Internet worms that exploited weaknesses in Microsoft-based products. But what is remarkable about Nimda and Code Red in not that they were innovative, but that they succeeded at all. This is because they each exploited weaknesses that had been well publicized for nearly a year! These worms were successful because vast numbers of systems were still unpatched and therefore were able to propagate them.

In a sentence: Security is often more about people than it is about technology. In this example, people frequently fail to take even the most basic security steps by keeping their system up-to-date with security patches.

Always look for, and read, all information available pertaining to any hot fix, patch, or service release. There may be important information in the release notes that can cause tremendous grief or sadness should you fail to understand everything about the update prior to installing it.

Network Hardening

All of the devices in a network are potential targets unless they are hardened. This means that they must be free of all known vulnerabilities in design and configuration.

The responsibility for hardening network devices is shared between the devices' respective manufacturers (they must produce OS's or firmware that is free from security flaws) and the network administrators who manage them. (They must configure them so that there are no weaknesses.)

Firmware updates

Virtually every sort of network device — routers, switches, hubs, bridges, firewalls, modems, base stations, and so on — contains some sort of software in the form of an operating system or firmware. Whatever it's called, chances are that from time to time a network device's OS or firmware will need to be patched or upgraded in order to stave off a potential security issue.

If you're reading this chapter sequentially, you've heard this before and you'll hear it again. Do test all updates on test devices in test environments prior to installing new software or firmware or making configuration changes. If you take your network down on account of an update procedure going bad, then you might say that the cure was worse than the disease.

Rather than spend a lot of time looking for security fixes from all of the vendors that typical IT shops support, a better approach might be to subscribe to their notifications of security information. One can also obtain information from vendor-neutral sources, such as BugTraq, CERT, or SecurityFocus.com. This assures that news of security fixes and other important issues will be pushed out to one's mailbox or other places frequently visited.

Device configuration

Network devices must be configured, again according to the general principles outlined at the beginning of this chapter: disable unnecessary services and remove guest or anonymous access. Consider permitting administration of each device only when physically connected to the device, not over the network. (This will be impractical when a device you must manage is across town or across the country.)

When possible, restrict over-the-network administrative access to only known specific administrative systems. In other words, configure the device so that only certain systems (usually by IP address) can connect to the device in order to manage it.

Configuration of any network device must be kept as simple as possible. Consider the core purpose of the device: Configure it for those purposes only and remove everything extraneous.

A good case-in-point here is the now-classic story of a security flaw in Microsoft's IIS (Internet Information Server, Microsoft's Web server software). Network engineers who managed newer Cisco routers figured they had nothing to worry about; however, some Cisco routers had Microsoft IIS imbedded within them, and they DID have the security flaw that, if exploited, could permit an intruder to take over the device. In most cases, the Microsoft IIS software could have been disabled or removed from Cisco routers.

Enabling & disabling services and protocols

Only those services and protocols that are absolutely necessary should be configured and present on network devices. For instance, a Cisco router that needs to route only TCP/IP should not be configured to route other protocols, such as IPX/SPX or AppleTalk.

Firewall configuration

Firewalls must be configured so that ONLY the network services and protocols that are absolutely necessary for the organization to function should be turned on. All other services and protocols must be turned off.

Firewalls should be configured according to the rule, "All services must be disabled by default, except for those which are explicitly enabled."

Fail open versus fail closed

Where possible, devices should be configured so that they "fail closed" instead of "fail open." Case in point: If a firewall should malfunction, it would be far better were it to block all traffic rather than permit all traffic. The former would be a mere inconvenience compared to the disaster that the latter would cause.

Access control lists

Access control lists, or ACLs, are configurations on network devices that determine which persons, protocols, or services are permitted in a given setting. For example, an ACL on a network device might control administrative access to the device. Or in the case of a Cisco router, an ACL is a simple firewall that is used to permit and deny network services and protocols (and also is used to determine who/what can access the router for administrative purposes).

Whatever the specific role of any ACL, it should be configured to deny everything except that which is explicitly permitted. This is the safest possible configuration that offers maximum protection in static and changing environments.

Application Hardening

All applications, utilities, and tools that run on a computer system or a network device must be hardened, or locked down, in order to reduce the exposure of intrusion. This is important because most security incidents result from poor configuration and the absence of security patches and updates. The remainder of this section will discuss the hardening of several popular types of applications.

Throughout this chapter, you see the theme of configuration minimalism and patching repeated over and over. This is not a new form of dripping-water torture, but simply our way of stressing the fundamentals of security applications.

Segregate vital applications/services

Security experts agree that an organization should consider installing a collection of vital applications and services on individual, separate servers, rather than install all of them on a single system. The reason for this is straightforward: Were vulnerability on any one application exploited, then there would be a great risk that all of the applications would be compromised.

If, on the other hand, all critical applications were installed each on its own server, then a compromise is more likely to be contained to just the compromised application.

Consider the following example. An enterprise built a server on which it installed a Web server, FTP server, e-mail server, and DNS server. An intruder discovered a flaw in the Web server and was able to take control of the system. After doing so, he destroyed the server's FTP, e-mail, and DNS services. Were the services on separate servers, it is likely that the intruder would have been unable to harm other services.

E-mail servers

E-mail servers are subject to many forms of abuse, ranging from break-in attempts to misuse. Aside from the general recommendations of installing patches and keeping permissions and access control to barest minimums, you also need to ensure the following:

- ✔ Prevent e-mail relaying. SPAMmers like to hide the true origins of their junk mail; one of the ways in which they do this is by relaying e-mail through mail servers that still permit relaying. An e-mail server discovered to permit relaying will soon be used to ferry millions of SPAM messages.

- ✔ Hide addressee information on Internet mail servers. You should make every effort to make it impossible for someone on the Internet to be able to access your e-mail server and harvest e-mail addresses from it. If a directory of e-mail recipients is on your Internet e-mail server, it should be configured so that no one (from the Internet) can obtain the contents of that directory.

- ✔ Message and mailbox quotas. Strict limits on individual message size as well as mailbox size should be set up and enforced. Otherwise, someone may be able to launch a simple "denial of service" attack on one individual or the entire server by sending hundreds or thousands of large messages to recipients on the server, with the intention of jamming up the e-mail server so that it does not work any more.

- ✔ Block SPAM. While the debate is still raging on whether SPAM is a real security issue or just an enormous annoyance, it floods our e-mail servers every day. In many larger organizations, the volume of SPAM e-mail is greater than legit e-mail. Consider purchasing a corporate-wide, server-centric, anti-SPAM product to cut down on this annoying problem.

FTP servers

Even in this day of ubiquitous Web access, FTP servers are still in frequent use and are unlikely to go away any time soon. FTP servers are used to upload or download individual files or groups of files, using either a Web client or an FTP client.

Like other application servers, FTP servers must be configured correctly in order to prevent security problems. Aside from keeping patch levels, and so on up-to-date, the following measures need to be taken care of on FTP servers:

✔ Restrict file system access to just one directory. An FTP client, like a file system browser (such as Windows Explorer), can browse a file system. Absolute care must be taken to restrict FTP users to only a single directory or limited set of directories.

✔ Turn on logging. Make sure your FTP server is configured to log every access and download/upload.

✔ Use a non-OS file system. Using the OS file system for FTP transfers will make you vulnerable to inappropriate access by an FTP user, whether an intruder discovers a new exploit, or if you have incorrectly configured file system access permissions. Further, an intruder might be able to upload lots of large files and fill up your OS file system — this would be a bad thing to happen, even on a good day.

✔ Use separate userids and passwords for each individual user. If you assign userids and passwords to groups of users, you will lose the ability to know precisely who performed a specific upload or download.

✔ Avoid anonymous FTP if possible. Anonymous FTP is useful for making files generally available for download to the general public. However, anonymous FTP upload will permit someone to attack your site by uploading so many large files until your system runs out of disk space.

DNS servers

In case it hasn't been mentioned before, you should keep your DNS server software updated with all available patches and service releases, particularly those addressing security.

A hacked DNS server is a bad thing; if a DNS server falls victim to an intruder, said intruder may be able to modify, remove, or corrupt the database. This could result in Web browsers being pointed to the wrong computer (imagine if someone made a clone of your favorite banking, auction, or bookstore Web site, and then attacked its DNS server to point all Web browsers to the clone instead of to the real site).

Here are some specific measures that should be taken to protect DNS servers.

✔ Restrict zone transfers to known systems. DNS servers perform "zone transfers" where one DNS server — usually the master — copies its database to one or more secondary servers. Master servers should be configured to send copies of their database *only* to known, registered secondary servers. And secondary servers should be configured to accept zone transfers *only* from known master servers.

✔ Restrict database access to a select few. Only a small number of trusted, trained administrators should have access to the DNS database.

NNTP servers

NNTP is the protocol used to transfer UseNet news content from one news server to another. Besides the usual good hygiene regarding keeping patches up-to-date and removal of unnecessary or unused services, NNTP servers should be configured to accept news updates only from known upstream NNTP servers, and likewise configured to send news only to known downstream servers.

File/print servers

File and print servers are the workhorses in many work environments. They control access to large server-based shared directories, as well as access to all network-connected printers.

In addition to the usual server hardening, file/print servers must be carefully configured so as to not accidentally permit more access than is intended. This can be an especially challenging task in large organizations containing not only hundreds, thousands, or tens of thousands of users, but sometimes an even greater number of groups and aliases. This can turn what should be a simple user-access task into the biggest pot of nightmare spaghetti imaginable.

Still, a few simple guidelines are in order.

- ✔ Keep all shared volumes separate from OS file systems.
- ✔ Avoid the temptation to give directory access to "Everyone."
- ✔ Explicitly block file and printer access from outside your corporate network. Otherwise, a security flaw or configuration error could result in resources being available to users on the Internet (probably something you don't want).
- ✔ Utilize quotas. Accidents as well as intrusions can result in all disk space being exhausted in the absence of a quota mechanism to limit the amount of resources that any individual is allowed to use.

DHCP servers

We have probably not yet mentioned that it is important to always keep security patches current on a system, and this is true of DHCP servers.

Further, it is important that DHCP servers be protected from attack by restricting administrative access, and by configuring the server to prevent intruders from reconfiguring the server or by exhausting its IP address pool.

Web servers

Web servers are among the most complex application services in common use today, so you should not be surprised to see a parade of security fixes being issued from your Web server software vendor. It is essential that security fixes be installed as soon as possible.

Web servers have ready access to database management systems, databases, file systems, software code, and of course static HTML content. Hence, Web servers generally have a large number of configuration parameters available, associated with security and also performance.

Web server software components

Web servers are often complex enough that they consist of several components that can each be installed or not. Any modules that are not used should be removed. This will prevent any potential intrusion via these modules, since they are simply not there to exploit.

Access to databases and file systems

A frequent security problem associated with Web servers and related databases and file systems is that system administrators (or Webmasters) give "wide open" database/file system access permissions to the Web server application. This is a potentially fatal mistake: If an intruder is able to exploit and take over a Web server, then nothing will stop the intruder from accessing any or all data in a database or file system.

Instead, the Web server should have access to only those data elements, files, directories, and functions that are *absolutely necessary* for the Web site to run. All other access should be turned off.

Database and Directory Service Hardening

Data repositories, whether they take the form of relational databases, directory service databases, or other vital information, all share a common set of principles when it comes to hardening. These principles have been discussed earlier in this chapter; they are

- ✔ Lock down access control using "denied unless explicitly permitted." No one without a legitimate business reason to access any data should be able to do so.

- ✔ Turn on access logging. Every legitimate access to data, as well as unsuccessful attempts, should be logged. At a minimum, such logs should contain: what, who, when, and where.

It should also be noted that, in most situations, there are multiple ways to access data in a database or directory. Every path must be completely locked down in order to prevent unauthorized and inappropriate access. For example, we could design an application that has extremely good security in its software but which also has poorly configured database permissions. While it might be difficult to break in to the data using the application, one could use ordinary data access tools to get to the data.

Databases and directory services

Databases are immensely complex and come with a great variety of tools that are used to manage and access data. If any of these facilities is poorly configured or unguarded, they may provide easy access paths to intruders who have no legitimate reason to access the database.

✔ Databases have tools used by the data base administrator (DBA) to manage tables, logs, and other elements. Access to these tools must be restricted to only the few persons with a true business reason to have them.

✔ Databases are accompanied by collections of components that are used by software developers to access data in the database. Access to these component libraries should be restricted to software developers. (Although this method alone would be a very poor strategy for protecting data!)

✔ Permissions on the databases themselves should be restricted as much as possible so that only legitimate users and processes can access them. And even then, users should only be able to access data that is specific to their job function.

✔ Almost without exception, databases are collections of files that reside in a system's file system. Access to these database files must be restricted to only those users and processes that have a good reason to access them.

Prep Test

1 An FTP service that permits a user to log in without a userid or password is called:

 A ○ Ambiguous FTP

 B ○ Anonymous FTP

 C ○ Guest FTP

 D ○ Incorrectly configured FTP

2 The most common recommendation for the installation of security patches is:

 A ○ Install immediately

 B ○ Install only after an intruder has exploited that feature

 C ○ Never install

 D ○ Install after one year

3 Removing unnecessary components and services is known as:

 A ○ Deepening

 B ○ Softening

 C ○ Layering

 D ○ Hardening

4 Guest accounts should be disabled or removed In order to:

 A ○ Prevent unauthorized login via a guest account

 B ○ Force the use of the administrator login for system maintenance

 C ○ Simplify access control administration

 D ○ Prevent a guest spoofing attack

5 The reason that unnecessary services should be removed is:

 A ○ This shortens the system's primary key.

 B ○ System performance is improved.

 C ○ Systems administration is simplified.

 D ○ A service that has been removed cannot be attacked.

6 **The principle advantage of "deny all unless explicitly permitted" is:**

A ○ Access control lists execute faster.

B ○ New users are automatically denied access.

C ○ Access control reports are inherently shorter.

D ○ New users are automatically granted access.

7 **The biggest risk from default passwords is:**

A ○ Intruders can try to guess default passwords and log in to accounts.

B ○ Intruders will be able to decrypt secret messages.

C ○ Intruders will be able to encrypt secret messages.

D ○ Intruders will be able to take over the system.

8 **Web servers are difficult to secure because:**

A ○ They are administered by a large group of individuals.

B ○ They are very complicated and have many configuration settings.

C ○ They are administered by untrained users.

D ○ No security patches are available.

9 **The principle disadvantage of "permit all unless explicitly denied" is**

A ○ Access control lists execute faster.

B ○ New users are automatically denied access.

C ○ Access control reports are inherently shorter.

D ○ New users are automatically granted access.

10 **Access logs should contain all of the following except:**

A ○ Why

B ○ Who

C ○ What

D ○ When

Answers

1 **B.** Anonymous FTP. Anonymous FTP accepts "ftp" or "anonymous" as the userid, and the user's e-mail address as the password. *Review "Application Hardening — FTP servers."*

2 **A.** Install immediately. Security patches should be installed as soon as they are available. Review *"OS/NOS Hardening."*

3 **D.** Hardening. The hardening procedure consists of several activities including the disabling or removal of unnecessary services. *Review "Hardening Basics."*

4 **A.** Prevent unauthorized login via a guest account. Intruders can try to log in using guest accounts because they frequently have default or easy-to-guess passwords such as "guest." *Review "Hardening Basics."*

5 **D.** A service that has been removed cannot be attacked. The removal of unnecessary services is one of the basic fundamentals of safe systems administration. *Review "Hardening Basics."*

6 **B.** New users are automatically denied access. "Deny unless permitted" by design denies all new users until they are specifically permitted. *Review "Hardening Basics."*

7 **A.** Intruders can try to guess default passwords and log in to accounts. If vendor-supplied default passwords are permitted to remain on a system, intruders who know the default passwords can try to log in to systems. *Review "Hardening Basics."*

8 **B.** They are very complicated and have many configuration settings. A Web server is a very complex piece of machinery. This complexity means that they have numerous configuration settings, many of which affect security. *Review "Application Hardening."*

9 **D.** New users are automatically granted access. The problem with the "permit all except explicitly denied" is that new users are automatically granted access, since their names will not ordinarily appear in the "explicitly denied" list. *Review "Hardening Basics."*

10 **A.** Why. An audit log should record who (who made the change), what (the detail on the change), and when (the time of day). But an audit log will not know why a particular change was performed. *See "Database and Directory Service Hardening."*

Part V
Cryptography

"We take network security very seriously here."

In this part . . .

The Cryptography domain comprises a very large part of the Security+ exam. Unfortunately, it is also one of the more complex subjects in information security. It encompasses symmetric algorithms, asymmetric algorithms, message authentication, digital certificates, public key infrastructure (PKI), key management functions, and key escrow and recovery.

Chapter 12

Cryptography Basics

Get ready for some spooky *Tales From the Crypt-O*! Well, maybe not spooky, but sometimes the subject of cryptography can be quite intimidating.

Cryptography (from the Greek, *kryptos* meaning *hidden* and *graphia* meaning *writing*) is the science of encrypting and decrypting communications to make them unintelligible for all but the intended recipient. In this chapter, I decrypt the subject of cryptography to help you prepare for the Security+ exam.

For the most part, the Security+ exam does not get into very technical details about a particular subject — cryptography is an exception. Study this chapter carefully and memorize specific characteristics about the algorithms discussed here.

Quick Assessment

1   _____ means that an action or occurrence can't be easily denied.

2   _____ describes the difficulty, in terms of time, effort, and resources, in breaking a cryptosystem.

3   Packets that are encrypted once at the original encryption source and then decrypted only at the final decryption destination describes what type of encryption?

4   DES, 3DES, AES, and IDEA are all examples of _____ key algorithms.

5   The Advanced Encryption Standard (AES) is based on what algorithm?

6   Asymmetric key cryptography uses a _____ and _____ key pair to encrypt and decrypt information.

7   Using asymmetric key cryptography, an open message format uses a sender's private key to protect _____.

8   A _____ is used to verify the authenticity and integrity of a message.

9   Message digests are produced using a _____.

10 MD5 produces a _____-bit message digest.

Answers

1 Nonrepudiation. *See "Concepts of Using Cryptography."*

2 Work factor. *Review "Work factor: Force x effort = work!"*

3 End-to-end. *Review "Encryption and decryption."*

4 Symmetric. *See "Symmetric key cryptography."*

5 Rijndael Block Cipher. *See "Advanced Encryption Standard."*

6 Public, private. See *"Asymmetric key cryptography."*

7 Authenticity. *See "Asymmetric key cryptography."*

8 Digital signature. *See "Digital signatures."*

9 One-way hashing function. *See "Message digests."*

10 128. *See "Message digests."*

Concepts of Using Cryptography

Cryptography can be used to achieve several goals of information security, including these:

- **Confidentiality:** Cryptography protects the confidentiality (or *secrecy*) of information. Even when the transmission or storage medium has been compromised, the encrypted information is practically useless to unauthorized persons without the proper keys for decryption.

- **Integrity:** Cryptography can ensure the integrity (or accuracy) of information through the use of either

  - Hashing algorithms
  - Message digests

- **Authentication:** Cryptography can be used for authentication and non-repudiation through

  - Digital signatures
  - Digital certificates
  - Public Key Infrastructure (PKI)

Nonrepudiation means that an action or occurrence can't be easily denied. For example, it's difficult for a user to deny sending an e-mail message that was digitally signed with that user's private key.

Don't confuse these three points with the CIA triad, which I discuss in Chapter 2. The *CIA triad* deals with confidentiality, integrity, and *availability*; cryptography does nothing to ensure availability.

Cryptography Basics

Cryptography today has evolved into a complex science (some say an art) presenting many great promises and challenges in the field of information security. In this section, I discuss several important terms and concepts, basic cryptographic operations, and the individual components of the cryptosystem. A *cryptosystem* is the hardware or software implementation that transforms plaintext into ciphertext (encryption) and back into plaintext (decryption).

Plaintext and ciphertext

A *plaintext* message is a message in its original readable format or a ciphertext message that has been properly *decrypted* (unscrambled) to produce the original readable plaintext message.

A *ciphertext* message is a plaintext message that has been transformed *(encrypted)* into a scrambled message that's unintelligible. This concept doesn't apply to messages from your boss that may also happen to be unintelligible!

Work factor: Force x effort = work!

Work factor describes the difficulty — in terms of time, effort, and resources — in breaking a cryptosystem. Given enough time, effort, and resources, any cryptosystem can be broken. The goal of all cryptosystems, then, is to achieve a work factor that sufficiently protects the encrypted information against a reasonable estimate of available time, effort, and resources. However, *reasonable* can be difficult to estimate with the rapid improvements in technology today.

Moore's Law is based on an observation that processing power seems to double about every 18 months. To compensate for Moore's Law, some *really* hard encryption algorithms are used. Today, encrypted information is valuable for perhaps only three months with encryption algorithms that theoretically take several hundred millennia to break, confident in the knowledge that tomorrow it will be mere child's play.

Block and stream ciphers

Ciphers are cryptographic transformations. The two main classes of ciphers are *block* and *stream*, which describe how the cipher operates on input data.

Block ciphers

Block ciphers operate on a single fixed block (typically 64 or 128 bits) of plaintext to produce the corresponding ciphertext. Advantages of block ciphers compared with stream ciphers are

- ✔ **Reusable cryptographic keys:** Key management is much easier.
- ✔ **Interoperability:** Block ciphers are more widely supported than stream ciphers.

Block ciphers are typically implemented in software.

Stream ciphers

Stream ciphers operate in real time on a continuous stream of data, typically bit-by-bit. Stream ciphers are generally faster than block ciphers and require less code to implement. However, the keys in a stream cipher are generally used only once and then discarded. Key management becomes a serious problem. Stream ciphers are typically implemented in hardware.

Encryption and decryption

Encryption (or *enciphering*) is the process of converting plaintext communications into ciphertext. *Decryption* (or *deciphering*) reverses that process, converting ciphertext into plaintext. Traffic on a network can be encrypted by using either *end-to-end* or *link encryption*.

End-to-end encryption

With *end-to-end encryption,* packets are encrypted once at the original encryption source and then decrypted only at the final decryption destination. The advantages of end-to-end encryption are its speed and overall security. However, in order for the packets to be properly routed, only the data is encrypted, not the routing information.

Link encryption

Link encryption requires that each node (for example, a router) has separate key pairs for its upstream and downstream neighbors. Packets are encrypted and decrypted at every node along the network path.

The following steps illustrate link encryption:

1. **Computer 1 encrypts a message by using secret key A and then transmits the message to Router 1.**

2. **Router 1 decrypts the message by using secret key A, re-encrypts the message by using secret key B, and then transmits the message to Router 2.**

3. **Router 2 decrypts the message by using secret key B, re-encrypts the message by using secret key C, and then transmits the message to Computer 2.**

4. **Computer 2 decrypts the message by using secret key C.**

The advantage of using link encryption is that the entire packet (including routing information) is encrypted. However, link encryption has these two disadvantages:

✔ **Latency:** Packets must be encrypted/decrypted at every node.

✔ **Inherent vulnerability:** If a node is compromised or a packet's decrypted contents are cached in a node, the message can be compromised.

Putting it all together: The cryptosystem

A *cryptosystem* is the hardware or software implementation that transforms plaintext into ciphertext (encryption) and back into plaintext (decryption).

An effective cryptosystem must have these properties:

- ✔ The encryption and decryption process is efficient for all possible keys within the cryptosystem's keyspace (for example, 64-bit or 128-bit).

- ✔ The cryptosystem is easy to use.

- ✔ The strength of the cryptosystem is dependent on the secrecy of the *cryptovariables* (or *keys*), not the secrecy of the algorithm. (Most cryptographic algorithms are public anyway.)

Cryptosystems typically comprise two elements:

- ✔ **Cryptographic algorithm:** This details the step-by-step procedures used to produce

    - Ciphertext (encipher)

    - Plaintext (decipher)

- ✔ **Cryptovariable:** The key to the cryptographic algorithm, the *cryptovariable* (or key) is a secret value applied to the algorithm. The strength and effectiveness of the cryptosystem is largely dependent upon the secrecy and strength of the cryptovariable.

An analogy of a cryptosystem is a deadbolt lock. A deadbolt lock can be easily identified, and its inner working mechanisms aren't closely guarded state secrets. What makes a deadbolt lock effective is the individual key that controls a specific lock on a specific door. However, if the key is weak (imagine only one or two notches on a flat key) or not well protected (left under your doormat), the lock won't protect your belongings. Similarly, if an attacker is able to determine what cryptographic algorithm (lock) was used to encrypt a message, it should still be protected because you're using a strong key (128-bit) that you have kept secret, not a 6-character password written on a scrap of paper left under your mousepad.

Not Quite the Metric System: Symmetric and Asymmetric Key Systems

Cryptographic algorithms are broadly classified as either symmetric or asymmetric key systems. Symmetric key systems are more widely implemented because these systems are typically less complex than asymmetric systems and are not as computationally intensive (meaning they are faster).

Symmetric key cryptography

Symmetric key cryptography uses a single key to both encrypt and decrypt information.

Symmetric key cryptography is also known as

- Symmetric algorithm
- Secret key
- Single key
- Private key

Two parties can exchange an encrypted message by following these steps:

1. **The sender encrypts the plaintext message with a secret key known only by the sender and the intended recipient.**

2. **The sender transmits the encrypted message to the intended recipient.**

3. **The recipient decrypts the message with the same secret key to obtain the plaintext message.**

For an attacker to read the message, the attacker must either

- Guess the secret key (for example, through a *brute-force* attack). See Chapter 4 for more on brute-force attacks.
- Intercept the secret key during the initial exchange

The following are the main disadvantages of symmetric systems:

- **Distribution:** Secure distribution of secret keys is absolutely required either through out-of-band methods (such as through an in-person exchange or some other secure method) or by using asymmetric systems.
- **Scalability:** A different key is required for each pair of communicating individuals.
- **Limited functionality:** Symmetric systems can't provide either
  - Authentication
  - Nonrepudiation

Symmetric systems have many advantages:

- **Speed:** Symmetric systems are much faster than asymmetric systems.
- **Strength:** Strength is gained when used with a large key.
- **Availability:** Many algorithms are available.

Symmetric key algorithms include

▶ DES

▶ Triple DES

▶ Advanced Encryption Standard (AES)

▶ International Data Encryption Algorithm (IDEA)

▶ RC5

Data Encryption Standard (DES)

In the early 1970s, the National Institute of Standards and Technology (NIST) solicited vendors to submit encryption algorithm proposals to be evaluated by the National Security Agency (NSA) in support of a national cryptographic standard. This new encryption standard was used for private-sector and sensitive but unclassified (SBU) government data. In 1974, IBM submitted a 128-bit algorithm originally known as *Lucifer*. After several modifications, the IBM proposal was endorsed by the NSA and formally adopted as the Data Encryption Standard (DES) in 1977.

DES is the most common symmetric key algorithm used today. It is a block cipher that uses a 56-bit key.

The *DES algorithm* is a symmetric (or private) key cipher consisting of an algorithm and a key. The algorithm is a 64-bit block cipher based on a 56-bit symmetric key. (It comprises 56 key bits + 8 parity bits . . . or think of it as 8 bytes with each byte containing 7 key bits and 1 parity bit.) During encryption, the original message (plaintext) is divided into 64-bit blocks. Operating on a single block at a time, each 64-bit plaintext block is split into two 32-bit blocks. Under control of the 56-bit key, 16 rounds of transpositions and substitutions are performed on each individual character to produce the resulting ciphertext output.

The original goal of the DES standard was to develop an encryption standard that would be viable for 10 to 15 years. Although DES far exceeded this goal, in 1999 the Electronic Frontier Foundation achieved the inevitable, breaking a DES key in only 23 hours.

Triple DES (3DES)

Triple DES (3DES) has effectively extended the life of the DES algorithm. In Triple DES, a message is

1. Encrypted by using one key

2. Encrypted again by using a second key

3. Encrypted again by using either the first key or a third key

The use of three separate 56-bit encryption keys produces an effective key length of 168 bits. But Triple DES doesn't just triple the work factor required to crack the DES algorithm. Because the attacker doesn't know whether he or she successfully cracked even the first 56-bit key (pick a number between 0 and 72 quadrillion!) until all three keys are cracked and the correct plaintext is produced, the workforce is more like 2^{56} x 2^{56} x 2^{56}, or 72 quadrillion x 72 quadrillion x 72 quadrillion. (Don't try this on a calculator; just trust me on this one.)

Double DES wasn't a significant improvement to DES. By using a meet-in-the-middle attack (see Chapter 4), it has been shown that the work to crack Double DES is only slightly greater than for DES. For this reason, Double DES isn't commonly used.

Using Triple DES would seem enough to protect even the most sensitive data for at least a few lifetimes, but a few problems exist with Triple DES.

✔ The performance cost is significant because of the complex computations it requires.

Although Triple DES is faster than many other symmetric encryption algorithms, it's still unacceptably slow and won't work with many applications requiring high-speed throughput of large volumes of data.

✔ A weakness in the implementation allows a cryptanalyst to reduce the effective key size to 108 bits in a brute-force attack.

Although a 108-bit key size still requires a significant amount of time to crack (theoretically several million millennia), it's still a weakness.

Advanced Encryption Standard (AES)

The *Advanced Encryption Standard (AES)* is a block cipher that will replace DES. In October 2000, NIST announced selection of the Rijndael Block Cipher to implement AES.

AES is based on the Rijndael Block Cipher.

Rijndael Block Cipher

The *Rijndael Block Cipher,* developed by Dr. Joan Daemen and Dr. Vincent Rijmen, has variable block and key lengths (128, 192, or 256 bits). It was designed to be

✔ Simple

✔ Resistant to known attacks

✔ Fast

Twofish Algorithm

The *Twofish Algorithm* was a finalist in the AES selection process. It is a symmetric block cipher that operates on 128-bit (instead of 64-bit) blocks, employing 16 rounds with key lengths up to 256 bits.

IDEA Cipher

The *International Data Encryption Algorithm (IDEA) cipher* evolved from the Proposed Encryption Standard and the Improved Proposed Encryption Standard originally developed in 1990. IDEA is a block cipher that operates on 64-bit plaintext blocks using a 128-bit key. IDEA performs eight rounds on 16-bit sub-blocks and can operate in four distinct modes similar to DES. The IDEA cipher provides stronger encryption than RC4 and Triple DES, but because it's patented, it's not widely used. It is used in Pretty Good Privacy (PGP), an encryption tool with e-mail support. For more on RC5, read the following section.

RC5

RC5 (Rivest Cipher No. 5) is part of a series of symmetric algorithms developed by RSA Data Security. RC5 is a block mode cipher that uses

- ✔ Variable-length key (0 to 2048 bits)
- ✔ Variable block size (32, 64, or 128 bits)
- ✔ Variable number of processing rounds (0 to 255)

Asymmetric key cryptography

Asymmetric key cryptography uses separate keys for encryption and decryption information. These keys are known as *public* and *private* key pairs.

Asymmetric key cryptography is also known as

- ✔ Asymmetric algorithm
- ✔ Public key

Secure message format

The secure message format guarantees the confidentiality of a message. When two parties want to exchange an encrypted message by using asymmetric key cryptography, they follow these steps:

1. **The sender encrypts the plaintext message with the intended recipient's public key and transmits the encrypted message**

   This produces a ciphertext message that can then be transmitted to the intended recipient.

2. **The recipient receives the message and decrypts the message with his private key.**

   Only the private key can decrypt the message. Without the private key

   - An attacker with only the public key can't decrypt the message.

   - The original sender can't decrypt the message.

Secure message format uses the recipient's private key to protect confidentiality.

Open message format

The *open message format* guarantees the authenticity but not the confidentiality of a message.

Open message format uses the sender's private key to protect authenticity.

If the sender wants to guarantee the authenticity of a message (or, more correctly, the authenticity of the sender), he can "sign" the message by using the following steps:

1. **The sender encrypts the plaintext message with his own private key.**

   This produces a ciphertext message that can then be transmitted to the intended recipient.

2. **The signed message is transmitted to the intended recipient.**

3. **To verify that the message is from the purported sender, the recipient applies the sender's public key, which is known to everyone.**

Of course, an attacker can verify the authenticity of the message, too.

Secure and signed message format

The secure and signed message format guarantees the confidentiality and authenticity of a message, which is accomplished by using the following steps:

1. **The sender encrypts the message first with the intended recipient's public key and then with his own private key.**

   This produces a ciphertext message that can then be transmitted to the intended recipient.

2. **The secure and signed message is transmitted to the intended recipient.**

3. **The recipient uses the sender's public key to verify the authenticity of the message and then uses his own private key to decrypt the message's contents.**

If an attacker intercepts the message, he can apply the sender's public key but then has an encrypted message that can't be decrypted without the intended recipient's private key. Thus, both confidentiality and authenticity are assured.

A secure and signed message format uses the sender's private key and the recipient's public key to protect confidentiality and authenticity.

A public and private key are mathematically related, but (theoretically) the private key can't be computed or derived from the public key. This property of asymmetric systems is based on the concept of a one-way function. A *one-way function* is a problem that's easy to compute in one direction but not in the reverse direction. In asymmetric key systems, a *trapdoor* (private key) resolves the reverse operation of the one-way function.

Because of the complexity of asymmetric key systems, they are more commonly used for key management (see Chapter 13) or digital signatures (discussed later in this chapter) than for encryption of bulk information. Often, a *hybrid* system is employed, using an asymmetric system to securely distribute the secret keys of a symmetric key system that's used to encrypt the data.

The main disadvantage of asymmetric systems is speed. Because of the types of algorithms that are used to achieve the one-way hash functions, very large keys are required. (A 128-bit symmetric key has the equivalent strength of a 2,304-bit asymmetric key.) This, in turn, requires more computational power, causing a significant loss of speed (up to 10,000 times slower than a comparable symmetric key system).

However, many significant advantages to asymmetric systems exist, including

- **Extended functionality:** Asymmetric key systems can provide both confidentiality and authentication; symmetric systems can provide only confidentiality.

- **Scalability:** This resolves cryptographic key management issues associated with symmetric key systems.

Asymmetric key algorithms include

- RSA
- Diffie-Hellman
- El Gamal

RSA

The RSA algorithm is a *key transport algorithm* based on the difficulty of factoring a number that is the product of two large prime numbers (typically 512 bits). Two users (for example, Thomas and Richard) can securely transport symmetric keys by using RSA like this:

1. **Thomas creates a symmetric key, encrypts it with Richard's public key, and then transmits it to Richard.**

2. **Richard decrypts the symmetric key by using his own private key.**

Diffie-Hellman key exchange

Diffie-Hellman is a *key agreement algorithm* based on discrete logarithms for secure key exchange. Two users (Thomas and Richard) can exchange symmetric keys by using Diffie-Hellman like this:

1. **Thomas and Richard obtain each other's public keys.**

2. **Thomas and Richard then combine their own individual private key with the public key of the other person, producing a symmetric key that's known only to the two users involved in the exchange.**

Diffie-Hellman key exchange is vulnerable to man-in-the-middle attacks in which an attacker intercepts the public keys during the initial exchange and substitutes his own private key to create a session key that decrypts the session. A separate authentication mechanism is necessary to protect against this type of attack, ensuring that the two parties communicating in the session are the legitimate parties.

El Gamal

El Gamal is an unpatented, asymmetric key algorithm based on the discrete logarithm problem used in Diffie-Hellman. It extends the functionality of Diffie-Hellman to include encryption and digital signatures.

Message Authentication

Message authentication guarantees the authenticity and integrity of a message by ensuring that:

✔ A message hasn't been altered (either maliciously or accidentally) during transmission.

✔ A message isn't a replay of a previous message.

✔ The message was sent from the origin stated (is not a forgery).

✔ The message is sent to the intended recipient.

Basic message authentication and integrity controls include checksums, CRC-values, and parity checks. More advanced message authentication is performed by using digital signatures and message digests.

Digital signatures and message digests are used for message authentication.

Digital signatures

The *Digital Signature Standard* (DSS), published by NIST in Federal Information Processing Standard (FIPS) 186-1, specifies two acceptable algorithms in its standard: the RSA Digital Signature Algorithm and the Digital Signature Algorithm (DSA, which is based on a modified El Gamal algorithm). Both algorithms use the SHA-1 Secure Hash Algorithm, which I discuss in the upcoming section "SHA-1."

A *digital signature* is a simple way to verify the authenticity (and integrity) of a message. Instead of encrypting a message with the intended receiver's public key, the sender encrypts it with his own private key. The sender's public key properly decrypts the message, authenticating the originator of the message. This is known as an *open message format* in asymmetric key systems, which I discuss in the section "Asymmetric key cryptography," earlier in this chapter.

However, it's often impractical to encrypt a message with the receiver's public key to protect confidentiality and then encrypt the entire message again by using the sender's private key to protect authenticity and integrity. Instead, a representation of the encrypted message is encrypted with the sender's private key to produce a digital signature. The intended recipient decrypts this representation by using the sender's public key and then independently calculates the expected results of the decrypted representation by using the same known one-way hashing algorithm. Read more about this in the following section, "Message digests." If the results are the same, the integrity of the original message is assured. This representation of the entire message is known as a *message digest*.

Message digests

To *digest* means to reduce or condense something. This is precisely what a message digest does. (Conversely, *indigestion* means to expand, as in gases . . . how do you spell *relief*?) A *message digest* is a condensed representation of a message; think *Reader's Digest.* Ideally, a message digest has these properties:

- ✔ The original message can't be re-created from the message digest.
- ✔ Finding a message that produces a particular digest shouldn't be computationally feasible.
- ✔ No two messages produce the same message digest.
- ✔ The message digest should be calculated by using the entire contents of the original message — it shouldn't be a representation of a representation.

Message digests are produced by using a one-way hash function.

Several types of one-way hashing algorithms (digest algorithms) are available, including

- ✔ MD5
- ✔ SHA-1
- ✔ HMAC

A *one-way function* ensures that the same key can't encrypt and decrypt a message in an asymmetric key system.

- ✔ One key encrypts the message (produces ciphertext).
- ✔ A second key (the trapdoor) decrypts the message (produces plaintext), effectively reversing the one-way function.

A *one-way hashing algorithm* produces a hashing value (or message digest) that can't be reversed; it can't be decrypted. No trapdoor exists for a one-way hashing algorithm. The purpose of a one-way hashing algorithm is to ensure integrity and authentication.

MD5

MD5 is a one-way hash algorithm developed by Ronald Rivest in 1991. It is actually part of a family (like the Jackson Family of pop music fame) of digest algorithms developed by Ronald Rivest beginning with MD (Jermaine). After some limited success with MD, individual variations were created beginning with MD2 (Michael). MD2 produced a 128-bit digest and was used extensively for many years; but eventually flaws were found, and a new replacement was needed. MD3 (Tito) was never taken seriously; and after a very short period in the limelight, MD4 (LaToya) was quickly exploited. However, unlike any of its predecessors, MD5 (Janet) is strong, fast, resilient, and sexy (ooops!) and is one of the most popular hashing algorithms in use today. MD5 takes a variable size input (message) and produces a fixed-size output (128-bit message digest). Messages are processed in 512-bit blocks using four rounds of transformation.

SHA-1

SHA-1 (Secure Hash Algorithm) functions very similar to the way that MD5 functions. In fact, Ronald Rivest was instrumental in its design. Like MD5, SHA-1 takes a variable size input (message) and produces a fixed-size (160-bit message digest versus MD5's 128-bit message digest). SHA-1 processes messages in 512-bit blocks and adds padding to a message length, if necessary, to produce a total message length that's a multiple of 512.

HMAC

The Hashed Message Authentication Code (HMAC) (or Checksum) further extends the security of the MD5 and SHA-1 algorithms through the concept of a *keyed digest*. HMAC creates a single message digest that incorporates

- ✔ A previously shared secret key
- ✔ The original message

Even if an attacker intercepts a message, modifies its contents, and calculates a new message digest, the result won't match the receiver's hash calculation because the modified message's hash doesn't include the secret key.

Prep Test

1 Cryptography can be used to achieve each of the following information security goals, except _____.

   A ○ Confidentiality

   B ○ Integrity

   C ○ Accountability

   D ○ Authentication

2 Which of these is not an advantage of symmetric key systems?

   A ○ Scalability

   B ○ Speed

   C ○ Strength

   D ○ Availability

3 All of these are examples of symmetric algorithms, except:

   A ○ DES

   B ○ Twofish

   C ○ IDEA

   D ○ Elliptic curve

4 DES is a(n) _____ key algorithm that uses a _____-bit key.

   A ○ Asymmetric; 56

   B ○ Symmetric; 56

   C ○ Asymmetric: 64

   D ○ Symmetric; 64

5 The Advanced Encryption Standard (AES) is based on what symmetric key algorithm?

   A ○ Twofish

   B ○ Knapsack

   C ○ Diffie-Hellman

   D ○ Rijndael

6 A message that's encrypted with the sender's private key only, for the purpose of authentication, is known as a(n):

A ○ Secure message format

B ○ Signed and secure message format

C ○ Open message format

D ○ Message digest

7 In asymmetric key systems, a _____ resolves the reverse operation of the one-way function.

A ○ Backdoor

B ○ Trapdoor

C ○ Public key

D ○ Digital signature

8 All these are examples of asymmetric key systems, except:

A ○ Diffie-Hellman

B ○ IDEA

C ○ RSA

D ○ El Gamal

9 Which of the following is not a message digest algorithm?

A ○ MD5

B ○ SHA-1

C ○ RC5

D ○ HMAC

Answers

1 **C.** Accountability. Cryptography can be used for confidentiality, integrity, and authentication. *Review "Concepts of Using Cryptography."*

2 **A.** Scalability. Symmetric key systems aren't scalable because of the difficulty of key management between individual pairs of communicating parties. *Review "Symmetric key cryptography."*

3 **D.** Elliptic curve. DES, Twofish, and IDEA are all symmetric key algorithms. Elliptic curve is an asymmetric key algorithm. *Review "Symmetric key cryptography."*

4 **B.** Symmetric; 56. DES is a 64-bit block cipher comprised of a 56-bit key and 8 parity bits. *Review "Data Encryption Standard (DES)."*

5 **D.** Rijndael. The Rijndael Block Cipher has been selected as the AES. Twofish was a finalist for the AES standard but wasn't selected. Knapsack and Diffie-Hellman are asymmetric key systems. *Review "Advanced Encryption Standard (AES)."*

6 **C.** Open message format. A secure message is encrypted with the receiver's public key to achieve confidentiality. A signed and secure message is encrypted with both the receiver's public key and the sender's private key. A message digest is produced by a one-way hashing function to digitally sign a message for authentication. *Review "Asymmetric key cryptography."*

7 **B.** Trapdoor. A trapdoor is a private key. *Review "Asymmetric key cryptography."*

8 **B.** IDEA. The International Data Encryption Algorithm (IDEA) is a symmetric key algorithm. *Review "Asymmetric key cryptography."*

9 **C.** RC5. RC5 is a symmetric key algorithm that uses a variable-length key. *Review "Message digests."*

Cryptography Basics

Chapter 13

Public Key Infrastructure (PKI)

A Public Key Infrastructure (PKI) enables secure e-commerce through the integration of public key cryptography, digital signatures, and other services necessary to ensure confidentiality, integrity, authentication, nonrepudiation, and access control.

Quick Assessment

1 A _____ is a secure credential that contains the owner's public key and identifies that owner.

2 _____ is a de facto standard that provides a standard syntax for certificate requests.

3 Most digital certificates are based on the _____ standard, which defines various content, configuration, and process requirements.

4 The _____ is a broad, high-level security policy that provides the basis for trust between organizations.

5 The four basic components of a PKI are the _____, _____, _____, and _____.

6 A _____ provides current status information about certificates issued by a CA.

7 A CRL *does* (or *does not*) contain expired certificates.

8 Ensuring that certificates and CRLs are available to users when requested is the primary function of the _____.

9 Two common trust models found in PKIs are _____ and _____.

10 In a hierarchical model, the central CA, located at the top of the hierarchy, is known as the _____.

Answers

1 Digital certificate. *See "Digital Certificates."*

2 PKCS #10. *Review "Digital Certificates."*

3 X.509. *See "Digital Certificates."*

4 Certificate Policy (CP). *Review "Policies and Procedures."*

5 Certification Authority (CA), Registration Authority (RA), Repository, and Archive. *See "PKI Components."*

6 Certificate Revocation List (CRL). *See "PKI Components."*

7 Does not. *See "PKI Components."*

8 Repository. *See "PKI Components."*

9 Hierarchical model and cross-certification model. *See "Trust Models."*

10 Root CA. *See "Trust Models."*

Digital Certificates

The basic element of a PKI is the *digital* (or *public-key*) *certificate.* A digital certificate is a secure credential that contains the owner's public key and identifies that owner. Most digital certificates are based on the X.509 standard (which defines various content, configuration, and process requirements) and the Abstract Syntax Notation 1 (ASN.1) standard for data syntax and encoding. Another important set of standards are the Public Key Cryptography Standards (PKCS), which are not really standards at all (the PKCS standards were developed by RSA Data Security, Inc.) but are still widely recognized and used in public key cryptography. The PKCS standards are numbered PKCS #1 through PKCS #12. Although they are all relevant to public-key cryptography, PKCS #7 and PKCS #10 are two of the more commonly known standards. PKCS #7 provides a general syntax for digital signatures, and PKCS #10 provides a standard syntax for certification requests.

A digital certificate typically includes the following information:

- ✔ Owner's name, company or organization, and contact information
- ✔ Owner's public key
- ✔ The certificate's activation date
- ✔ The certificate's expiration date
- ✔ What the certificate can be used for
- ✔ The name of the trusted party that issued the certificate (known as the *issuer*)
- ✔ A unique serial number assigned by the issuer

The issuer of the digital certificate digitally signs the contents of the certificate by using its own private key. The issuer's public key can be used to verify that the certificate is authentic and that its contents have not been altered. The owner's public key is then used to verify the identity of the individual named on the certificate. See Figure 13-1 for an example of a digital certificate.

Figure 13-1:
An example
of a digital
certificate.

Policies and Procedures

Two important elements associated with a PKI are the *Certificate Policy* (CP) and the *Certification Practice Statement* (CPS). The CP and CPS must be formalized within an organization to ensure a level of trust beyond the organization. Although both documents are similar in format, they each have a separate, distinct purpose.

The Certificate Policy (CP) is a very broad, high-level security policy (see Chapter 17 for a complete discussion of policies and procedures) that provides the basis for trust between organizations. (The CA is discussed in the next section.) CPs are defined in the X.509 standard as "a named set of rules that indicates the applicability of a certificate to a particular community and/or class of application with common security requirements" and are fully described in RFC 2527. The CP is represented by an Object Identifier (OID) in an X.509 Version 3 digital certificate.

Certification Practice Statements (CPSs) provide the detailed nuts and bolts of the process through which certificates are issued, maintained, and revoked by a Certification Authority (CA). A CPS is generally more detailed than a CP, but it may not necessarily be published in its entirety (if certain information is deemed sensitive).

Certificate Policies (CPs) are analogous to policies and standards, and Certification Practice Statements (CPSs) are analogous to procedures (see Chapter 16 for more information about policies, standards, and procedures).

The relationship between CP and CPS can be described as follows:

- The CP tells "what must be done" by the CA.
- The CPS tells "how it will be done" by the Certification Authority (CA) and/or Registration Authority (RA).

Together, the CP and CPS provide information which can help an organization determine what level of trust is appropriate for a given certificate or CA.

PKI Components

The four basic components of a PKI are the Certification Authority (CA), Registration Authority (RA), Repository, and Archive. These components may all be incorporated into a single system or deployed across multiple systems in multiple locations.

Certification Authority (CA)

The Certification Authority (CA) comprises hardware, software, and the personnel administering the PKI. The CA issues certificates to users and/or other CAs, maintains and publishes status information and Certificate Revocation Lists (CRLs), and maintains archives.

When a CA issues a digital certificate to a user, the CA is certifying that the user identified on the certificate and any additional information on the certificate is accurate and that the stated uses for the certificate are authorized. The certificate contains the user's public key as well as the CA's digital signature (which permits you to validate the authenticity of the CA).

When a CA issues a digital certificate to another CA, it is certifying that the CA identified on the certificate is trustworthy and that any certificates the identified CA issues are likewise trustworthy.

A *Certificate Revocation List* (CRL) provides current status information about the certificates issued by a CA. A CRL is usually published on the Internet and signed with the CA's digital signature to ensure authenticity. The CRL normally contains the serial numbers of digital certificates that have been revoked, the date they were revoked, and the reason. Before trusting a certificate, users should ensure they have the latest CRL from the CA. Expired certificates are not included in the CRL, which contains only certificates that have been revoked prior to their expiration date.

The most critical function of a CA is to protect its private key. If a CA's private key were compromised, fraudulent certificates could be issued by an attacker, thereby invalidating the entire PKI. The CA's private key must be protected when it is being used as well as when it is stored.

Registration Authority (RA)

The Registration Authority (RA) also comprises hardware, software, and the personnel administering the PKI. The RA can be thought of as a subset of the CA. In larger organizations, it may not be possible or desirable to have one centralized CA responsible for issuing and revoking all digital certificates. These responsibilities can be delegated by the CA to one or more RAs.

The RA is responsible for validating the information on a certificate request at the time of the request. An individual may present appropriate credentials to an RA in person, and the request is then sent to the CA for a certificate to be issued. Alternatively, the request may be originated by the CA, and verification is then sent to the RA. After verification by the RA, the CA then issues the certificate.

Repository

A *repository* (or *certificate directory*) is a system that stores a CA's certificates and CRLs and distributes them to authorized parties. The main purpose of the repository is to ensure that certificates and CRLs are available to users when requested. The main security issues for a repository are ensuring secure updates and availability. If an attacker is able to update the repository with bad information or crash the system, the lack of availability of the system will result in a denial-of-service attack because users would be unable to verify certificates.

Archive

An *archive* (or *key recovery server*) is responsible for long-term storage of archived information from the CA. Maintaining archives is important to ensure that certificates can be verified, even after they have expired or been revoked. This may be necessary at some later date, for example, to determine whether a digital signature on a contract was valid and authorized at the time it was executed. An archive also ensures that encrypted information can be recovered if a private key is ever lost by storing components that make it possible to re-construct a lost private key and decrypt the information.

Trust Models

The two most common trust models found in PKIs are the *hierarchical model* and the *cross-certification model*. Each of these models can be employed exclusively or in a hybrid configuration.

In a hierarchical model, a single CA (known as the *root CA*) delegates issuing authority to subordinate RAs. Because all of the users in the PKI trust the root CA, certificates issued by various RAs in the hierarchy can automatically be trusted.

In a cross-certification model, two organizations that want to trust each other issue cross-certification certificates. A certificate must be issued for each direction in the trust relationship. (Company A issues a certificate to Company B, and Company B issues a certificate to Company A.) This concept is similar to trust relationships in Windows NT.

Key Management Functions

Like physical keys, encryption keys must be safeguarded. Most successful attacks against encryption exploit vulnerabilities in key management functions rather than some inherent weakness in the encryption algorithm. The following are the major functions associated with key management:

- ✔ **Key generation:** Keys must be generated randomly on a secure system, and the generation sequence itself shouldn't provide potential clues regarding the contents of the keyspace. Generated keys shouldn't be displayed in the clear. Key pairs may be generated either on an end-user's system or on a trusted third-party system.

✔ **Key distribution:** Keys must be securely distributed. This is a major vulnerability in symmetric key systems. Using an asymmetric system to securely distribute secret keys is one solution. See Chapter 12 for a complete discussion of symmetric and asymmetric systems.

✔ **Key installation:** Key installation is often a manual process. This process should ensure that the key isn't compromised during installation, incorrectly entered, or too difficult to be used readily.

✔ **Key storage:** Keys must be stored on protected or encrypted storage media, or the application using the keys should include safeguards that prevent extraction of the keys.

✔ **Key control:** Key control addresses the proper use of keys. Different keys have different functions and may be approved for only certain levels of classification.

✔ **Key disposal:** Keys (and any distribution media) must be properly disposed of, erased, or destroyed so that the key's contents are not disclosed, possibly providing an attacker insight into the key management system.

Prep Test

1 _____ provides a standard syntax for certification requests:

A ○ PKCS #7
B ○ PKCS #10
C ○ ASN.1
D ○ X.509

2 A digital certificate typically includes all of the following, except:

A ○ Owner's name
B ○ Owner's public key
C ○ Owner's private key
D ○ Certificate activation date

3 The Certificate Policy (CP) is represented in an X.509 Version 3 digital certificate by a(n) _____.

A ○ Digital signature
B ○ Message digest
C ○ Unique serial number
D ○ Object identifier (OID)

4 The Certification Practices Statement (CPS) is analogous to _____.

A ○ Policies
B ○ Procedures
C ○ Standards
D ○ Baselines

5 The four main components of a Public Key Infrastructure (PKI) include all the following except:

A ○ Directory Service
B ○ Certificate Authority
C ○ Repository
D ○ Archive

6 **A CRL normally contains all of the following information, except:**

A ○ Serial number of revoked certificates

B ○ Revocation date

C ○ Reason

D ○ Expiration date

7 **The _____ is responsible for storing a CA's certificates and CRLs and distributing them to authorized parties.**

A ○ CA

B ○ RA

C ○ Repository

D ○ Archive

8 **The _____ ensures that encrypted information can be recovered if a private key is lost.**

A ○ CA

B ○ RA

C ○ Repository

D ○ Archive

9 **In a _____ trust model, a single CA delegates issuing authority to subordinate RA's.**

A ○ Hierarchical

B ○ Cross-certification

C ○ Client-server

D ○ Master-slave

10 **_____ is a key management function that addresses the proper use of cryptographic keys.**

A ○ Key generation

B ○ Key installation

C ○ Key storage

D ○ Key control

Answers

1 **B.** PKCS #10. PKCS #7 provides a general syntax for digital signatures. ASN.1 provides a standard for data syntax and encoding. X.509 defines various content, configuration, and process requirements. *Review "Digital Certificates."*

2 **C.** Owner's private key. A digital certificate typically includes the owner's name, owner's public key, activation date, expiration date, authorized uses, issuer's name, and serial number. *Review "Digital Certificates."*

3 **D.** Object identifier (OID). The CP is represented by an Object Identifier (OID) in an X.509 Version 3 digital certificate. *Review "Policies and Procedures."*

4 **B.** Procedures. Certification Practice Statements (CPSs) are analogous to procedures. *Review "Policies and Procedures."*

5 **A.** Directory Service. The four basic components of a PKI are the Certificate Authority (CA), Registration Authority (RA), Repository, and Archive. *Review "PKI Components."*

6 **D.** Expiration date. A CRL does not contain information about expired certificates. *Review "PKI Components."*

7 **C.** Repository. A repository (or certificate directory) is a system that stores a CA's certificates and CRLs and distributes them to authorized parties. *Review "PKI Components."*

8 **D.** Archive. An archive (or key recovery server) is responsible for long-term storage of archived information from the CA. *Review "PKI Components."*

9 **A.** Hierarchical. In a hierarchical model, a single CA (known as the *root CA*) delegates issuing authority to subordinate RAs. *Review "Trust Models."*

10 **D.** Key control. Key control addresses the proper use of keys. *Review "Key Management Functions."*

Part VI
Operational/ Orgaizational Security

The 5th Wave   By Rich Tennant

"Hey Philip! I think we're in. I'm gonna try linking directly to the screen, but gimme a disguise in case it works. I don't want all of New York to know Jerry DeMarco of 14 Queensberry, Bronx, NY, hacked into the Times Square video screen."

In this part . . .

The Operational and Organizational Security domain includes physical security, disaster recovery, business continuity, privilege management, forensics, risk identification, education, and documentation.

Chapter 14

Physical Security

In This Chapter

▶ Understanding threats to physical security

▶ Planning and designing a secure facility

▶ Identifying physical access controls, technical and administrative controls, and environmental and life safety controls

*P*hysical security has traditionally been the realm of building managers and security force personnel. In recent years, a general trend has begun emerging that places at least some responsibility for physical security on information systems security personnel. As security systems become more and more advanced and more integrated with other information systems, this trend is likely to continue. View this not as a burden, but an opportunity — the opportunity to strut your stuff and say cool, confident-sounding stuff like, "I'm your worst nightmare: I'm a geek with a badge!" How cool is that!

Quick Assessment

1 Fire requires what three elements to burn?

2 There is a greater potential for _____ in low humidity environments, which may damage sensitive electronic equipment.

3 _____ is a type of electrical noise that is caused by the different charges between three electrical wires (hot, neutral, and ground).

4 _____ is a type of electrical noise that is caused by electrical components, such as fluorescent lighting.

5 An electrical anomaly that results in a momentary rush of power is known as a _____.

6 _____ cabling releases toxic chemicals when it burns and thus cannot be used in the area below raised floors or above drop ceilings.

7 Finger scan systems, hand geometry systems, and retina and iris pattern systems are all examples of _____.

8 Two general types of fire suppression systems are _____ and _____.

9 _____ is a commonly used colorless, odorless gas that is most effective against electrical fires.

10 _____ is a fire extinguishing agent that suppresses a fire by disrupting the chemical reaction necessary for a fire to burn.

Answers

1   Heat, oxygen, and fuel. *See "Physical Security Threats."*

2   Electrostatic discharge (ESD). *Review "Physical Security Threats."*

3   Electromagnetic interference (EMI). *Review "Physical Security Threats."*

4   Radio frequency interference (RFI). *See "Physical Security Threats."*

5   Spike. *See "Physical Security Threats."*

6   PVC. *See "Designing a secure facility."*

7   Biometric access controls. *See "Physical controls."*

8   Water sprinkler systems and gas discharge systems. *See "Fire detection and suppression."*

9   Carbon dioxide (CO_2). *See "Fire detection and suppression."*

10   Halon. *See "Fire detection and suppression."*

Physical Security Threats

Threats to physical security come in many forms, including the following:

- ✔ Natural disasters
- ✔ Emergency situations
- ✔ Man-made threats

All possible threats must be identified in order to perform a complete and thorough risk analysis and to develop an appropriate and effective control strategy.

Saving human lives is the first priority in any life-threatening situation.

Some of the more-common threats to physical security include

- ✔ **Fire:** Threats from fire can be devastating and lethal. Proper precautions, preparation, and training save lives and limit the spread of fire and damage. Hazards associated with fires include

  - Smoke

  - Explosions

  - Building collapse

  - Release of toxic materials or vapors

  - Water damage

  Fire requires three elements to burn: *heat, oxygen,* and *fuel.* These three elements are sometimes referred to as the *fire triangle.* (See Figure 14-1.) Fire suppression and extinguishing systems fight fires by removing one of these three elements or by temporarily breaking up the chemical reaction between these three elements: that is, separating the fire triangle. Fires are classified according to the fuel type, as listed in Table 14-1.

Table 14-1 Fire Classes and Suppression/Extinguishing Methods

Class	Fuel	Extinguishing Method
A	Common combustibles (paper, wood, furniture, or clothing)	Water or soda acid
B	Burnable fuels (gasoline or oil)	CO_2, soda acid, or Halon
C	Electrical fires (computers and electronics)	CO_2 or Halon
D	Special fires (chemical or grease fires)	May require total immersion or other special techniques

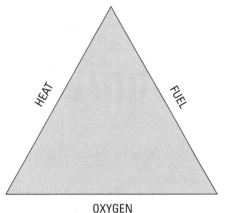

✓ **Water:** Water damage (and damage from liquids in general) can occur from many different sources including

- Pipe breakage
- Firefighting efforts
- Leaking roofs
- Spilled drinks
- Flooding

Wet computers and other electrical equipment pose a potentially lethal hazard.

✓ **Vibration and movement:** Causes may include

- Earthquakes
- Landslides
- Explosions

Equipment may also be damaged by

- Sudden or severe vibrations
- Falling objects
- Equipment racks tipping over

Vibrations or movement may weaken structural integrity, causing a building collapse.

✓ **Severe weather:** This includes

- Hurricanes
- Tornadoes
- High winds
- Severe thunderstorms and lightning

- Rain
- Snow
- Sleet
- Ice

Such forces of nature may cause

- Fires
- Water damage and flooding
- Structural damage
- Loss of communications and utilities
- Personnel hazards

✔ **Electricity:** Sensitive equipment can be damaged or affected by electrical hazards and anomalies, including

- **Electrostatic discharge (ESD):** The ideal humidity range for computer equipment is from 40 to 60 percent. Higher humidity causes condensation and corrosion. Lower humidity increases the potential for ESD (commonly referred to as static electricity). A static charge of as little as 40 volts (V) can damage sensitive circuits, and 2,000V can cause a system shutdown. The minimum discharge that can be felt by humans is 3,000V, and discharges of over 25,000V are possible.

- **Electrical noise:** This includes Electromagnetic Interference (EMI) and Radio Frequency Interference (RFI). EMI is generated by the different charges between the three electrical wires (hot, neutral, and ground). RFI is caused by electrical components, such as fluorescent lighting and electric cables.

- **Electrical anomalies:** These are listed in Table 14-2.

Table 14-2	Electrical Anomalies
Electrical Event	*Definition*
Blackout	Total loss of power
Fault	Momentary loss of power
Brownout	Prolonged drop in voltage
Sag	Short drop in voltage
Inrush	Initial power rush
Spike	Momentary rush of power
Surge	Prolonged rush of power

- **Lightning strikes:** Approximately 10,000 fires are started every year by lightning strikes in the United States alone, despite the fact that only 20 percent of all lightning ever reaches the ground. Lightning can heat the air in immediate contact with the stroke to 54,000 degrees Fahrenheit (F) and can discharge 100,000 amperes of electrical current.

- **Magnetic fields:** Monitors and storage media (including floppy disks and hard drives) can be permanently damaged or erased by magnetic fields.

✔ **Sabotage/theft/vandalism:** Both internal and external threats must be considered. A heightened security posture is prudent during such situations as

- Labor disputes

- Corporate downsizing

- Hostile terminations

- Bad publicity

- Demonstrations/protests

- Civil unrest

- Cancellation of popular TV shows, such as *Star Trek, Survivor,* and *Dr. Phil*

✔ **Equipment failure:** Equipment failures are inevitable. The effects can be mitigated by

- Maintenance and support agreements

- Ready spare parts

- Redundant systems

✔ **Loss of communications and utilities:** These include

- Voice and data

- Electricity

- Heating, ventilation, and air conditioning (HVAC)

Loss of communications and utilities may be due to any of the physical security threats listed previously, as well as human error.

✔ **Personnel loss:** This can be due to

- Illness

- Injury

- Death

- Transfer

- Labor disputes

- Resignations

- Terminations

The effects of a personnel loss can be mitigated through good security practices, such as

- Documented procedures

- Job rotations

- Cross training

- Redundant functions

Facility Requirements Planning

Astute organizations involve security professionals during the design, planning, and construction of new or renovated facilities. Proper facility requirements planning during the early stages of construction helps ensure that a new building or data center is adequate, safe, and secure — all of which can help an organization avoid costly mistakes later.

Choosing a secure location

Location, location, location! Although this bit of conventional business wisdom may be less important to profitability in the age of e-commerce, it's still a critical factor in physical security. Important factors when considering a location include

- **Climatology and natural disasters:** Although an organization is unlikely to choose a geographic location based on the likelihood of hurricanes or earthquakes, these factors must be considered when designing a safe and secure facility. Other factors may be

    - Floodplain avoidance

    - Location of evacuation routes

    - Adequacy of civil and emergency preparedness

- **Local considerations:** Is the location in a high crime area? Are hazards, such as hazardous materials storage, railway freight lines, or flight paths for the local airport, nearby? Will local air and noise (including vibration) pollution affect your systems?

- **Visibility:** Will your employees and facilities be targeted for crime and vandalism? Is the site near another high visibility organization that may attract undesired attention?

Keeping a low profile is generally better; avoid using external building markings if possible.

✔ **Accessibility:** Will on-call employees have to drive for an hour to respond when needed? Consider

- Local traffic patterns

- Convenience to airports

- Proximity to emergency services (police, fire, and medical facilities)

- Availability of adequate housing

✔ **Utilities:** Where is the facility located in the power grid? Is electrical power stable and clean? Is sufficient fiber-optic cable already in place to support telecommunications requirements?

✔ **Joint tenants:** Will you have full access to all necessary environmental controls? Can (and should) boundary protection costs and responsibilities be shared between joint tenants?

Designing a secure facility

Many of the physical and technical controls in this chapter should be considered during the initial design of a secure facility. Doing so often reduces the costs and improves the overall effectiveness of these controls. Other building design considerations include

✔ **Exterior walls:** Ideally, exterior walls should be able to withstand high winds (tornadoes and hurricanes/typhoons). If possible, windows should be avoided throughout the building, particularly on lower levels. Metal bars over windows on lower levels may be necessary. Windows should be

- Fixed (cannot be opened)

- Shatterproof

- Sufficiently opaque to conceal inside activities

✔ **Interior walls:** Interior walls adjacent to secure or restricted areas must

- Extend from the floor to the ceiling (through raised flooring and drop ceilings)

- Comply with applicable building and fire codes

Walls adjacent to storage areas (such as closets containing janitorial supplies, paper, media, or other flammable materials) must meet minimum fire ratings, which are typically higher than for other interior walls.

Ideally, Kevlar (bulletproof) walls protect the most sensitive areas.

✔ **Floors:** Flooring (both slab and raised) must be capable of bearing loads in accordance with local building codes (typically 150 pounds per square foot). Additionally, raised flooring must have a nonconductive surface and be properly grounded.

✔ **Ceilings:** Weight bearing and fire ratings must be considered.

Drop ceilings may temporarily conceal water leaks; conversely, drop ceilings can reveal leaks while impeding water damage.

✔ **Doors:**

- Doors must be of sufficient strength and design to resist forcible entry and have a fire rating equivalent to adjacent walls.

- Emergency exits must remain unlocked from the inside and should be clearly marked and monitored or alarmed.

- Electronic lock mechanisms and other access control devices should fail *open* in an emergency to permit emergency exit.

Many doors swing out to facilitate emergency exit, so their hinges are located on the outside. These hinges must prevent an intruder from easily lifting hinge pins and removing the door.

✔ **Lighting:** Exterior lighting for all physical spaces and buildings in the security perimeter (including entrances and parking areas) should be sufficient to provide personnel safety as well as to discourage prowlers and casual intruders.

✔ **Wiring:** All wiring, conduits, and cable runs must comply with building and fire codes and be properly protected. *Plenum* cabling must be used below raised floors and above drop ceilings. (Plenum cabling uses a coating other than standard PVC, because PVC releases toxic chemicals when burning.)

✔ **Electricity and HVAC:** Electrical load and HVAC requirements must be carefully planned to ensure sufficient power is available in the right locations and that proper climate ranges (temperature and humidity) are maintained. I discuss additional controls in "Environmental and life-safety controls," later in this chapter.

✔ **Pipes:** Shutoff valves should be located and appropriately marked for pipes for

- Water

- Steam

- Gas

Drains should have *positive flow* (carry drainage away from the building).

Physical Security Controls

Physical security controls include a combination of

- ✔ Physical controls
- ✔ Technical controls
- ✔ Environmental and life safety controls
- ✔ Administrative controls

Physical controls

Physical controls are systems and techniques used to restrict access to a security perimeter and provide boundary protection. These include

- ✔ Fencing
- ✔ Security guards
- ✔ Dogs
- ✔ Security badges
- ✔ Biometric access controls

Fencing

Fencing is the primary means for securing an outside perimeter or external boundary. Fencing controls physical access. Fencing includes

- ✔ Fences and walls
- ✔ Gates, doors, and turnstiles
- ✔ Mantraps

  A *mantrap* is a physical access control method consisting of a pair of locked doors or turnstiles. If detected, an intruder can be contained between the doors or turnstiles.

The main disadvantages of fencing are

- ✔ Cost
- ✔ Appearance

Security guards

Although modern surveillance equipment, biometric access controls, and intrusion detection systems (IDS) may seem to diminish the role of security guards, these tools increase the need for skilled physical security personnel capable of operating advanced technology and applying discerning judgment. The major advantages of security guards include

- **Discernment:** Guards can apply human judgment to situations.
- **Visibility:** Guards provide a visible deterrent, response, and control capability.
- **Dual functions:** Guards can also perform receptionist and visitor escort functions.

Some disadvantages include

- **Unpredictability:** Pre-employment screening and bonding doesn't assure reliability or integrity.
- **Imperfections:** Along with human judgment comes the element of human error.
- **Cost:** Maintaining a full-time security force (including training) or out-sourcing these functions can be expensive.

Dogs

Like human guards, dogs provide a highly visible deterrent, response, and control capability. (Cats are generally less effective, unless it's a really big cat — like a tiger!) Dogs are typically more loyal and reliable than humans, with more acute smell and hearing. However, the use of guard dogs is typically restricted to an outside security perimeter. Other considerations include

- Limited judgment capability
- Cost and maintenance
- Potential liability issues

Security badges

Security badges (or access cards) are used for identification and authentication of authorized personnel entering a secure facility or area.

A *photo identification card* (also referred to as a *dumb card*) is a simple ID card with a facial photograph of the bearer. Typically, no technology is embedded in these cards for authentication purposes. A security guard determines whether entry is permitted by the bearer.

Smart cards are digitally encoded cards that contain an integrated chip (IC) or magnetic stripe (possibly in addition to a photo). Smart cards, and their associated access control systems, can be programmed to

✔ Permit multilevel access

✔ Restrict access to some periods (day and time)

✔ Record access information, such as day and time

Biometric access controls

Biometrics provides the only absolute method for positively identifying an individual based on some unique physiological or behavioral characteristic of that individual. (Something you are.) I discuss biometrics extensively in Chapter 3. Although here I am referring to *physical* access control devices (rather than *logical* access control devices, as in Chapter 3), the underlying concepts and technologies are the same. To review, the major biometric systems in use today include

✔ Finger scan systems

✔ Hand geometry systems

✔ Retina pattern

✔ Iris pattern

✔ Voice recognition

✔ Signature dynamics

Technical controls

Technical controls include

✔ Monitoring and surveillance

✔ Intrusion detection

✔ Alarms that alert personnel to physical security threats and allow them to respond appropriately

Surveillance

Visual surveillance systems include photographic and electronic equipment that are

✔ **Preventive:** When used to monitor live events, these systems are a preventive control.

✔ **Detective:** When used to record live events, they're a detective control.

✔ **Deterrent:** The visible use of these systems also provides a deterrent.

Companies use electronic systems, such as closed-circuit television (CCTV), to extend and improve the monitoring and surveillance capability of security guards. Photographic systems, including videocassette recorders, are used to record events for later analysis or as evidence for prosecution.

Intrusion detection

Intrusion detection in the physical security domain refers to systems that detect attempts to gain unauthorized physical access to a building or area. Modern intrusion detection systems (IDS) commonly use sensors and/or motion detectors to detect a break-in attempt.

Alarms

Alarms are activated when a condition is detected. Examples of systems employing alarms include

✔ Fire and smoke detectors

✔ Motion sensors and intrusion detection systems (IDS)

✔ Metal and explosives detectors

✔ Access control systems (physical and logical)

✔ Climate control monitoring systems

Environmental and life safety controls

These are the controls necessary for maintaining a safe and acceptable operating environment for computers and personnel. These include electrical power, HVAC, and fire detection and suppression.

Electrical power

General considerations for electrical power include

✔ Dedicated feeder(s) from one or more utility substations or power grids

✔ Adequate physical access controls for electrical distribution panels and circuit breakers

An Emergency Power Off (EPO) switch should be installed near major systems and exit doors to shut down power in case of fire or electrical shock.

A backup power source, such as a diesel power generator, should be established. Backup power should only be provided for such critical facilities and systems as

✔ Emergency lighting

✔ Fire detection and suppression

> ✔ Mainframes, servers, and essential workstations
>
> ✔ HVAC
>
> ✔ Physical access control systems
>
> ✔ Telecommunications equipment.

Protective controls for electrostatic discharge (ESD) include

> ✔ Proper humidity levels (40 to 60 percent)
>
> ✔ Proper grounding
>
> ✔ Antistatic flooring, carpeting, and floor mats

Protective controls for electrical noise include

> ✔ Power line conditioners and surge protectors
>
> ✔ Proper grounding
>
> ✔ Shielded cabling

An Uninterruptible Power Supply (UPS) is perhaps the most important protection against electrical anomalies. A UPS provides clean power to sensitive systems and a temporary power source during electrical outages (blackouts); Ensuring that the UPS provides adequate battery power for a sufficient amount of time to properly shut down the protected systems is important.

A UPS should not be used as a backup power source. A UPS — even a building UPS — is designed to provide temporary power, typically for 10 to 30 minutes, in order to allow a proper shutdown of protected systems.

Surge protectors and surge suppressors provide only minimal protection for sensitive computer systems and are more commonly (and dangerously) used to overload an electrical outlet or as a daisy-chained extension cord. Don't be lured into a false sense of security by these units — check them regularly for proper use and operation and don't accept them as a viable alternative to a UPS.

HVAC

Heating, ventilation, and air conditioning (HVAC) systems maintain the proper environment for computers and personnel. HVAC requirements planning involves complex calculations based on such factors as the average BTUs (British Thermal Units) produced by the estimated computers and personnel occupying a given area, the size of the room, insulation characteristics, and ventilation systems.

The ideal temperature range for computer equipment is between 50 and 80 degrees F. At temperatures as low as 100 degrees F, magnetic storage media can be damaged.

The ideal humidity range for computer equipment is between 40 and 60 percent.

- ✔ Higher humidity causes condensation and corrosion.
- ✔ Lower humidity increases the potential for ESD or static electricity.

Doors and side panels on computer equipment racks should be kept closed (and locked, for physical access control) to ensure proper airflow for cooling and ventilation.

Heating and cooling systems should be properly maintained and air filters cleaned regularly to reduce dust contamination and fire hazards.

Most gas discharge systems automatically shut down HVAC systems prior to discharging, but a separate EPO switch should be installed near exits to facilitate a manual emergency shutdown.

Ideally, HVAC equipment should be dedicated, controlled, and monitored. If the systems aren't dedicated or independently controlled, proper liaison with the building manager is necessary to ensure that escalation procedures are effective and understood. Monitoring systems should alert the appropriate personnel when operating thresholds are exceeded.

Fire detection and suppression

Fire detection and suppression systems are some of the most essential life safety controls for protecting facilities, equipment, and most important, human lives.

Detection systems

The three main types of fire detection systems are the following:

- ✔ **Heat-sensing:** These devices either sense temperatures exceeding a predetermined level (*fixed-temperature detectors*) or rapidly rising temperatures (*rate-of-rise detectors*). The former are more common and exhibit a lower false alarm rate.

- ✔ **Flame-sensing:** These devices either sense the flicker (or pulsing) of flames or the infrared energy of flames. These systems are relatively expensive but provide an extremely rapid response time.

- ✔ **Smoke-sensing:** These devices either sense variations in light intensity (*photoelectric sensors*) or disturbances in the normal ionization current of radioactive materials (*radioactive sensors*). These systems are typically used as early warning devices in ventilation systems.

Suppression systems

The two primary types of fire suppression systems are these:

- **Water sprinkler systems:** Water extinguishes fire by removing the heat element from the fire triangle and is most effective against Class A fires. Water is the primary fire-extinguishing agent for all business environments. Although water can potentially damage equipment, it's one of the most effective, inexpensive, readily available, and least harmful (to humans) extinguishing agents available.

- **Gas discharge systems:** Gas discharge systems may be portable (such as a CO_2 extinguisher) or fixed (beneath a raised floor). These systems are typically classified according to the extinguishing agent that's employed. These systems include

  - **Carbon dioxide (CO_2):** CO_2 is a colorless, odorless gas that extinguishes fire by removing the oxygen element from the fire triangle. (Refer to Figure 14-1.) CO_2 is most effective against Class B and C fires.

    Because CO_2 removes oxygen, use of CO_2 flooding systems is potentially lethal and best suited for unmanned areas or with a delay action (with manual override) in manned areas.

    CO_2 is used in portable fire extinguishers, which should be located near all exits and within 50 feet (15 meters) of any electrical equipment. All portable fire extinguishers (CO_2, water, and soda acid) should be clearly marked (the extinguisher type and the appropriate fire classes) and periodically inspected. All personnel should receive training on proper fire extinguisher use.

  - **Soda acid:** This includes a variety of chemical compounds that extinguish fires by removing the fuel element (suppressing the flammable components of the fuel) of the fire triangle. (Refer to Figure 14-1.) Soda acid is most effective against Class A and B fires. It is not used for Class C fires because of the highly corrosive nature of many of the chemicals used.

  - **Halon:** Halon systems suppress fire by separating the elements of the fire triangle (a chemical reaction) and are most effective against Class B and C fires. (Refer to Figure 14-1.) Halon doesn't damage computer equipment, leaves no liquid or solid residue, mixes thoroughly with the air, and spreads extremely fast. However, Halon in concentrations above ten percent is harmful if inhaled, and it degrades into toxic chemicals (hydrogen fluoride, hydrogen bromide, and bromine) when used on fires with temperatures above 900 degrees F.

    New Halon systems can't be installed. Because of Halon's ozone-depleting characteristics, the Montreal Protocol of 1987 prohibits the further production and installation of Halon systems.

Administrative controls

These include the policies and procedures necessary to ensure that physical access, technical controls, and environmental and life-safety controls are properly implemented and achieve an overall physical security strategy.

Restricted areas

Areas in which sensitive information is handled or processed should be formally designated as restricted areas with additional security controls implemented.

- ✔ Restricted areas should be clearly marked.
- ✔ All employees should know the difference between authorized and unauthorized personnel.

Visitors

Visitor policies and escort requirements should be clearly defined in the organizational security policy. All visitors should be required to

- ✔ Present proper identification to a security guard or receptionist
- ✔ Sign a visitor log
- ✔ Complete a nondisclosure agreement, if appropriate
- ✔ Wear a conspicuous badge that clearly

    - Identifies them as a visitor
    - Indicates whether an escort is required

        If an escort is required, the assigned escort should be identified by name and account for the visitor at all times while on the premises.

    Color-coded badges often are used to indicate a visitor.

Emergency procedures

Emergency procedures must be

- ✔ Clearly documented
- ✔ Readily accessible (often posted in appropriate areas)
- ✔ Periodically updated
- ✔ Routinely practiced in training and drills

Additional copies of emergency procedures may also be kept at secure off-site facilities. Emergency procedures should include

✔ Emergency system shutdown procedures

✔ Evacuation plans and routes

✔ Business continuity plan/disaster recovery plans (BCP/DRP)

General housekeeping

Good housekeeping practices are an important aspect of physical security controls.

✔ Implementing and enforcing a no-smoking policy reduces

  • Fire hazards

  • Contamination of sensitive systems

✔ Cleaning dust and ventilation systems

  • Maintains a cleaner computing environment

  • Reduces static electricity and fire hazards

✔ Keeping work areas clean and trash emptied

  • Reduces fire hazards (combustibles)

  • Helps identify and locate sensitive information that has been improperly handled

Prep Test

1 **The three elements necessary for a fire to burn include all these except:**

A ○ Fuel

B ○ Oxygen

C ○ Heat

D ○ Nitrogen

2 **Electrical fires are classified as what type of fire and use what extinguishing methods?**

A ○ Class B; CO_2, or soda acid

B ○ Class B; CO_2, or Halon

C ○ Class C; CO_2, or Halon

D ○ Class A; water, or soda acid

3 **A prolonged drop in voltage describes what electrical anomaly?**

A ○ Brownout

B ○ Blackout

C ○ Sag

D ○ Fault

4 **What type of cabling should be used below raised floors and above drop ceilings?**

A ○ CAT-5

B ○ Plenum

C ○ PVC

D ○ Water-resistant

5 **Dogs perform a similar physical security function as human guards but have which distinct advantage over human guards?**

A ○ Can also perform receptionist and visitor escort functions

B ○ Can operate highly sophisticated surveillance systems

C ○ Don't need uniforms

D ○ Are generally more reliable

6 A _____ is used to provide temporary power sufficient to properly shut down critical systems in an electrical outage.

A ○ Surge suppressor

B ○ Backup diesel power generator

C ○ Uninterruptible Power Supply (UPS)

D ○ Surge protector

7 The ideal temperature and humidity range for computer equipment is

A ○ 50 to 80 degrees F; 70 to 90 percent

B ○ 50 to 80 degrees C; 40 to 60 percent

C ○ 50 to 80 degrees F; 60 to 80 percent

D ○ 50 to 80 degrees F; 40 to 60 percent

8 Portable CO_2 fire extinguishers are classified as what type of extinguishing system?

A ○ Gas discharge systems

B ○ Water sprinkler systems

C ○ Deluge systems

D ○ Preaction systems

9 Which of these extinguishing agents fights fires by separating the elements of the fire triangle?

A ○ Water

B ○ Soda acid

C ○ CO_2

D ○ Halon

10 Production of Halon has been banned for what reason?

A ○ It is toxic at temperatures above 900 degrees F.

B ○ It is an ozone-depleting substance.

C ○ It is ineffective.

D ○ It is harmful if inhaled.

Answers

1 **D.** Nitrogen. The fire triangle consists of fuel, oxygen, and heat. *Review "Physical Security Threats."*

2 **C.** Class C; CO_2 or Halon. Class B fires are burnable fuels that can be extinguished with CO_2, soda acid, or Halon. Class A fires are common combustible materials. *Review "Physical Security Threats."*

3 **A.** Brownout. A *blackout* is a total loss of power, a *sag* is a short drop in voltage, and a *fault* is a momentary loss of power. *Review "Physical Security Threats."*

4 **B.** Plenum. CAT-5 cabling can be either plenum or PVC coated. PVC cabling releases toxic vapors when burned. Both PVC and plenum coatings are water resistant. *Review "Designing a secure facility."*

5 **D.** Are generally more reliable. Properly trained guard dogs are generally more reliable than human guards. *Review "Physical controls."*

6 **C.** Uninterruptible Power Supply (UPS). Surge protectors and surge suppressors are the same thing and provide no protection against electrical outages. A backup generator can be used to provide temporary power for an extended period of time and is generally used to continue operations. *Review "Electrical power."*

7 **D.** 50 to 80 degrees F; 40 to 60 percent. Humidity ranges above 80 percent cause condensation and corrosion, ranges below 60 percent increase the potential for ESD. 50 to 80 degrees C (122 to 176 degrees F) is bad for both computers and humans! *Review "HVAC."*

8 **A.** Gas discharge systems. Water sprinkler systems are fixed systems that discharge water. Deluge systems are types of water sprinkler systems. *Review "Suppression systems."*

9 **D.** Halon. Water fights fires by removing the heat element. Soda acid fights fires by suppressing the fuel element. CO_2 fights fires by removing the oxygen element. *Review "Suppression systems."*

10 **B.** It is an ozone-depleting substance. Halon does release toxic chemicals at temperatures above 900 degrees F and is harmful if inhaled in concentrations greater than 10 percent, but these are not the reasons production was banned. Halon is one of the most effective fire-extinguishing agents currently available. *Review "Suppression systems."*

Chapter 15

Business Continuity and Disaster Recovery

*T*his chapter discusses technological and procedural ways in which information systems can be made more reliable. The chapter leads off with a section on backups, recovery, and a number of technology solutions available for making applications highly available.

Next, the fascinating world of Business Continuity Planning and Disaster Recovery Planning are explored; this is among the most gripping and engaging material in this book. The steps used in developing Business Continuity Plans and Disaster Recovery Plans are described, as are the various "touch points" between the two. The chapter concludes with an emotional description of a few of the ways in which Business Continuity Planning and Disaster Recovery Planning efforts impact and assist one another.

Quick Assessment

1 Three basic backup types are _____, _____, and _____.

2 The primary purpose of clusters is to increase _____.

3 Redundant power supplies and system boards are examples of _____.

4 The report that lists business functions in order of priority is _____.

5 The report that lists business functions at risk is _____.

6 An alternate data processing facility that consists of only an empty computer room is known as a _____.

7 In order to be effective, the Business Continuity Strategy must be _____.

8 The two parts of emergency response teams are _____ and _____.

9 A formal "paper review" of the Recovery Plan is known as a _____.

10 The report that estimates the greatest possible survivable outage is _____.

Answers

1   Full, incremental, differential. *Review "Making Technology Reliable."*

2   Reliability. *See "Making Technology Reliable."*

3   Fault tolerance. *See "Making Technology Reliable."*

4   Criticality Assessment. *Review "Business Continuity Planning."*

5   Vulnerability Assessment. *Learn more in the section on "Business Continuity Planning."*

6   Cold site. *See "Business Continuity Planning."*

7   Documented or supported. *See "Business Continuity Planning."*

8   Salvage, recovery. *Review "Disaster Recovery Planning."*

9   Structured walkthrough. *See "Disaster Recovery Planning."*

10   Maximum Tolerable Downtime. *See "Business Continuity Planning."*

Making Technology Reliable

There are a great number of calamities that beset computer systems and render them inoperable. The next section in this chapter will discuss these events in detail; this section will discuss how technology can make systems more available.

Backup and recovery

It has long been recognized that computer hardware — including those components that store information — are subject to failure. Human error can also damage or destroy information. A key component of any computer facility's operations includes regular backups of important information, just in case anything bad may happen.

Backups

The procedure of copying a computer's stored information from one device to another is known as a *backup*. Generally, information on hard disks is copied to magnetic tapes or optical discs.

The idea here is that, in the event the computer's hard disk fails, or if human error causes irreparable damage to store data, then the data copied to tape or optical disc can be copied back to the computer's hard disk and processing can resume.

Media rotation schemes

Experience has revealed that damage to data when caused by human error is sometimes not discovered for a long time — days, weeks, or longer. To counter this possibility, organizations have adopted a scheme of rotating backup media (the tapes or optical discs) so that several "generations" of backed-up data exist and can be recovered if necessary.

For example, data on a computer may be backed up weekly. But rather than using the same set of backup tapes each week, the organization may use several sets, labeled "week 1," "week 2," "week 3," "week 4." This would allow the organization to be able to recover data from any of four backup sets.

Full, incremental, and differential backups

In many cases, the entire collection of data on a hard disk need not be backed up each time, since only a small portion of data changes from day to day. This has led to some different techniques for backing up data.

- ✔ **Full backup.** All data on a hard disk or file system is backed up.

- ✔ **Differential backup.** All data on the hard disk or file system that has changed since the last full backup is backed up. All data that is unchanged since the last full backup is not backed up.

- ✔ **Incremental backup.** All data on the hard disk or file system that has changed since the last backup (whether full, incremental or differential) is backed up. Unchanged data is not backed up.

The differential and incremental backups were developed so that backups could run faster and consume fewer tapes. But the presence of multiple sets of backup media present some challenges during data recovery that will be discussed next.

Secure recovery

Once in a while, an organization finds that it must recover data from backup tapes. This can occur for a variety of reasons; some scenarios are described here.

- ✔ **Human error.** Someone made a mistake that caused data to be damaged or destroyed. Once it is determined precisely which data — which file(s) and from which backup set(s) — needs to be restored, it is copied from backup tape(s) back to the computer's hard disks.

- ✔ **Hardware failure.** A hardware component on the computer system has failed, causing data to be unreachable. The failed components are replaced, and data from the most recent backup tape(s) copied to the hard disks.

- ✔ **Security incident.** A hacker or intruder has broken in to a system and damaged parts of he computer's operating system as well as some company data. Similarly, a computer virus or worm may have success-fully attacked the system, causing indeterminate damage. In either case, it is difficult (if possible at all) to determine exactly what has been damaged.

   In the case of a security incident, a different recovery procedure is needed in order to completely eradicate the effects of the incident. The safest way to proceed is to completely erase all information on the com-puter and re-install the operating system from its original release media (not a backup tape, which could also be damaged from the incident). Next, applications should likewise be installed from their respective release media, and finally data files recovered from the last known unaf-fected backup set.

Off-site storage

Imagine a fire raging through a computer room. The computer is destroyed by the fire, smoke, or water. Probably the first thing you think of is to get the room cleaned up and get some new computers. Next, you need to copy data from backup tapes to the new computers, and you're back on the air. Walk over to the rack or cabinet where the backup tapes are kept, and. . . . Oops! They are also destroyed.

It is for this reason that backup media must be stored in a different location from the computers. And by different location we don't mean the next room, or down the hall, but far away: across town in a very secure location.

Off-site storage facilities must be strategically chosen. Here are several points that must be considered:

- Hardened to withstand earthquakes and other calamitous natural events.
- Fortified and guarded to withstand attacks or raids.
- Dependable processes in order that backup media are issued only to authorized personnel.
- Away from floodplains and seashores.
- Close to a major airport or other transportation center, in the event that backup media needs to be transported to a different city.
- Close enough to the computer center so that backup media can be returned within an hour or two.

Most cities have one or more commercial off-site storage companies that can fill all of these needs.

High availability architectures

The demands of today's computing applications, among them e-commerce and other online transaction systems, require that these systems continue running despite events such as hardware failure and periodic maintenance. A number of architectures and methods have been developed that make applications "highly available."

Fault tolerance

Fault tolerance is a generic term that refers to the features or designs of a computer system that make it far less likely to stop running in the event of a hardware failure. Some typical fault tolerant features are

✔ Redundant power supplies. A production computer system can be equipped with two to six power supplies. In the event that a power supply fails, the failed power supply can be unplugged, and a replacement power supply plugged in, all while the computer system keeps running.

✔ Multiple processor modules. A computer system can have two or more independent processor boards, so in the event that any component on a processor board fails, the computer will keep running (although slower). Like redundant power supplies, the faulty processor module can be replaced while the computer keeps running.

✔ Redundant disks. Usually known as RAID (Redundant Array of Independent Disks), production computers can have large collections of disks, controlled in such a manner where the failure of one or more disks will not affect the computer's operations.

✔ Other redundant components. Fault tolerant computers generally have two or more of everything besides what we have mentioned previously. They also have two or more connections of every sort: network, SCSI, Fibre Channel, console, and whatever else the computer may use to communicate with storage devices and over networks.

Fault tolerance is not only a function of the physical computer itself, but also how the computer's operating system deals with events such as failed processor boards and network connections.

Clusters

A *cluster* is a set of two or more computers that are equipped and configured to operate as one virtual computer. This is not unlike fault tolerance, in that the objective is the continuous availability of an application. The main difference is that the application's availability is assured not through the architecture of a single computer system, but instead through the use of two or more computers that back each other up. In the event that one computer fails, one or more other computers in the cluster are ready to take over processing at a moment's notice.

Computers in a cluster have special cluster controlling software that keeps track of each computer's configuration and availability. The cluster software controls which computer(s) in the cluster will be "active" (currently processing transactions), "standby" (ready to process transactions), or "unavailable" (down or offline for one reason or another). The process of a standby computer changing status to active is called a "failover."

A number of software vendors produce and sell software that is used to build computer clusters. Figure 15-1 shows an example of clusters.

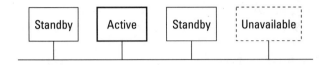

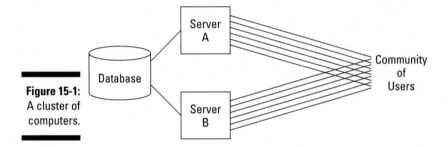

Figure 15-1:
A cluster of
computers.

Load sharing

The strict definition of load sharing speaks more to performance than to reliability. In load sharing, two or more computers share a common task, each sharing its part of the total load "side by side."

Building load sharing into a cluster of computers is commonplace; in a cluster, more than one computer can be in "active" status. The systems that are active are configured to share the entire workload. Figure 15-2 and Figure 15-3 are examples of load sharing.

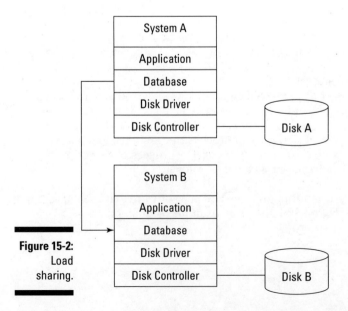

Figure 15-2:
Load
sharing.

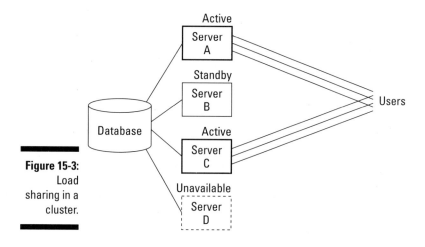

Figure 15-3:
Load
sharing in a
cluster.

Data replication

A frequent characteristic of a cluster is not just a collection of computers, but also a collection of separate storage subsystems. Storage subsystems — which are really just collections of disks in a separate cabinet — are not immune to failure, so it is wise to duplicate not only computers but storage subsystems.

But after some thought one has to wonder, how does the data on one storage subsystem (call it an active subsystem) get copied to the other (call it a standby subsystem)? There are three common methods: mirroring, transaction replication, and batch copying.

Mirroring

When two or more storage subsystems are mirrored, commands to store, change or remove data on one storage subsystem are performed on other storage subsystems in parallel. The commands that are duplicated are usually at the "disk block" or "hardware" level; for example, store thus-and-so data at block number X, change thus-and-so data at block number Y, and so forth.

When two storage subsystems are so connected, one is said to be a mirror of the other. They are identical in every way. (See Figure 15-4.)

When a failure in the active storage subsystem occurs, the standby subsystem is ready to take over immediately. Its entire contents are identical to the former active subsystem.

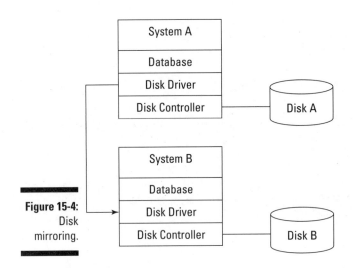

Figure 15-4:
Disk
mirroring.

Transaction replication

Transaction replication, at first glance, is the same as disk mirroring. The difference is in the details.

In transaction replication, commands to perform transactions — usually at the "database" level; for example, store such-and-such value for item XYZ in table C.

Like disk mirroring, the standby storage system contains the same information as the active system and can take over active status at any time.

Batch copying

Batch copying refers to a method of buffering transactions and copying them to other systems in batches, for instance every ten to fifteen minutes. Thus, the other systems are not completely up-to-date, but lag behind active servers by several minutes or more.

BCP & DRP Overview

Business Continuity Planning (BCP) and Disaster Recovery Planning (DRP) are two separate but closely related disciplines, both having to do with an organization's response to a disaster and its plans for continuing business operations despite a disaster.

The difference between BCP and DRP

Business Continuity Planning is concerned with the resources, processes, and equipment needed to continue operating critical portions of a business when any kind of a disaster has struck.

Disaster Recovery Planning is concerned with the resources, processes, and equipment needed to restore business facilities (buildings, and so on) when a disaster has struck.

During a disaster, BCP and DRP teams spring into action. BCP teams keep critical functions rolling, while DRP teams work to restore the original facilities in order to return to business as usual.

BCP & DRP events

There are a wide variety of events that can disrupt the critical functions in an organization. We'll discuss them within two major categories: natural and man-made.

Natural disasters

A few examples of natural disasters are

- Earthquakes
- Floods
- Range or forest fires
- Tsunamis
- Tornadoes, cyclones, and hurricanes
- Landslides

Man-made disasters

Some examples of man-made disasters are

- Sabotage
- War
- Strikes and other mass absences of employees
- Hazardous materials spills

There are any numbers of disasters that can find their root causes in either man-made or natural events. They are

- ✔ Utility (power, gas, steam) outages
- ✔ Communications outages
- ✔ Transportation outages (roadways, air, rail)
- ✔ Mass evacuations

Whether man-made or natural, disasters have a single theme: They can sometimes cause significant disruption of business operations. The remainder of this chapter discusses Business Continuity Planning and Disaster Recovery Planning, the two separate but similar business processes that work to keep the business running and get things back to normal as soon as possible.

Business Continuity Planning

As we touched upon earlier, BCP is entirely concerned with keeping the business running even though a disaster has occurred. *How* this is done is explained in this section in some detail.

The scope of the BCP project

When an organization decides to undertake a business continuity planning project, it usually does so with the intention of assuring that the core of the organization's business functions are included in the project. The success of the effort is highly dependent upon the team's ability to properly manage the scope of the project and also upon the business expertise of each member of the team.

The BCP project team must be able to wisely discern any requests to add to the scope of the project. While scope creep and scope leap can cause death by choking, there may be instances where an addition to the scope of a BCP project is vital to its success.

Here are a couple of examples so that you will have a concrete idea of what we're talking about.

Suppose that a BCP project at a savings and loan was underway, and someone noted that Accounts Receivable was inadvertently left out of the project. They argued that, without the ability to accept payments, the institution would quickly falter. This is an example of an addition of scope that was needed.

Imagine another BCP project, this time at a long-distance telephone company, where someone proposed that product marketing be added to the scope of its initial business continuity planning project. In this instance the project team should reject this motion, because product marketing, while important to the long-term success of the organization, was not really all that critical in the context of a disaster.

Business Impact Assessment

The initial work that must be performed in a BCP project is called the Business Impact Assessment, or BIA. The purpose of the BIA is to describe the impact that various kinds of disasters will have on business operations.

The BIA contains both quantitative and qualitative information. For instance, a disaster threatens the value of the organization's brand(s) and reputation — clearly a qualitative impact. But a disaster will also have some predictable financial impact — a quantitative impact.

The BIA contains several sections: the Vulnerability Assessment, the Criticality Assessment, a statement of Maximum Tolerable Downtime, and a Resource Requirements statement. Each of these is explained here.

Vulnerability Assessment

The Vulnerability Assessment identifies significant vulnerabilities in an organization's operations. It looks at each part of an organization's daily operations and points out those that, if interrupted, would cause great harm to the organization's viability.

Criticality Assessment

The Criticality Assessment is a rank-ordered listing of all of an organization's business operations, ordered by how critical each operation is to the business. For instance, Billing would rank high in most Criticality Assessments, while Holiday Party Planning would rank low.

The Criticality Assessment also charts the impact of each business operation based upon the *duration* of possible interruptions.

Maximum Tolerable Downtime

Maximum Tolerable Downtime is an extension of the interruption duration component in the Criticality Assessment. Maximum Tolerable Downtime states, for each business function, the longest that the function can be unavailable before the viability of the entire organization is threatened.

For example, imagine that the online bookseller Amazon.com loses its Internet connectivity that completely takes Amazon.com off the air. How long could such an outage occur before the very survival of Amazon.com is in question? One hour? One day? One week? Whatever the value is estimated to be, one would figure that an outage longer than this direction would cause the business to fail altogether.

Resource Requirements

The Resource Requirements portion of the Business Impact Assessment defines the resources required to sustain critical business operations during a disaster. These resources are most often people, but also equipment, communications facilities, and information.

Developing the Recovery Plan

When the Business Impact Assessment has been completed the BCP project team will have a clear idea of which business functions are the most important, which ones tolerate how much downtime, and what resources are required to support each. At this point, it is possible to begin to put together the Recovery Plan, a statement that describes, in detail, the procedures that must be followed in order to keep the most critical business functions going.

Emergency response

Emergency response teams — the persons who will be keeping business operations running — must be identified for each type of disaster. It is important to know who will be doing what.

All emergency response procedures must be completely documented; in all likelihood, they will be more thoroughly than even the normal daily non-emergency procedures. This is because the people who will be carrying out business procedures during an emergency may not be as familiar with the procedures as are those who perform them under normal circumstances.

Emergency communication

During a disaster, communications will be more important than during normal business conditions, since there will be a higher number of unexpected and unusual events and situations that people need to know about.

During a disaster, all organization personnel need to be kept informed about a great number of things: where and when to report to work, what functions they will need to perform, with whom they will work, and other things pertinent to the emergency conditions that will exist at the time.

An organization operating under disaster conditions will need to pay careful attention to external organizations with whom it is communicating and/or doing business. The organization needs to convey accurate information that will help external entities accommodate any changes that may be in effect during the emergency. Remember that the organization during an emergency is doing the best it can to keep normal operations going; communication with all affected and assisting parties will be absolutely essential at this time.

Utilities

During normal business conditions, public utilities, such as electricity, natural gas, oil, and steam, play vital roles in supporting the organization's needs. During an emergency, an organization may have greater-than-normal utility consumption needs that will need to be worked out in advance of an actual emergency.

Organizations that are particularly dependent upon energy will need to make other special arrangements in advance of an emergency if the organization wants to succeed in keeping business operations running during periods of crisis. For instance, an organization may need to consider the use of permanent or temporary on-site electric/diesel generators or perhaps "dual entrance" utilities where a single location will have multiple utility entrances at opposite ends of the building or facility.

These decisions will be based upon the results of the Criticality Assessment and Maximum Tolerable Downtime reports. If an organization is highly dependent upon the constant supply of utility services during an emergency, then it will have to invest in facilities, such as generators and other alternate energy supplies, in order to keep vital systems running continuously.

Logistics

The BCP planning team will have to consider any and all situations that may beset the organization and plan accordingly in order to have all necessary supplies, materials, personnel, and documentation present in order to keep the business running. Logistics has to do with the tactical planning and organization required to keep vital functions running as much as possible.

Fire protection

The BCP team must understand the organization's fire fighting capability in data centers and all of its facilities. An important issue to be aware of is the state of fire fighting ability during a widespread emergency if public utilities have been cut off. For instance, without large quantities of water, buildings that could otherwise be occupied may be closed if local fire departments lose the water supplies required to fight structure fires.

Data processing continuity

Because information technology lies at the heart of so many organizations, its information technology capabilities may require a good deal of attention. In the event that a disaster temporarily immobilizes a data center, the organization must develop detailed plans concerning how its IT capabilities will be maintained. Generally, BCP projects manage this issue by recommending the use of one or more alternate sites where IT operations will continue. The various kinds of alternate sites are discussed here.

- **Cold site.** This is an empty data center, equipped only with floor space and environmental systems, such as, air conditioning and utilities. This is the least expensive alternate site, but requires a lot of advance planning and takes a long time to get up and running. Computers must be moved in and installed, communications circuits must be ordered, to name a few.

- **Warm site.** This is a cold site except that it is installed with computers and communications capabilities. A warm site can assume full capabilities more quickly than a cold site.

- **Hot site.** A hot site is a completely equipped and configured data center with computers, communications facilities, like a warm site. However, the computers in the hot site already have the organization's software programs and databases installed and are ready at a moment's notice to take over IT operations. A hot site is the most expensive to maintain, because of the continuous effort required to maintain readiness.

- **Multiple data centers.** Many larger organizations have data centers in more than one city. They can and should take advantage of these already existing data centers and develop hot-site-like capabilities where computers and staff in one data center can immediately assume the operations performed by other data centers.

Business Continuity Strategy

Once the Business Impact Assessment has been completed, the BCP project team has a clear idea of which business functions are most vulnerable and which are most critical to continuing business operations. Next, the *Business Continuity Strategy* can be developed.

The Business Continuity Strategy describes in great detail all of the resources that are to be used, and the procedures to be followed, to continue each critical business operation that is interrupted by a disaster.

Teams of experts

As the BCP project moves into the Business Continuity Strategy phase, the BCP project team must carefully choose who will develop the strategy statement. The people chosen must have deep knowledge and expertise in the business process(es) they are documenting.

Choosing the right persons to develop the Business Continuity Strategy documents is only half the job here. Because of the time commitment required to finish these documents, it is tempting to choose lesser-qualified individuals who have more time to spare. The result will be a Strategy document that may be inaccurate or incomplete.

Coordinating resources and tasks

The teams that develop the different parts of the organization's Business Continuity Strategy must frequently examine each other's work in order to ensure that there are no resource conflicts. During emergency conditions, there will probably be fewer resources than would normally be available; resources that are double- or triple-allocated are going to cause problems during an emergency. It is better to reconcile scarce resources in the planning phase than in the execution phase.

The teams must also examine each other's Strategy documents to make sure that emergency business processes work well with one another. Since there will be fewer than the usual number of resources conducting business operations, it is more important than ever that the processes work just right since there will be fewer people available to cover the gaps.

Documenting the strategy

The emergency business processes that are developed in the Business Continuity Strategy must be documented as thoroughly and accurately as possible. Remember that the people carrying out the emergency procedures may not be those who do so during normal business conditions. And even if they are, there may be enough differences in procedures that every step and every move must be clearly defined and described.

Disaster Recovery Planning

The development of Business Contingency Plans and Disaster Recovery Plans are similar. Both efforts utilize carefully chosen project teams, must both identify critical business processes, and require executive support.

The BDP and DRP teams will use the Criticality Assessment, since this identifies the organization's most critical business functions. The Criticality Assessment prioritizes business functions, which in turn will drive priorities in both the BCP and DRP planning efforts.

Recovery plan development

While the BCP plans to keep business operations going, the DRP plans concentrate on restoring or replacing damaged facilities so that critical business functions can resume their operations there.

The BCP plan identifies emergency response teams that must be prepared for disasters that are likely to strike. Members of these teams must be trained in a wide variety of disciplines and skill such as water and smoke damage, structural damage, hazardous materials, and flooding.

Facilities documentation

In order for emergency response teams to be able to properly respond during disasters, they must have up-to-date information available for all corporate facilities. For example, the teams need to know about utility entrances (locations for water shutoff, electrical panels), fire suppression systems, and emergency supplies. They will also need to know which companies maintain various systems in each facility, as well as contact information for specialized emergency assessment personnel, such as civil and mechanical engineers. But all of these capabilities depend upon accurate information.

Salvage and recovery

Emergency response teams are generally broken into two parts: salvage and recovery. Each is explained here.

Salvage teams are responsible for restoring damaged facilities to full functionality. The steps most often associated with this effort are: assessment, salvage, cleaning, and restore to readiness.

Recovery teams assist BCP teams with logistical assistance and supplies needed to get alternate operations sites running.

The organization must carefully and fully estimate the costs involved with salvage and recovery, as these activities tend to be quite expensive. The need for financial readiness cannot be overemphasized.

Communications

The DRP emergency response team is responsible for communicating with the organization's employees, who must know where to report for work and where to find information about their jobs and responsibilities during an emergency.

Recovery plan testing

There are a number of ways to test a disaster recovery plan. The common methods are described here.

- ✔ **Checklist.** This is just a read-through of the disaster recovery plan by subject matter experts in the organization. The purpose of this test is to watch for easily identifiable omissions or errors.

- ✔ **Structured Walkthrough.** This is a more formal "checklist"-type test, but it is performed by several experts gathered in one place, usually with a moderator or facilitator who guides the team through various scenarios.

- ✔ **Simulation.** All identified disaster recovery team members rehearse the procedures that would be performed in an actual disaster. In a simulation, the teams do not actually perform real "live" business processes but only pretend to do so.

- ✔ **Parallel.** This type of test closely resembles the "real thing," in that emergency personnel actually perform business operations. However, real live business operations continue to operate.

- ✔ **Interruption.** This is the most extreme, costly, and risky type of disaster recovery test. In an interruption test, some portion of live production business operations are actually stopped, while emergency response teams perform actual recovery procedures.

DRP and BCP Working Together

In a few places in this chapter, we hinted at some intersection points that exist between BCP and DRP efforts. We'll spell them out here.

Both the Business Continuity Planning and Disaster Recovery Planning teams utilize the results of the Business Impact Assessment, in particular the Vulnerability Assessment and Criticality Assessment. These two documents describe the organization's most critical business functions and their respective vulnerabilities. The BCP and DRP teams each utilize these reports in order to set their own priorities and develop details in their respective response plans.

The recovery team within the DRP effort provides the Business Continuity Plan's response teams with needed supplies and other logistical support. Recall that the BCP response team is concentrating on the continuance of business operations; the DRP recovery team keeps the BCP response team stocked with supplies that are needed to support their work.

Prep Test

1 A recovery test that involves a review of procedures is known as a
_____?

A ○ Simulation
B ○ Parallel
C ○ Serial
D ○ Checklist

2 A _____ contains computer equipment but no communications facilities.

A ○ Standby site
B ○ Cold site
C ○ Hot site
D ○ Warm site

3 The characteristic of a computer's architecture that includes redundant components is known as _____?

A ○ Clustering
B ○ High availability
C ○ Failover
D ○ Fault tolerance

4 The type of backup that saves files changed since the last backup is known as a(n) _____?

A ○ Complete backup
B ○ Incremental backup
C ○ Differential backup
D ○ Full backup

5 The primary purpose of off-site storage is _____?

A ○ To provide better protection of backup data than is possible at the main site.
B ○ To maximize data recovery time in case of a disaster.
C ○ To have data stored in a location away from the data center.
D ○ To give other organizations an opportunity to access the saved data.

6 Which of the following is NOT an example of a natural disaster?

   A ○ Tsunami
   B ○ Strikes
   C ○ Lightning
   D ○ Flood

7 Clustering, Fault Tolerance, and Load Sharing are all examples of
_____.

   A ○ Redundancy
   B ○ Data replication
   C ○ Failovers
   D ○ High availability architectures

8 Mirroring is used to _____.

   A ○ Provide buffered data replication
   B ○ Copy data from one storage subsystem to another
   C ○ Create a clone of a critical system
   D ○ Copy a backup set for off-site storage

9 The report that identifies the most important functions in an organization
is the _____?

   A ○ Business Impact Assessment
   B ○ Criticality Assessment
   C ○ Vulnerability Assessment
   D ○ Function-Point Assessment

10 In what way are the BCP and DRP plans related?

   A ○ Both use the Function Point Analysis.
   B ○ They share the same emergency procedures.
   C ○ One project team produces both.
   D ○ Both use the Criticality Assessment.

Answers

1 **D**. Checklist. A checklist review is a paper review of disaster recovery procedures. *Review "Disaster Recovery Planning."*

2 **D**. Warm site. A warm site is a fully equipped data center with computers, but it has no communications facilities or software. *Review "Business Continuity Planning."*

3 **D**. Fault Tolerance. This includes features such as redundant power supplies, system boards, and network adaptors. *Review "Making Technology Reliable."*

4 **B**. Incremental backup. An incremental backup saves only those files that have changed since the last backup. *Review "Making Technology Reliable."*

5 **C**. To have data stored in a location away from the data center. The purpose of off-site storage is to provide for a safe place for data storage that is apart from the main data center. *Review "Making Technology Reliable."*

6 **B**. Strikes. Any sort of a deliberate, organized massive employee absence is a man-made disaster. *Review "BCP & DRP Overview."*

7 **D**. High availability architectures. High availability architectures are those that increase the reliability of an application. *Review "Making Technology Reliable."*

8 **B**. Copy data from one storage subsystem to another. Mirroring is a "block level" method used to maintain a copy of a storage subsystem. *Review "Making Technology Reliable."*

9 **B**. Criticality Assessment. The Criticality Assessment provides a list of business functions, ranked in order of importance. *Review "Business Continuity Planning."*

10 **D**. Both use the Criticality Assessment. The BCP and DRP teams are primarily separated, but both use the Criticality Assessment in order to ensure that they are concentrating on the business' most critical functions. *See "Business Continuity Planning."*

Chapter 16

Security Management

Security management involves the various practices and processes that ensure an effective security strategy. The most technical security solutions are of limited effectiveness if not deployed as part of a comprehensive security strategy. Building that strategy begins here — with security management.

Quick Assessment

1 The four main types of policies are _____, _____, _____, and _____.

2 The concept of _____ ensures that no single individual has complete authority and control of a critical system or process.

3 The individual that is ultimately responsible for the safeguarding of assigned information assets is the _____.

4 The concept of _____ means an individual requires specific information to perform his or her assigned job function.

5 A risk comprises a _____ and a _____.

6 A _____ is defined as the absence or weakness of a safeguard in an asset.

7 The three main elements of risk management are _____, _____, and _____.

8 The two major types of risk analysis are _____ and _____.

9 Transferring the potential loss associated with a risk to a third party is known as _____.

10 A _____ is a control or countermeasure that reduces risk associated with a specific threat.

Answers

1 Senior management, regulatory, advisory, and informative. *See "Policies."*

2 Separation of duties and responsibilities. *Review "General Security Policies and Practices."*

3 Information owner. *Review "Roles and responsibilities."*

4 Need to know. *See "Need-to-know."*

5 Threat, vulnerability. *See "Principles of Risk Management."*

6 Vulnerability. *See "Principles of Risk Management."*

7 Identification, analysis, and control. *See "Principles of Risk Management."*

8 Quantitative, qualitative. *See "Risk analysis."*

9 Risk assignment (or transference). *See "Risk control."*

10 Safeguard. *See "Risk control."*

Policy and Procedures

Policies, standards, guidelines, and procedures are the blueprints for a successful information security program. They

- ✔ Present governing rules and regulations
- ✔ Provide valuable guidance and decision support
- ✔ Help establish legal authority

Too often, technical security solutions are implemented without first creating the necessary policies, standards, guidelines, and procedures. This results in often expensive and ineffective controls that aren't uniformly applied and don't support an overall security strategy.

Policies

A *security policy* forms the basis of an organization's information security program. RFC 2196, *The Site Security Handbook*, defines a security policy as "a formal statement of rules by which people who are given access to an organization's technology and information assets must abide."

The four main types of policies are

- ✔ **Senior Management:** A high-level management statement of an organization's security objectives, organizational and individual responsibilities, ethics and beliefs, and general requirements and controls.
- ✔ **Regulatory:** Highly detailed and concise policies usually mandated by federal, state, industry, or other legal requirements.
- ✔ **Advisory:** Not mandatory, but highly recommended often with specific penalties or consequences for failure to comply. Most policies are considered to be in this category.
- ✔ **Informative:** Purpose is only to inform with no explicit requirements for compliance.

Standards, guidelines, and procedures are supporting elements of a policy and provide specific implementation details of the policy.

Standards

Standards are specific, mandatory requirements that further define and support higher-level policies. For example, a standard may require the use of a specific technology, such as a minimum requirement for encryption of sensitive data using 3DES, without specifying the exact product to be implemented.

Baselines are similar to and related to standards. A baseline can be useful for identifying a consistent basis for an organization's security architecture, taking into account system-specific parameters, such as different operating systems. After consistent baselines are established, appropriate standards can be defined across the organization.

Guidelines

Guidelines are similar to standards but are recommendations rather than compulsory requirements. For example, a guideline may provide tips or recommendations for determining the sensitivity of a file and whether encryption is required.

Procedures

Procedures provide detailed instructions on how to implement specific policies and meet the criteria defined in standards. Procedures may include Standard Operating Procedures (SOPs), run books, and user guides. For example, a procedure may be a step-by-step guide for encrypting sensitive files using a specific software encryption product.

General Security Policies and Practices

General security policies and practices that should be considered and implemented where appropriate are discussed in the following sections.

Separation of duties and responsibilities

The concept of *separation* (or *segregation*) *of duties and responsibilities* ensures that no single individual has complete authority and control of a critical system or process. This practice promotes security in the following ways:

- Reduces opportunity for waste, fraud, or abuse
- Provides two-man control (or dual-control, two-person integrity)
- Reduces dependence on individuals

Job rotations

Job rotations (or rotation of duties) are another effective security control with many benefits to an organization. Similar to the concept of separation of duties and responsibilities, job rotations involve regularly transferring key personnel into different positions or departments within an organization. Job rotations benefit an organization in the following ways:

- ✔ Reduces opportunity for waste, fraud, or abuse
- ✔ Reduces dependence, through cross-training opportunities, on individuals; also promotes professional growth
- ✔ Reduces monotony and/or fatigue for individuals

Background checks/security clearances

Pre- and post-employment background checks can provide an employer with valuable information about an individual being considered for a job or position within an organization. Such checks can give an immediate indication of an individual's integrity and can help screen out unqualified applicants.

Basic background checks should be conducted for all personnel with access to sensitive information or systems within an organization. A basic background check should include

- ✔ **Reference checks:** Personal, professional, and prior employers
- ✔ **Verification of data in employment applications and resumes:** Social Security numbers, education, professional/technical certifications, military records, and previous employment
- ✔ **Other Records:** Court, local law enforcement, and motor vehicle records

Personnel who fill more sensitive positions should undergo a more extensive pre-employment screening and background check, possibly including

- ✔ **Credit records**
- ✔ **Drug testing**
- ✔ **Special background investigation:** FBI and INTERPOL records, field interviews with former associates, or a personal interview with a private investigator

Periodic post-employment screenings (such as credit records and drug testing) may also be necessary, particularly for personnel with access to financial data or personnel being considered for promotions to more sensitive or responsible positions.

Employment agreements

Various employment agreements should be signed when an individual joins an organization or is promoted to a more sensitive position within an organization. Typical employment agreements include non-compete/non-disclosure agreements and acceptable use policies.

Hiring and termination practices

Hiring and termination practices should be formalized within an organization to ensure fair and uniform treatment and to protect the organization and its information assets.

Standard hiring practices should include background checks and employment agreements (as I discuss in the preceding section "Background checks/security clearances"), as well as a formal indoctrination and orientation process. This process may include formal introductions to key organizational personnel, creating user accounts and assigning IT resources (PCs and notebook computers), assigning security badges and parking permits, and a general policy discussion with human resources personnel.

Formal termination procedures should be implemented to help protect the organization from potential lawsuits, property theft/destruction, unauthorized access, or workplace violence. Procedures should be developed for various scenarios including resignations, termination, layoffs, accident or death, immediate departures versus prior notification, and hostile situations. Termination procedures may include

✔ Surrendering keys, security badges, and parking permits

✔ Conducting an exit interview

✔ Security escort to desk and/or from premises

✔ Returning company materials (notebook computers, mobile telephones, pagers)

✔ Changing door locks and system passwords

✔ Formal turnover of duties and responsibilities

✔ Removing network/system access and disabling user accounts

✔ Policies regarding retention of e-mail, personal files, and employment records

✔ Notification of customers, partners, vendors, and contractors, as appropriate

Job descriptions

Concise job descriptions that clearly identify an individual's responsibility and authority, particularly on information security issues, help

- ✔ Reduce confusion and ambiguity
- ✔ Provide legal basis for an individual's authority or actions
- ✔ Demonstrate negligence or dereliction in carrying out assigned duties

Roles and responsibilities

The true axiom that information security is everyone's responsibility is too often put into practice as *Everyone is responsible, but no one is accountable.* To avoid this pitfall, specific roles and responsibilities for information security should be defined in an organization's security policy, individual job or position descriptions, and third-party contracts. These roles and responsibilities should apply to employees, consultants, contractors, interns, and vendors. Several broad categories for information security roles and common responsibilities include the following.

Management

Senior-level management is often responsible for information security at several levels, including the role as an information owner, which I discuss in the next section. However, in this context, management has a responsibility to demonstrate a strong commitment to an organization's information security program. This can be achieved through the following actions:

- ✔ **Corporate information security policy:** This should include a statement of support from management and should also be signed by the CEO or COO.
- ✔ **Lead-by-example:** A CEO who refuses to carry a mandatory identification badge or who bypasses system access controls sets a poor example that others may emulate.
- ✔ **Cashola:** Pay exorbitant salaries to your security staff and praise them daily!

Owner

An *information owner* is normally assigned at an executive or senior-management level within an organization, such as director or vice president. An information owner doesn't legally *own* the information that he's been assigned; the information owner is ultimately *responsible* for the safeguarding of assigned information assets and may have *fiduciary responsibility* or be held *personally liable* for negligence in protecting these assets under the concept of due care. *Due care* refers to the steps that an organization takes to implement the best security practices. Closely related to, but distinctly different from the concept of due care, is *due diligence*. Due diligence is the prudent management and execution of due care.

The concepts of *due care* and *due diligence* are related but distinctly different:

- ✔ **Due care:** The steps that an organization takes to implement security best practices.
- ✔ **Due diligence:** The prudent management and execution of due care.

Typical responsibilities of an information owner may include

- ✔ Determining information classification levels for assigned information assets
- ✔ Maintaining inventories and accounting for assigned information assets
- ✔ Periodically reviewing classification levels of assigned information assets for possible downgrading, destruction, or disposal
- ✔ Delegating day-to-day responsibility (but not accountability) and functions to a custodian

Custodian

An *information custodian* is the individual with day-to-day responsibility for protecting information assets. IT systems or network administrators often fill this role. Typical responsibilities may include

- ✔ Performing regular backups and restoring data when necessary
- ✔ Ensuring that directory and file permissions are properly implemented and provide sufficient protection
- ✔ Assigning new users to appropriate permission groups and revoking user privileges, when required

The distinction between owners and custodians, particularly regarding their different responsibilities, is an important concept in information security management. The information owner is the individual that has ultimate responsibility for the security of the information, whereas the information custodian is the individual responsible for the day-to-day security administration.

Users

An *end-user* (or user) includes just about everyone within an organization. Users aren't specifically designated. They can be broadly defined as anyone with authorized access to an organization's internal information or information systems. Typical user responsibilities include

- ✔ Complying with all security requirements defined in organizational policies, standards, and procedures, applicable legislative or regulatory requirements, and contractual requirements (such as non-disclosure agreements and service-level agreements)

- ✔ Exercising due care in safeguarding organizational information and information assets

- ✔ Participating in information security training and awareness efforts

- ✔ Reporting any suspicious activity, security violations, security problems, or security concerns to appropriate personnel

Need-to-know

The concept of *need-to-know* means an individual requires specific information to perform his or her assigned job function. The concept of need-to-know is used together with clearance levels and data classification systems to protect systems and information. In order for access to be granted, an individual must have a clearance level at or above the classification level of the system or information to be accessed *and* have a specific need -to know that information.

Password management

Password management policies are critical for ensuring that critical passwords are not inadvertently compromised and systems secured by passwords are kept secure. These policies may include various password controls (see Chapter 3 for more details) and policies regarding when system password changes should be made (at regular intervals or specific events, such as departing system administrators).

Service Level Agreements (SLAs)

A *Service Level Agreement* (SLA) is a document similar to a contract (and in many cases formalized as a contract) that provides a defined standard for service. An SLA protects both the customer and the service provider. For example, in the case of a help desk or customer service center, an SLA might define customer service hours, the level of support provided, and a normal response time (for example, within 4 hours). An SLA between a customer site and a telecommunications provider might define maintenance windows, acceptable limits for outage periods, and a minimum quality or level of service.

Privacy

Clearly defined policies and procedures regarding privacy are extremely important to ensure that organizations comply with applicable privacy laws. Privacy laws are enacted to protect information collected and maintained on individuals from unauthorized disclosure or misuse.

Two important pieces of privacy legislation in the United States are the Federal Privacy Act of 1974, which protects records and information maintained by U.S. government agencies about U.S. citizens and residents, and the U.S. Health Insurance Portability and Accountability Act of 1996, which protects individual medical records and mandates various security requirements.

Another important aspect of privacy is the expectation of privacy (or lack thereof) in the use of corporate e-mail. Many organizations explicitly state that an individual has no right or expectation of privacy when using corporate e-mail systems. E-mail is provided for official business use, and as such, is the property of the company and therefore subject to monitoring.

Code of Ethics

Ethics (or moral values) are not easily defined and a fine line often hovers between ethical and unethical activity. Ethical activity doesn't necessarily equate to illegal activity. And what may be acceptable in some organizations, cultures, or societies may be unacceptable or even illegal in others.

Ethical standards can be based on a common or national interest, individual rights, laws, tradition, culture, or religion. One helpful distinction between laws and ethics is that laws define what we *must* do and ethics define what we *should* do.

Many organizations define a *Code of Ethics* for employees or professionals to abide by. Although such codes are typically written to address very general situations, they are often applicable for ethical questions regarding the use of computer resources.

Principles of Risk Management

The business of information security is all about risk management. A *risk* comprises a threat and a vulnerability, defined as follows:

 ✔ **Threat:** Any natural or man-made circumstance or event that could have an adverse or undesirable impact, minor or major, on an organizational asset.

 ✔ **Vulnerability:** The absence or weakness of a safeguard in an asset that makes a threat potentially more harmful or costly, more likely to occur, or likely to occur more frequently.

Threat + Vulnerability = Risk

An *asset* is a resource, process, product, or system that has some value to an organization and must therefore be protected. Assets may be *tangible* (computers, data, software, records) or *intangible* (privacy, access, public image, ethics), and may likewise have a *tangible value* (purchase price) or *intangible value* (competitive advantage).

Risk can never be completely eliminated. Given sufficient time, resources, motivation, and money, any system or environment, no matter how secure, can eventually be compromised. Some threats or events, such as natural disasters, are entirely beyond our control and largely unpredictable. Therefore, the main goal of risk management is *risk mitigation:* reducing risk to a level that's acceptable to an organization. Risk management comprises the following three main elements:

 ✔ Identification

 ✔ Analysis

 ✔ Control

Risk identification

A preliminary step in risk management is risk identification. Risk identification involves identifying specific elements of the three components of risk: assets, threats, and vulnerabilities.

Asset valuation

Identifying an organization's assets and determining its value is a critical step in determining the appropriate level of security required for an asset. The value of an asset to an organization can be both *quantitative* (cost) and *qualitative* (importance). An inaccurate or hastily conducted asset valuation process can have the following consequences for controls:

 ✔ Poorly chosen or improperly implemented

 ✔ Not cost-effective

 ✔ Protect the wrong asset

A properly conducted asset valuation process has several benefits to an organization:

- Supports quantitative and qualitative risk assessments, business impact assessments, and security auditing
- Facilitates cost/benefit analysis and supports management decisions regarding selection of appropriate safeguards
- Can be used to determine insurance requirements, budgeting, and replacement costs
- Helps demonstrate due care and limit personal liability

Threat analysis

Threat analysis involves the following four steps:

1. **Define the actual threat.**

2. **Identify possible consequences to the organization if the threat is realized.**

3. **Determine the probable frequency of a threat.**

4. **Assess the probability that a threat will actually materialize.**

For example, a company with a major distribution center located along the Gulf Coast of the United States may be concerned about hurricanes. Possible consequences may include power outages, wind damage, and flooding. Based on climatology, the company can determine that an annual average of three hurricanes pass within 50 miles of its location between June and September and that a high probability exists of a hurricane actually affecting the company's operations during this period. During the remainder of the year, the threat of hurricanes is a low probability.

The number and types of threats that an organization must consider can be overwhelming, but can generally be categorized as:

- **Natural:** Earthquakes, floods, hurricanes, lightning, fire, and so on.
- **Man-made:** Unauthorized access, data entry errors, strikes/labor disputes, theft, terrorism, social engineering, malicious code and viruses, and so forth

Vulnerability assessment

A *vulnerability assessment* provides a valuable baseline for determining appropriate and necessary safeguards. For example, a denial-of-service threat may exist based on a vulnerability found in Microsoft's implementation of

Domain Name System (DNS). However, if an organization's DNS servers have been properly patched or the organization uses a Unix-based BIND (Berkeley Internet Name Domain) server, the specific vulnerability may already have been adequately addressed, and no additional safeguards may be necessary for that threat.

Risk analysis

The next element in risk management is risk analysis. A *risk analysis* brings together all the elements of risk management (identification, analysis, and control) and is critical to an organization for developing an effective risk management strategy. The two major types of risk analysis are *quantitative* and *qualitative*.

Quantitative risk analysis

A *quantitative risk analysis* attempts to assign an objective numeric value (cost) to the components (assets and threats) of the risk analysis.

A fully quantitative risk analysis requires all elements of the process, including asset value, impact, threat frequency, safeguard effectiveness, safeguard costs, and uncertainty and probability, to be measured and assigned a numeric value. However, assigning a value to every component associated with a risk (safeguard effectiveness and uncertainty) is not possible, and some qualitative measures must be applied.

Achieving a purely quantitative risk analysis is impossible.

Qualitative risk analysis

A *qualitative risk analysis* is scenario-driven and doesn't attempt to assign numeric values to the components (assets and threats) of the risk analysis.

Qualitative risk analysis is more subjective than a quantitative risk analysis and, unlike a quantitative risk analysis, it's possible to conduct a purely qualitative risk analysis. The challenge of a qualitative risk analysis is developing real scenarios that describe a threat and potential losses to organizational assets.

Risk control

A properly conducted risk analysis provides the basis for selecting appropriate safeguards and countermeasures. A *safeguard* is a control or countermeasure that reduces risk associated with a specific threat. The absence of a safeguard against a threat creates a vulnerability and increases the risk.

Safeguards counter risks through one of three general remedies:

- **Risk reduction:** Mitigating risk by implementing the necessary security controls, policies, and procedures to protect an asset. This can be achieved by altering, reducing, or eliminating the threat and/or vulnerability associated with the risk.

  This is the most common risk control remedy.

- **Risk assignment (or transference):** Transferring the potential loss associated with a risk to a third party, such as an insurance company.

- **Risk acceptance:** Accepting the loss associated with a potential risk. This is sometimes done for convenience (not prudent) but more appropriately when the cost of other countermeasures is prohibitive and the potential risk probability is low.

Security Awareness

Security awareness is an often-overlooked factor in an information security program. Although security is the focus of security practitioners in their day-to-day functions, it's often taken for granted that common users possess this same level of security awareness. As a result, users can unwittingly become the weakest link in an information security program. Several key factors are critical to the success of a security awareness program:

- **Senior-level management support.** Under ideal circumstances, senior management is seen attending and actively participating in training efforts.

- **Clear demonstration of how security supports the organization's business objectives.**

- **Clear demonstration of how security is important to all individuals and their job functions.**

- **Current levels of training and understanding of the intended audience taken into account.** Training that's too basic will be ignored; training that's too technical will not be understood.

- **Action and follow-up.** A glitzy presentation that's forgotten as soon as the audience leaves the room is useless. Find ways to incorporate the lessons with day-to-day activities and follow-up plans.

The three main components of an effective security awareness program are a *general awareness program, formal training,* and *education.*

Awareness

A *general awareness program* provides basic security information and ensures that everyone understands the importance of security. Awareness programs may include the following elements:

- ✔ **Indoctrination and orientation:** New employees and contractors should receive a basic indoctrination and orientation. During the indoctrination, they may receive a copy of the corporate information security policy, be required to acknowledge and sign acceptable use statements and non-disclosure agreements, and meet immediate supervisors and pertinent members of the security and IT staff.

- ✔ **Presentations:** Lectures, video presentations, and interactive computer-based training (CBTs) are excellent tools for disseminating security training and information. Employee bonuses and performance reviews are sometimes tied to participation in these types of security awareness programs.

- ✔ **Printed materials:** Security posters, corporate newsletters, and periodic bulletins are useful for disseminating basic information such as security tips and promoting awareness of security.

Training

Formal training programs provide more in-depth information than an awareness program and may focus on specific security-related skills or tasks. Such training programs may include

- ✔ **Classroom training:** Instructor-led or other formally facilitated training, possibly at corporate headquarters or a company training facility.

- ✔ **On-the-job training:** May include one-on-one mentoring with a peer or immediate supervisor.

- ✔ **Technical or vendor training:** Training on a specific product or technology provided by a third-party.

- ✔ **Apprenticeship or qualification programs:** Formal probationary status or qualification standards that must be satisfactorily completed within a specified time period.

Education

An *education program* provides the deepest level of security training focusing on underlying principles, methodologies, and concepts.

An education program may include

- ✔ **Continuing education requirements:** Continuing Education Units (CEUs) are becoming popular for maintaining high-level technical or professional certifications.

- ✔ **Certificate programs:** Many colleges and universities offer adult education programs with classes on current and relevant subjects for working professionals.

- ✔ **Formal education or degree requirements:** Many companies offer tuition assistance or scholarships for employees enrolled in classes that are relevant to their profession.

Documentation

Documentation, documentation, documentation. We all know we should do it. Few actually do. But complete and up-to-date documentation of your critical systems and configurations is an essential component of information security. Important documentation includes

- ✔ **Systems architecture.** This includes logical and physical diagrams and system configurations. These documents are critical for understanding your systems, identifying vulnerabilities, troubleshooting, and disaster recovery.

- ✔ **Change documentation.** A formal change management and configuration control process is important for maintaining availability and stability of production systems and for keeping documentation current. The change control process includes proposal, design, review, approval, and implementation.

- ✔ **System logs.** Maintaining and regularly reviewing system logs helps identify unauthorized access attempts, system abuse, and impending system problems.

- ✔ **Inventories.** Complete asset inventories help identify losses due to theft or disasters and also provide a good accounting of what assets need to be protected.

Data classification

Information and data, in all their various forms, are valuable business assets. As with other more tangible assets, the information's value determines the level of protection required by the organization. Applying a single protection standard uniformly across all an organization's assets is neither practical nor desirable. A data classification scheme helps an organization to assign a value to its information assets based on its sensitivity to loss or disclosure as well as to determine the appropriate level of protection. Appropriate safeguards regarding the use, handling, reproduction, transport, retention, storage, and destruction of information can then be implemented based on classification levels. Additionally, data classification schemes may be required for regulatory or other legal compliance.

Commercial data classification

Commercial data classification schemes are typically implemented to protect information that has a monetary value, to comply with applicable laws and protect privacy, and to limit liability. Criteria by which commercial data is classified include

- **Value:** This is the most common classification criteria in commercial organizations. Classification is based on monetary or some other intrinsic value.

- **Age/useful life:** Information that loses value over time, becomes obsolete or irrelevant, or becomes common/public knowledge should be classified accordingly.

- **Regulatory requirements:** Private information, such as medical records subject to HIPAA (Health Insurance Portability and Accountability Act of 1996) regulations and educational records subject to the Privacy Act) may have legal requirements for protection. Classification of such information may be based not only on compliance but also liability limits.

Descriptive labels are often applied to company information, such as *Confidential and Proprietary* and *Internal Use Only*. However, the organizational requirements for protecting information labeled as such is often not formally defined or is unknown. Organizations should formally identify standard classification levels as well as specific requirements for labeling, handling, storage, and destruction/disposal.

Government data classification

Government data classification schemes are generally implemented to

- Protect national interests or security
- Comply with applicable laws
- Protect privacy

One of the more common systems, used within the U.S. Department of Defense (DoD), consists of five broad categories for information classification:

- ✔ **Unclassified.** The lowest government data classification level is unclassified. Unclassified information isn't sensitive, and unauthorized disclosure won't cause any harm to national security.

- ✔ **Sensitive but Unclassified (SBU).** Generally includes information of a private or personal nature. Examples include test questions, disciplinary proceedings, and medical records.

- ✔ **Confidential.** Information that could cause damage to national security if compromised. Confidential information is the lowest level of "classified" government information.

- ✔ **Secret.** Information that could cause *serious* damage to national security if compromised. Secret information must normally be accounted for throughout its life cycle to destruction.   •

- ✔ **Top Secret.** Information that could cause *grave* damage to national security if compromised. Top Secret information may require additional safeguards such as special designations and handling restrictions.

Prep Test

1 Specific, mandatory requirements that further define and support higher-level policies are

- **A** ○ Guidelines
- **B** ○ Regulations
- **C** ○ Standards
- **D** ○ Procedures

2 Most security policies are categorized as:

- **A** ○ Informative
- **B** ○ Regulatory
- **C** ○ Mandatory
- **D** ○ Advisory

3 A baseline is a type of:

- **A** ○ Policy
- **B** ○ Guideline
- **C** ○ Procedure
- **D** ○ Standard

4 The practice of regularly transferring personnel into different positions or departments within an organization describes the following employment security practice is

- **A** ○ Separation of Duties
- **B** ○ Re-assignment
- **C** ○ Lateral Transfers
- **D** ○ Job Rotations

5 The individual responsible for assigning information classification levels for assigned information assets is

- **A** ○ Management
- **B** ○ Owner
- **C** ○ Custodian
- **D** ○ User

6 The individual with day-to-day responsibility for protecting information assets is the:

A ○ Information owner

B ○ End-user.

C ○ Information custodian

D ○ Management

7 The three main elements of risk management include all of the following except:

A ○ Identification

B ○ Analysis

C ○ Control

D ○ Accountability

8 A _____ is a control or countermeasure that reduces risk associated with a specific threat.

A ○ Safeguard

B ○ Threat

C ○ Vulnerability

D ○ Asset

9 Which of the following is not considered a general remedy for risk management?

A ○ Risk reduction

B ○ Risk acceptance

C ○ Risk assignment

D ○ Risk avoidance

10 Which of the following government data classification levels describes information, which, if compromised, could cause serious damage to national security?

A ○ Top Secret

B ○ Secret

C ○ Confidential

D ○ Sensitive but Unclassified

Answers

1 **C.** Standards. Guidelines are similar to standards but are recommendations rather than requirements. Regulations could be considered one of the four main types of policies. Procedures are detailed instructions for implementing specific policies. *Review "Policy and Procedures."*

2 **D.** Advisory. Although not mandatory, advisory policies are highly recommended and may provide penalties for failure to comply. *Review "Policy and Procedures."*

3 **D.** Standard. A baseline takes into account system-specific parameters to help an organization identify appropriate standards. *Review "Policy and Procedures."*

4 **D.** Job Rotations. Separation of duties is related to job rotations but is distinctly different. Re-assignment and lateral transfers are functionally equivalent to job rotations but aren't necessarily done for the same reasons and aren't considered security employment practices. *Review "Job rotations."*

5 **B.** Owner. Although an information owner may be in a management position and is also considered a user, the information owner role has the responsibility for assigning information classification levels. An information custodian is responsible for day-to-day security tasks. *Review "Roles and responsibilities."*

6 **C.** Information custodian. IT systems or network administrators often fill this role. *Review "Roles and responsibilities."*

7 **D.** Accountability. identification, analysis, and control are all elements of risk management. *Review "Principles of Risk Management."*

8 **A.** Safeguard. A safeguard is a control that is implemented to reduce risk associated with a specific threat. *Review "Risk control."*

9 **D.** Risk avoidance. Although risk avoidance is a valid concept, it's impossible to achieve and therefore not considered a general remedy for risk management. *Review "Risk control."*

10 **B.** Secret. Top Secret information leaks could cause *grave damage.* Confidential information breaches could cause *damage.* Sensitive but Unclassified information doesn't have a direct impact on national security. *Review "Data classification."*

Chapter 17

Computer Forensics and Incident Response

*C*omputer forensics is the science of conducting a computer crime investigation to determine what has happened, to find out who is responsible and to collect legally admissible evidence for use in a computer crime case.

Closely related to, but distinctly different from investigations, is incident response. The purpose of an investigation is to determine what happened, to determine who is responsible, and to collect evidence. *Incident response* determines what happened, contains and assesses damage, and restores normal operations.

Investigations and incident response must often be conducted simultaneously in a well-coordinated and controlled manner to ensure that the initial actions of either activity don't destroy evidence or cause further damage to the organization's assets. For this reason, Computer Incident (or Emergency) Response Teams (CIRT or CERT, respectively) need to be properly trained and qualified to secure a crime scene or incident while preserving evidence. Ideally, the CIRT includes individuals who conduct the investigation.

An analogy to this would be an example of a police patrolman who discovers a murder victim. It's important that the patrolman quickly assess the safety of the situation and secure the crime scene; but at the same time, he or she must be careful not to destroy any evidence. The homicide detective's job is to gather and analyze the evidence. Ideally, the homicide detective would be the individual who discovers the murder victim, allowing her or him to assess the safety of the situation, secure the crime scene, and begin collecting evidence.

Quick Assessment

1 Identify the four major categories of evidence.

2 Visual or audio surveillance tapes generated during or after a crime are considered what type of evidence?

3 The _____ is an important test for determining the admissibility of documentary evidence in a case.

4 Two types of opinions that may be admitted as demonstrative evidence are _____ and _____.

5 A duplicate or copy of evidence is considered _____ evidence.

6 _____ evidence supports or substantiates other evidence presented in a case.

7 _____ evidence is evidence that is not based on personal, firsthand knowledge of the witness but rather was obtained through other sources.

8 In order for evidence to be admissible in a case, it must be _____, _____, and _____.

9 The _____ provides accountability and protection for evidence throughout its entire life cycle.

10 _____ focuses on containing the damage following an incident and returning to normal operations.

Answers

1 Direct, real (or physical), documentary, demonstrative. *See "Types of evidence."*

2 Real (or physical). *Review "Types of evidence."*

3 Hearsay rule. *Review "Types of evidence."*

4 Expert and nonexpert. *See "Types of evidence."*

5 Secondary. *See "Types of evidence."*

6 Corroborative. *See "Types of evidence."*

7 Hearsay. *See "Rules of evidence."*

8 Relevant, reliable, legally permissible. *See "Admissibility of evidence."*

9 Chain of custody (or chain of evidence). *See "The chain of custody and the evidence life cycle."*

10 Incident response. *See "Incident Response."*

Conducting Investigations

A computer crime investigation should begin immediately upon report of an alleged computer crime or incident. Initially, any incident should be handled as a computer crime investigation until a preliminary investigation determines otherwise. The general steps to be followed in the investigative process are the following:

- ✔ **Detect and contain:** Early detection is critical to a successful investigation. Unfortunately, passive or reactive detection techniques (such as the review of audit trails and accidental discovery) are usually the norm in computer crimes and often leave a cold evidence trail. Containment is essential to minimize further loss or damage.

- ✔ **Notify management:** Management must be notified of any investigation as soon as possible. Knowledge of the investigation should be limited to as few people as possible and should be on a need-to-know basis. Out-of-band communications methods (reporting in person) should be used to ensure that sensitive communications about the investigation are not intercepted.

- ✔ **Begin preliminary investigation:** This is necessary to determine whether a crime has actually occurred. Most incidents are honest mistakes, not criminal conduct. This step includes

    - Reviewing the complaint or report

    - Inspecting damage

    - Interviewing witnesses

    - Examining logs

    - Identifying further investigation requirements

- ✔ **Initiate disclosure determination:** The first and most important thing to determine is whether disclosure of the crime or incident is required by law. Next, determine whether disclosure is desired. This should be coordinated with a public relations or public affairs official of the organization.

- ✔ **Conduct the investigation:**

    - **Identify potential suspects.** This includes insiders and outsiders to the organization. One standard discriminator to help determine or eliminate potential suspects is the MOM test: Did the suspect have the motive, opportunity, and means to commit the crime?

    - **Identify potential witnesses.** Determine who is to be interviewed and who will conduct the interviews. Be careful not to alert any potential suspects to the investigation; focus on obtaining facts, not opinions, in witness statements.

- **Prepare for search and seizure.** This includes identifying the types of systems and evidence to be searched for or seized, designating and training the search and seizure team members (CIRT), obtaining and serving proper search warrants (if required), and determining potential risk to the system during a search and seizure effort.

- **Report findings:** The results of the investigation, including evidence, should be reported to management and turned over to appropriate law enforcement officials or prosecutors.

Evidence

Evidence is information presented in a court of law to confirm or dispel a fact that's under contention. A case can't be brought to trial without sufficient evidence to support the case. Thus, properly gathering evidence is one of the most important and most difficult tasks of the investigator.

Types of evidence

Sources of legal evidence that can be presented in a court of law generally fall into one of four major categories:

- **Direct evidence:** This is oral testimony or a written statement based on information gathered through the witness's five senses (an eyewitness account) that proves or disproves a specific fact or issue.

- **Real (or physical) evidence:** These are tangible objects from the actual crime, such as these:
  - Tools and weapons
  - Stolen or damaged property
  - Visual or audio surveillance tapes

Physical evidence from a computer crime is rarely available.

- **Documentary evidence:** Most evidence presented in a computer crime case is documentary evidence, such as the following;
  - Originals and copies of business records
  - Computer-generated and computer-stored records
  - Manuals
  - Policies
  - Standards

- Procedures

- Log files

Business records, including computer records, are traditionally considered hearsay evidence by most courts because these records cannot be proven accurate and reliable. One of the most significant obstacles for a prosecutor to overcome in a computer crime case is seeking the admission of computer records as evidence.

✔ **Demonstrative evidence.** Used to aid the court's understanding of a case. Opinions are considered demonstrative evidence and may be either

- **Expert:** Based on personal expertise and facts

- **Nonexpert:** Based on facts only

Other examples of demonstrative evidence include models, simulations, charts, and illustrations.

Other types of evidence that may fall into at least one the preceding major categories include

✔ **Best evidence:** Original, unaltered evidence. In court, this is preferred over secondary evidence.

Data extracted from a computer satisfies the best evidence rule and may normally be introduced into court proceedings as such.

✔ **Secondary evidence:** A duplicate or copy of evidence, such as

- Tape backup

- Screen capture

- Photograph

✔ **Corroborative evidence:** Supports or substantiates other evidence presented in a case.

✔ **Conclusive evidence:** Incontrovertible and irrefutable: the smoking gun.

✔ **Circumstantial evidence:** Relevant facts that can't be directly or conclusively connected to other events but about which a reasonable inference can be made.

Rules of evidence

Important rules of evidence for computer crime cases include the best evidence rule and the hearsay evidence rule.

Best evidence rule

The best evidence rule, defined in the Federal Rules of Evidence, states that "to prove the content of a writing, recording, or photograph, the original writing, recording, or photograph is [ordinarily] required."

However, an exception to this rule is defined in the Federal Rules of Evidence:

> "If data are stored in a computer or similar device, any printout or other output readable by sight, shown to reflect the data accurately, is an "original."

This means that data extracted from a computer — that is a fair and accurate representation of the original data — satisfies the best evidence rule and may normally be introduced into court proceedings as such.

Hearsay rule

Hearsay evidence is that evidence that is not based on personal, firsthand knowledge of the witness; it was obtained through other sources. Under the Federal Rules of Evidence, hearsay evidence is normally not admissible in court. This rule exists to prevent unreliable statements by witnesses from improperly influencing the outcome of a trial.

Business records, including computer records, have traditionally, and perhaps mistakenly, been considered hearsay evidence by most courts because these records cannot be proven accurate and reliable. One of the most significant obstacles for a prosecutor to overcome in a computer crime case is seeking the admission of computer records as evidence.

A prosecutor may be able to introduce computer records as best evidence, not hearsay evidence.

Several courts have acknowledged that the hearsay rules are applicable to *computer-stored* records containing human statements but are not applicable to *computer-generated* records untouched by human hands.

Perhaps the most successful and commonly applied test of admissibility for computer records in general, has been the *business records exception*, established in the Federal Rules of Evidence, for records of regularly conducted activity, meeting these criteria:

1. **Made at or near the time of occurrence of the act**

2. **Made by a person with knowledge or from information transmitted by a person with knowledge**

3. **Made and relied upon during the regular conduct of business, as verified by the custodian or other witness familiar with their use**

4. **Kept for motives that tend to assure their accuracy**

5. **In the custody of the witness on a regular basis (as required by the chain of evidence)**

We discuss chain of evidence in the "Chain of custody and the evidence life cycle" section, later in this chapter.

Admissibility of evidence

Because computer-generated evidence can often be easily manipulated, altered, or tampered, and because it's not easily and commonly understood, this type of evidence is usually considered suspect in a court of law. In order to be admissible, evidence must be:

- ✔ **Relevant:** It must tend to prove or disprove facts that are relevant and material to the case.

- ✔ **Reliable:** It must be reasonably proven that what is presented as evidence is what was originally collected and that the evidence itself is reliable. This is accomplished, in part, through proper evidence handling and the chain of custody. (We discuss this in the "Chain of custody and the evidence life cycle" section, later in this chapter.)

- ✔ **Legally permissible:** It must be obtained through legal means. Evidence that's not legally permissible may include evidence obtained through these means:

  - **Illegal search and seizure:** Law enforcement personnel must obtain a prior court order; however, non-law enforcement personnel, such as a supervisor or system administrator, may be able to conduct an authorized search under some circumstances.

  - **Illegal wiretaps or phone taps:** Anyone conducting wiretaps or phone taps must obtain a prior court order.

  - **Entrapment or enticement:** *Entrapment* encourages someone to commit a crime that the individual may have had no intention of committing. Conversely, *enticement* lures someone toward some evidence (a honey pot, if you will) after that individual has already committed a crime. Enticement is not necessarily illegal but does raise ethical arguments and may not be admissible in court.

  - **Coercion:** Coerced testimony or confessions are not legally permissible.

  - **Unauthorized or improper monitoring:** Active monitoring must be properly authorized and conducted in a standard manner; users must be notified that they may be subject to monitoring.

The chain of custody and the evidence life cycle

The *chain of custody* (or *chain of evidence*) provides accountability and protection for evidence throughout its entire life cycle and includes the following information, which is normally kept in an evidence log:

- **Persons involved (Who):** Identify

  - Any and all individual(s) who discovered, collected, seized, analyzed, stored, preserved, transported, or otherwise controlled the evidence

  - Any witnesses or other individuals present during any of the above actions

- **Description of evidence (What):** Ensure that all evidence is completely and uniquely described.

- **Location of evidence (Where):** Provide specific information about the evidence's location when it is discovered, analyzed, stored, or transported.

- **Date/Time (When):** Record

  - The date and time that evidence is discovered, collected, seized, analyzed, stored, or transported

  - The date and time information for any log entries associated with the evidence

- **Methods used (How):** Provide specific information about how evidence is discovered, collected, stored, preserved, or transported.

Any time that evidence changes possession or is transferred to a different media type, it must be properly recorded in the evidence log to maintain the chain of custody.

Law enforcement officials must strictly adhere to chain of custody requirements. This adherence is recommended for anyone else involved in collecting or seizing evidence. Security professionals and incident response teams must fully understand and follow the chain of custody no matter how minor or insignificant a security incident may initially appear.

Even properly trained law enforcement officials sometimes make crucial mistakes in evidence handling. Most attorneys won't understand the technical aspects of the evidence that you may present in a case, but they know evidence-handling rules and will scrutinize and attack your actions in this area. Improperly handled evidence, no matter how conclusive or damaging, usually is inadmissible in court.

The *evidence life cycle* describes the phases of evidence from its initial discovery to its final disposition.

The evidence life cycle has these five stages:

- Collection and identification
- Analysis
- Storage, preservation, and transportation
- Presentation in court
- Return to victim (owner)

Collection and identification

Collecting evidence involves taking that evidence into custody. Unfortunately, evidence can't always be collected and must instead be seized. Many legal issues are involved in seizing computers and other electronic evidence. The publication *Searching and Seizing Computers and Obtaining Electronic Evidence in Criminal Investigations* (July 2002), published by the United States Department of Justice (DOJ) Computer Crime and Intellectual Property Section (CCIPS) provides comprehensive guidance on this subject. Find this publication available for download at `www.cybercrime.gov`.

In general, law enforcement officials can search and/or seize computers and other electronic evidence under any of four circumstances:

- **Voluntary or consensual:** The owner of the computer or electronic evidence can freely surrender the evidence.

- **Subpoena:** A court can issue a subpoena to an individual, ordering that individual to deliver the evidence to the court.

- **Search warrant or Writ of Possession:** The court can issue a *search warrant* to a law enforcement official, allowing that official to search and seize specific evidence. A *Writ of Possession* is a similar order issued in civil cases.

- **Exigent circumstances:** If probable cause exists and the destruction of evidence is imminent, it may be searched or seized without a warrant.

When evidence is collected, it must be properly marked and identified. This ensures that it can later be properly presented in court as actual evidence gathered from the scene or incident. The collected evidence must be recorded in an evidence log with the following information:

- **A description** of the particular piece of evidence including any specific information, such as make, model, serial number, physical appearance, material condition, and preexisting damage

- **The name(s)** of the person(s) who discovered and collected the evidence

✔ **The exact date and time, specific location, and circumstances** of the discovery/collection

Additionally, the evidence must be marked, using these guidelines:

✔ **Mark the evidence:** If possible without damaging the evidence, mark the actual piece of evidence with the collecting individual's initials, the date, and the case number (if known). Seal the evidence in an appropriate container and again mark the container with the same information.

✔ **Use an evidence tag:** If the actual evidence cannot be marked, attach an evidence tag with the same information as mentioned previously, seal the evidence and tag in an appropriate container, and again mark the container with the same information.

✔ **Seal evidence:** Seal the container with evidence tape and mark the tape in a manner that will clearly indicate any tampering.

✔ **Protect evidence:** Use extreme caution when collecting and marking evidence to ensure that it's not damaged. If you're using plastic bags for evidence containers, be sure that they're static-free.

Always collect and mark evidence in a consistent manner so that you can easily identify evidence and describe your collection and identification techniques to an opposing attorney in court, if necessary.

Analysis

Analysis involves examining the evidence for information pertinent to the case. Analysis should be conducted with extreme caution — by properly trained and experienced personnel only — to ensure that the evidence is not altered, damaged, or destroyed.

Storage, preservation, and transportation

Evidence that's not properly protected may be inadmissible in court, and the party responsible for collection and storage may be liable.

✔ All evidence must be properly stored in a secure facility and preserved to prevent damage or contamination from such hazards as

- Intense heat or cold
- Extreme humidity
- Water
- Magnetic fields
- Vibration

✔ During transportation, care must be taken to ensure that evidence is not lost, damaged, or destroyed.

Presentation in court

Evidence to be presented in court must continue to follow the chain of custody and be handled with the same care as at all other times in the evidence life cycle. This process continues throughout the trial until all testimony related to the evidence is completed and the trial is over.

Return to victim (owner)

After the conclusion of the trial or other disposition, evidence is normally returned to its proper owner. However, under some circumstances, some evidence, such as contraband, drugs, or paraphernalia, may be ordered destroyed. Any evidence obtained through a search warrant is legally under the control of the court, possibly requiring the original owner to petition the court for its return.

Incident Response

Incident response begins before an incident has actually occurred. Preparation is the key to a quick and successful response. A well-documented and regularly practiced incident response plan ensures effective preparation. The plan should include

- ✔ **Response procedures:** Detailed procedures that address different contingencies and situations should be included.

- ✔ **Response authority:** Roles, responsibilities, and levels of authority for all members of the CIRT must be clearly defined.

- ✔ **Available resources:** People, tools, and external resources (consultants and law enforcement agents) that are available to the CIRT should be identified. Training should include use of these resources, when possible.

- ✔ **Legal review:** The incident response plan should be evaluated by appropriate legal counsel to determine compliance with applicable laws and to determine whether they're enforceable and defensible.

Additional steps in incident response include

- ✔ **Determination:** This is similar to the detection and containment step in the investigative process and includes defining what constitutes a security incident for your organization. Upon determination that an incident has occurred, it's important to immediately begin detailed documentation of every action taken throughout the incident response process.

✔ **Notification:** This step and specific procedures are identical to the notification of management step in the investigative process, but this level of notification includes the disclosure determination step from the investigative process.

  • All contact information should be documented before an incident.

  • All notifications and contacts during an incident should be documented in the incident log.

✔ **Containment:** Like the detection and containment step in the investigative process, this step minimizes further loss or damage. This may include

  • Eradicating a virus

  • Denying access

  • Disabling services

✔ **Assessment:** This includes determining

  • Scope and cause of damage

  • Responsible or liable party

✔ **Recovery:** This may include

  • Rebuilding systems

  • Repairing vulnerabilities

  • Improving safeguards

  • Restoring data and services

This step should complement a business continuity plan (BCP) with priorities for recovery properly identified.

✔ **Evaluation:** This is the final phase of an incident response plan and includes the lessons learned. *Lessons learned* should include both what failed and what worked.

Investigations and incident response have similar steps but different purposes:

  ✔ Investigation is the gathering of evidence for possible prosecution.

  ✔ Incident response contains the damage and returns to normal operations.

Prep Test

1 **A standard discriminator to help determine or eliminate potential suspects questions whether the suspect had all of these, except:**

   A ○ Motive

   B ○ Opportunity

   C ○ Means

   D ○ Assistance

2 **_____ evidence is evidence that is gathered based on an eyewitness account that proves or disproves a specific fact or issue.**

   A ○ Direct

   B ○ Physical

   C ○ Documentary

   D ○ Real

3 **Tangible objects from an actual crime are classified as _____ evidence.**

   A ○ Direct

   B ○ Physical

   C ○ Documentary

   D ○ Demonstrative

4 **Most evidence presented in a computer crime case is typically what type of evidence?**

   A ○ Direct

   B ○ Physical

   C ○ Documentary

   D ○ Demonstrative

5 **Opinions are considered what type of evidence?**

   A ○ Direct

   B ○ Real

   C ○ Documentary

   D ○ Demonstrative

6 Which of these is not considered one of the four major categories of evidence?

   A ○ Circumstantial evidence

   B ○ Direct evidence

   C ○ Demonstrative evidence

   D ○ Real evidence

7 In order to be admissible in a court of law, evidence must be:

   A ○ Conclusive

   B ○ Relevant

   C ○ Incontrovertible

   D ○ Immaterial

8 What term describes the evidence-gathering technique of luring an individual toward some evidence after that individual has already committed a crime; is this considered legal or illegal?

   A ○ Enticement/Legal

   B ○ Coercion/Illegal

   C ○ Entrapment/Illegal

   D ○ Enticement/Illegal

9 In a civil case, the court may issue an order allowing a law enforcement official to seize specific evidence. This order is known as a(n):

   A ○ Subpoena

   B ○ Exigent Circumstances Doctrine

   C ○ Writ of Possession

   D ○ Search warrant

Answers

1 **D.** Assistance. The MOM test: Did the suspect have the motive, opportunity, and means to commit the crime? *Review "Conducting Investigations."*

2 **A.** Direct. Direct evidence is oral testimony or a written statement based on information gathered through the witness's five senses. *Review "Types of evidence."*

3 **B.** Physical. Physical (or real) evidence includes tangible objects from the actual crime, such as tools or weapons used and stolen or damaged property. *Review "Types of evidence."*

4 **C.** Documentary. Documentary evidence includes originals and copies of business records, computer-generated and computer-stored records, manuals, policies, standards, procedures, and log files. *Review "Types of evidence."*

5 **D.** Demonstrative. Demonstrative evidence is used to aid the court's understanding of a case and includes expert or nonexpert opinions. Review *"Types of evidence."*

6 **A.** Circumstantial evidence. Circumstantial evidence is a type of evidence but is not considered one of the four main categories of evidence. Circumstantial evidence may include circumstantial, direct, or demonstrative evidence. *Review "Types of evidence."*

7 **B.** Relevant. The tests for admissibility of evidence include relevance, reliability, and legal permissibility. *Review "Admissibility of evidence."*

8 **A.** Enticement/Legal. Entrapment is the act of encouraging someone to commit a crime that the individual may have had no intention of committing. Coercion involves forcing or intimidating someone to testify or confess. Enticement does raise ethical arguments but is not normally illegal. *Review "Admissibility of evidence."*

9 **C.** Writ of Possession. A subpoena requires the owner to deliver evidence to the court. The exigent circumstances doctrine provides an exception to search and seizure rules for law enforcement officials in emergency or dangerous situations. A search warrant is issued in criminal cases. *Review "Collection and identification."*

Part VII
The Part of Tens

The 5th Wave
By Rich Tennant

"Someone want to look at this manuscript I received on e-mail called 'The Embedded Virus That Destroyed the Publisher's Servers When the Manuscript Was Rejected'?"

In this part . . .

Part VII of this book is the Part of Tens. Yes, it would have been really neat if Part X could have been the Part of Tens, but in order to do that we would have to number the parts out of order (Part VI, Part X, and Part VII, which would be really confusing) or we would have to include useless filler material (which would waste your valuable time, my less than valuable time, and our editor's incredibly valuable time!).

In this part, we included tips on preparing for the big day (your test day, not your wedding day), great security books and Web sites, and information on other security certifications as part of your professional development path, once you've passed the Security+ certification!

Chapter 18

Ten Test Day Tips

*Y*our date with destiny has finally arrived! You've studied diligently and are psyched for the exam! Still, butterflies are wreaking havoc on your stomach. My advice: Avoid eating butterflies on the day of your exam! Here's some other advice to help you get through the Security+ exam!

Check Your Biorhythm

Prometric and VUE testing centers are conveniently located throughout the world. You can schedule an exam time that is best for you, whether you're a morning person or someone that peaks later in the day. You can even schedule an exam for the middle of the night. (Well, you'd have to take it in Alaska during winter!) Many testing centers are also open on Saturdays. So if you just can't focus your energy for two hours during your hectic workweek, I can't think of a better way to spend a Saturday morning!

Arrive Early

Plan to be in the testing center at least 15 minutes early. This ensures that you have sufficient time to sign in, relax, and meditate before your exam. It also gives you some breathing room for unforeseen contingencies, such as the following:

✔ Getting lost

✔ Sitting in traffic

✔ Looking for parking

✔ Answering sudden calls of nature

If you're late, you may lose your seat and forfeit your exam fee.

Bring ID and Your Confirmation Letter

You will have to prove your identity to the test administrator. You probably won't have time for "Six Degrees of Kevin Bacon" and the test administrator probably wouldn't go for it anyway. Be safe. Bring the following:

✔ A picture ID (such as your driver's license or passport)

✔ A major credit card (with *your* name!)

After you register and pay for your exam, you receive a confirmation letter (normally via e-mail). Print it out and bring it with you. If, for some reason, the testing center does not have your exam properly scheduled (it does happen!), you can save yourself valuable time and needless hassles by presenting the confirmation letter (so you don't have to convince the test administrator that you are in the right place, at the right time, for the right exam).

Review Your Notes One More Time

In the final moments immediately before you go into the testing area, review your notes, the Cheat Sheet at the front of this book, the Instant Answer icons, review questions, fortune cookie fortunes, and anything else you may want to recall for the exam.

Use Scratch Paper

The test administrator will offer you scratch paper (some places may have an erasable white board instead) to use during the exam. Use it!

Write down any lists, tables, or other difficult-to-remember information (see the preceding section) as soon as you go into the exam room (before you begin the exam). This is perfectly legal and is highly recommended.

Just remember: You have to give the scratch paper back after the exam.

When in Doubt . . . Guess!

This isn't the SAT, so guessing won't hurt you! Answer every question you can to the best of your ability; but when all else fails, just be sure to answer every question.

Mark questions that you want to think about — you'll have an opportunity at the end of the test to review them. With any luck, a question later in the exam will remind you of the correct answer for an earlier question you weren't sure of.

Fortunately, every question on the Security+ exam has only four answer choices and only one correct answer. This means you've got a 25 percent chance of getting a question right. If you can eliminate at least one bogus answer, then you've increased your odds to 33 percent. Eliminate two wrong answers and you've got a 50-50 shot. But if you don't answer the question, you've got a 100 percent chance of getting it wrong!

Go with Your Instincts

In general, your first guess on a multiple-choice question is your best guess. When you're reviewing questions at the end of the exam, avoid the temptation to change your original answer to a question unless you've got a compelling reason to do so, like this:

✔ A later question gave you a hint about the correct answer.

✔ You spot an obvious mistake.

✔ The correct answer suddenly jumps out at you.

Steady as She Goes!

You have 2 hours to answer 125 questions. This gives you slightly less than a minute per question. Although this might seem like a lot of pressure, you should have no trouble finishing the exam within the allotted time. Most questions will probably only take you 20-30 seconds to answer. Maintain a steady pace and don't get hung up on any single question. If you're unsure of an answer or want to think about a question a little longer, make a best effort guess, mark it for review, then come back to it after you've completed the rest of the exam.

If you do find yourself running out of time, reserve the last five minutes of your exam for guessing. Whatever you do, don't leave a question unanswered. (See the earlier section on guessing.)

Use All of Your Time

When you get to the end of your exam, you may find that you have plenty of time left on the clock. Use it!

- ✔ Look for questions you may have left unanswered (whether intentional or accidental).

- ✔ Review questions you marked for more consideration to be sure that you have the best answer.

- ✔ If you have time, go through the entire exam again and make sure that you haven't made easy mistakes (such as knowing the right answer and marking the wrong answer).

Be careful not to second-guess yourself out of a correct answer.

Chapter 19

Ten Great Books for the Security Professional

In This Chapter

▶ Ten highly recommended information security books

▶ And why!

*I*nformation security is a hot topic, and new books on this important subject are being published every day. Some are better than others. The following list contains ten excellent books on a variety of subjects in information security. Many outstanding information security books have been writtenThe following short list contains ten books that I highly recommend.

✔ *Information Security: Protecting the Global Enterprise* by Donald L. Pipkin (Prentice Hall PTR, $39.99).

  Step-by-step guidance for important security management practices.

✔ *Computer Security Basics* by Deborah Russell and G.T Gangemi Sr. (O'Reilly and Associates, $29.95).

  Much of the information is outdated, but it still is an excellent reference for security basics.

✔ *Security Engineering: A Guide to Building Dependable Distributed Systems* by Ross Anderson (John Wiley & Sons, $59.99).

  Excellent in-depth coverage of some very complex subjects.

✔ *Designing Network Security* by Merike Kaeo (Cisco Press, $50.00).

  Information security Cisco-style! In addition to very technology-specific information, this book also describes basic fundamentals (for example, authentication, authorization, accounting, cryptography, PKI, and security policy) in a very clear and concise manner.

✔ *Building Internet Firewalls,* 2nd Edition, by Elizabeth D. Zwicky, Simon Cooper, D. Brent Chapman, and Deborah Russell (O'Reilly and Associates, $49.95).

Principles of deploying firewalls to implement an effective security strategy (and how to build one).

✔ *RSA Security's Official Guide to Cryptography* by Steve Burnett and Stephen Paine (RSA Press, $59.99).

Thorough coverage of a complex subject in an easily understood format.

✔ *Fighting Computer Crime: A New Framework for Protecting Information* By Donn B. Parker (John Wiley & Sons, $39.99).

Introduces new ways of thinking about information security.

✔ *Incident Response: Investigating Computer Crime* by Kevin Mandia and Chris Prosise (Osborne/McGraw-Hill, $39.99).

Thorough coverage of investigations and evidence gathering.

✔ *The CERT Guide to System and Network Security Practices* by Julia H. Allen (Addison-Wesley, $39.99).

Securing your systems and network, step-by-step.

✔ Two books from the SANS Institute:

- *Network Intrusion Detection: An Analyst's Handbook* by Stephen Northcutt and Judy Novak (New Riders, $45.00).

- *Intrusion Signatures and Analysis* by Stephen Northcutt, Mark Cooper, Matt Fearnow, and Karen Frederick (New Riders, $39.99).

Chapter 20

Ten Security Web Sites

Carnegie-Mellon SEI CERT Coordination Center

`www.cert.org`

The Carnegie-Mellon Software Engineering Institute (SEI) CERT Coordination Center includes

✓ Vulnerabilities

✓ Incidents and fixes

✓ Security practices and evaluations

✓ Survivability research and analysis

✓ Training and education resources

Common Vulnerabilities and Exposures (CVE)

`http://cve.mitre.org`

The Common Vulnerabilities and Exposures (CVE) is a list of standardized names for vulnerabilities and other information security exposures. You can download the CVE dictionary from the `cve.mitre.org` Web site.

Foundstone

www.foundstone.com

The Foundstone Web site contains

- White papers
- Articles
- Advisories
- Excellent (free) security tools

The folks there also offer the crème de la crème of good guy hacking classes: Ultimate Hacking: Hands-On.

Guide to Computers and the Law

www.hg.org/compute.html

This Web site, sponsored by Hieros Gamos, includes a comprehensive guide to U.S. and international laws and regulations relevant to the computer industry.

INFOSYSSEC

www.infosyssec.org

Dubbed "The Security Portal for Information System Security Professionals," this comprehensive site provides one-stop shopping with hundreds (possibly thousands) of resources and links for the information security professional.

Network Security Library

www.secinf.net

The Network Security Library is an excellent source of free online books, articles, FAQs, and How-Tos. Subjects include

- Windows
- Unix

- ✔ Netware
- ✔ Firewalls
- ✔ Ids
- ✔ Security policy
- ✔ The Internet
- ✔ The NCSC and DOD Rainbow Series
- ✔ Harmless hacking

Simovits

`www.simovits.com/trojans/trojans.html`

A database of trojans sorted by

- ✔ Ports
- ✔ Trojan common name
- ✔ Trojan filename
- ✔ File size
- ✔ Actions
- ✔ Affected systems
- ✔ Country of origin
- ✔ Programming language

The SANS Institute

`www.sans.org`

The SANS (SysAdmin, Audit, Network, and Security) Institute hosts the SANS/FBI Top Twenty Vulnerabilities list. This list, co-sponsored by the FBI's National Infrastructure Protection Center (NIPC), helps organizations prioritize security efforts by listing and describing the top twenty Internet security vulnerabilities in three categories:

- ✔ General vulnerabilities
- ✔ Windows vulnerabilities
- ✔ Unix vulnerabilities

The Web site also includes links to

- The Global Information Assurance Certification (GIAC) program
- Sans conference schedules
- An extremely helpful security digest
- The SANS online bookstore
- Projects
- Resources
- Security links
- Sample security policies
- White papers
- GIAC student practical assignments
- Security tools

The Shmoo Group

www.shmoo.com

The Shmoo Group hosts news mail archives with such subjects as

- Checkpoint's Firewall-1
- Firewalls
- Bugtraq
- Intrusion detection systems.

It is also the new home for the securitygeeks news site.

WindowSecurity.com

www.securitysearch.net

Contains such resources as

- Anti-virus information
- Security articles and tutorials
- Message boards
- White papers

Chapter 21

Ten Other Security Certifications

*T*he Security+ certification provides an excellent start in the exciting field of information security. After the Security+ certification, you may consider additional certifications to complement your professional career development as you continue to gain skills and experience.

Check Point

www.checkpoint.com/services/education/certification

The Check Point Certified Professional Program provides product-focused certifications based on the most popular firewall product on the market today: Check Point FireWall-1. Certifications exams are available at Prometric and VUE testing centers and include

✓ Check Point Certified Security Administrator (CCSA)

✓ Check Point Certified Security Expert (CCSE)

✓ Check Point Certified Security Expert Plus (CCSE Plus)

Cisco

www.cisco.com

The Cisco Security Specialist 1 certification tests an individual's knowledge and skill at using various Cisco security products. Cisco Security Specialist certification requires CCNA (Cisco Certified Network Associate) certification and four additional exams:

- Managing Cisco Network Security (MCNS)
- Cisco Secure PIX Firewall Advanced (CSPFA)
- Cisco Secure Intrusion Detection System (CSIDS)
- Cisco Secure VPN (CSVPN)

Finally, the mother of all certifications, the Cisco Certified Internetworking Expert (CCIE), offers a security track requiring satisfactory completion of a two-hour, 100-question multiple choice qualification exam and a one-day hands-on lab.

CIW

www.ciwcertified.com

The Certified Internet Webmaster (CIW) is a vendor-neutral certification program. The CIW Security Analyst Specialization requires the candidate to have earned MCSE, CNE, CCNP or CCIE, LPI Level 2, or SAIR Level 2 LCE certification and pass the CIW Security Professional Exam.

DRII

www.dr.org

The Disaster Recovery Institute International (DRII) provides three levels of certification in business continuity planning and disaster recovery:

- Associate Business Continuity Planner (ABCP)
- Certified Business Continuity Planner (CBCP)
- Master Business Continuity Professional (MBCP)

ISACA

www.isaca.org

The Information Systems Audit and Control Association and Foundation (ISACA) administers two security certifications: the Certified Information Systems Auditor (CISA) and Certified Information Security Manager (CISM).

Requirements for CISA certification include successful completion of the CISA examination and a minimum of five years of professional experience in information systems auditing, control, or security.

The CISM certification is a new certification beginning in June 2003. Topics that will be tested include information security governance, risk management, IS program management, IS management, and response management.

(ISC)₂

www.isc2.org

The International Information Systems Security Certification Consortium (ISC)₂ offers the Systems Security Certified Practitioner (SSCP) and Certified Information Systems Security Professional (CISSP) certifications. The CISSP certification is perhaps the most respected and coveted security certification in the industry today. It requires a minimum of four years of information security experience (or three years with a college degree or equivalent life experience). The CISSP examination is a grueling 6-hour, 250-multiple-choice-question exam, covering the following 10 domains of information security:

- ✔ Access Control Systems & Methodology
- ✔ Applications & Systems Development
- ✔ Business Continuity Planning & Disaster Recovery Planning
- ✔ Cryptography
- ✔ Law, Investigation & Ethics
- ✔ Operations Security
- ✔ Physical Security
- ✔ Security Architecture & Models
- ✔ Security Management Practices
- ✔ Telecommunications, Network & Internet Security

Microsoft

www.microsoft.com

Although Microsoft does not offer a security certification, several security-relevant exams are available in the MCSE electives (listed at www.microsoft.com), including

✔ Designing Security for a Microsoft Windows 2000 Network

✔ Implementing and Supporting Microsoft Proxy Server 2.0

✔ Installing, Configuring, and Administering Microsoft ISA Server 2000, Enterprise Edition

SAIR Linux and GNU

www.linuxcertification.com

Like Microsoft certifications, SAIR (Software Architecture Implementation and Realization) Linux and GNU certifications offer security-relevant exams in the course of certification requirements. Three levels of SAIR certification are available:

✔ **Level I:** SAIR Linux and GNU Certified Administrator (LCA)

✔ **Level II:** SAIR Linux and GNU Certified Engineer (LCE)

✔ **Level III:** Master SAIR Linux and GNU Certified Engineer (MLCE)

These certifications each require successful completion of four exams in the following system usage areas:

✔ Linux Installation

✔ Network Connectivity

✔ System Administration

✔ Security, Ethics, and Privacy

SANS/GIAC

www.sans.org or www.giac.org

The Global Information Assurance Certification (GIAC) was founded by the SANS (Systems Administration, Networking, and Security) Institute in 1999. Candidates for GIAC certification must first complete a written practical assignment. Passing assignments are posted on the SANS Web site and qualify the individual to take a technical certification to complete GIAC certification. GIAC currently offers ten individual certifications:

✔ GIAC Security Essentials Certification (GSEC)

✔ GIAC Certified Firewall Analyst (GCFW)

✔ GIAC Certified Intrusion Analyst (GCIA)

✔ GIAC Certified Incident Handler (GCIH)

✔ GIAC Certified Windows Security Administrator (GCWN)

✔ GIAC Certified UNIX Security Administrator (GCUX)

✔ GIAC Information Security Officer - Basic (GISO-Basic)

✔ GIAC Systems and Network Auditor (GSNA)

✔ GIAC Certified Forensic Analyst (GCFA)

✔ GIAC Security Leadership Certificate (GSLC)

✔ GIAC IT Security and Audit Kickstart (GIAK)

A more advanced certification, the GIAC Security Engineer (GSE), is available for candidates who have completed the GSEC, GCFW, GCIA, GCIH, GCWN, and GCUX certifications and excel in at least one of the subject area modules.

GIAC examination costs range from $250 (if taken with SANS online or conference training) to $425 (if taken independently).

SCP

www.securitycertified.net

The Security Certified Program (SCP) offers two certifications for IT professionals: SCNP (Security Certified Network Professional) and SCNA (Security Certified Network Architect).

The SCNP certification consists of two exams, focusing on firewalls and intrusion detection. Corresponding courses for this program include Network Security Fundamentals (NSF) and Network Defense and Countermeasures (NDC).

The SCNA certification also consists of two exams, focusing on PKI and biometrics. The first exam is titled Advanced Security Implementation (ASI) and covers material from two corresponding courses: PKI and Biometrics Concepts and Planning (PBC) and PKI and Biometrics Implementation (PBI). The second exam, The Solutions Exam (TSE), is a comprehensive, scenario-based exam covering the entire SCP curriculum.

Part VIII
Appendixes

The 5th Wave   By Rich Tennant

"A centralized security management system sounds fine, but then what would we do with the dogs?"

In this part . . .

The Appendixes include a practice test and instructions for the CD-ROM that accompanies this book.

Appendix A

Practice Exam

• •

*T*his 50-question practice exam tests your knowledge on all of the Security+ test objectives that are covered in this book. By using this exam, which is similar to the real one, you can identify weak areas that you need to review. At the end of the practice exam, you will find the correct answers, along with explanations and the chapter where the topic is covered.

Exam Questions

1 **The process of an individual providing his userid is known as:**

   A ○ Authentication
   B ○ Identification
   C ○ Authorization
   D ○ Assertion

2 **A device that forwards packets based upon IP address is known as a:**

   A ○ router.
   B ○ firewall.
   C ○ switch.
   D ○ bridge.

3 **An intruder used a sniffer to record a userid and password transmitted over a network. The intruder will now attempt to log in using the userid and password he stored. This type of an attack is known as a:**

   A ○ Hack attack.
   B ○ Crack attack.
   C ○ Replay attack.
   D ○ Password guessing attack.

4 **A packet filter performs all of the following EXCEPT:**

   A ○ Examines each packet's headers.
   B ○ Blocks or permits traffic both inbound and outbound.
   C ○ Blocks or permits traffic based on address and port.
   D ○ User authentication.

5 **RADIUS is used for:**

   A ○ VPN key exchange.
   B ○ Session encryption.
   C ○ User authentication.
   D ○ SSL key exchange.

6 **Cryptography is used for all of the following EXCEPT:**

   A ○ Integrity.
   B ○ Confidentiality.
   C ○ Availability.
   D ○ Authentication.

7 S/MIME, MOSS, and PEM are examples of:

- **A** ○ E-Mail security mechanisms.
- **B** ○ Browser security mechanisms.
- **C** ○ Cryptographic algorithms.
- **D** ○ E-Mail hash functions.

8 Fire, water, and smoke are:

- **A** ○ The products of combustion.
- **B** ○ Three physical security threats.
- **C** ○ The sources of combustion.
- **D** ○ Best fought with a fire suppression system.

9 The level of security provided by FTP is:

- **A** ○ None.
- **B** ○ Both authentication and encryption.
- **C** ○ Encryption only.
- **D** ○ Authentication only.

10 The main purpose for disabling unused services is to:

- **A** ○ Reduce a system's disk space consumption.
- **B** ○ Improve a system's performance.
- **C** ○ Reduce the risk of compromise to the system.
- **D** ○ Simplify system administration tasks.

11 The four categories of security policies are:

- **A** ○ Prevention, response, investigative, conclusion.
- **B** ○ Informative, regulatory, mandatory, advisory.
- **C** ○ Mandatory, optional, preventative, responsorial.
- **D** ○ Compliance, physical, logical, environmental.

12 The "best evidence" rule states that:

- **A** ○ Evidence must be gathered by a forensic pathologist.
- **B** ○ Computer evidence is inadmissible because it cannot be verified as accurate.
- **C** ○ A copy is as good as the original.
- **D** ○ Evidence should be original and not a copy.

13 **The effect that a disaster would have on business operations is described in a:**

   A ○ Business Impact Assessment.

   B ○ Vulnerability Assessment.

   C ○ Risk Assessment.

   D ○ Recovery Plan.

14 **Access control policy determined by the user is known as:**

   A ○ Mandatory Access Control.

   B ○ Discretionary Access Control.

   C ○ User-Determined Access Control.

   D ○ Limited Access Control.

15 **CAT-5 cable is rated at what maximum bandwidth:**

   A ○ 16Mbps.

   B ○ 10Mbps.

   C ○ 100Mbps.

   D ○ 1Gbps.

16 **SYN flood attacks are successful when they:**

   A ○ Overwhelm a system's NIC.

   B ○ Force a routing table change.

   C ○ Penetrate the system's kernel layer.

   D ○ Overwhelm a system's available resources.

17 **A firewall that maintains a state table of all current sessions is known as a(n):**

   A ○ Proxy server.

   B ○ Application-level gateway.

   C ○ Packet filter.

   D ○ Circuit-level gateway.

18 **SSH is a secure replacement of:**

   A ○ Telnet and rlogin.

   B ○ Telnet.

   C ○ SMTP.

   D ○ SMTP and POP3.

19 **A disadvantage of symmetric key cryptography is:**

   A ○ Scalability: in a large organization there would be too many secret keys.

   B ○ Confidentiality: any third party can easily decrypt messages.

   C ○ Strength: symmetric cryptography has fallen out of favor.

   D ○ Usability: most users do not understand symmetric key cryptography.

20 **PGP is used to:**

A ○ Block traffic at the firewall.

B ○ Filter SPAM.

C ○ Encrypt, decrypt, and sign messages or files.

D ○ Control access to confidential directories and files.

21 **Which of the following is NOT a biometric access control:**

A ○ Palm scan

B ○ Body scan

C ○ Retina scan

D ○ Fingerprint scan

22 **The level of security provided by TFTP is:**

A ○ None.

B ○ Both authentication and encryption.

C ○ Encryption only.

D ○ Authentication only.

23 **A listing of administrative events or transactions is known as a(n):**

A ○ Audit list.

B ○ Event list.

C ○ Event trail.

D ○ Audit trail.

24 **Confidential and unclassified are two examples of:**

A ○ Access controls.

B ○ Security clearances.

C ○ Government data classification.

D ○ Mandatory access controls.

25 **The admissibility of evidence is based upon:**

A ○ Whether it was collected and stored by law enforcement.

B ○ Its relevance, reliability, and legality.

C ○ Whether or not it was generated or stored on a computer.

D ○ Whether both sides in a trial have had an opportunity to review it.

26 **The Criticality Assessment is:**

A ○ The rank-ordered list of critical business functions.

B ○ The criticism of vulnerabilities that threaten business processes.

C ○ Used to prioritize vulnerabilities.

D ○ The statement of threat of the occurrence times the probability.

27 Access control that is controlled by the system is known as:

A ○ Centralized Access Control

B ○ Discretionary Access Control

C ○ Mandatory Access Control

D ○ Bell La Padula Access Control

28 The maximum rated distance for UTP type cable is:

A ○ 155m.

B ○ 100ft.

C ○ 1000m.

D ○ 100m.

29 Systematically trying every possible password in order to break in to a user account is known as a:

A ○ Smurf attack.

B ○ Brute force attack.

C ○ Dictionary attack.

D ○ Birthday attack.

30 One advantage of a proxy server is:

A ○ All client systems will automatically know how to use it.

B ○ It is an appliance that requires no configuration.

C ○ It prevents direct communication between two computers.

D ○ It is compatible with all modern browsers.

31 CHAP, PAP, and EAP are examples of:

A ○ Remote access authentication protocols.

B ○ Remote access key exchange protocols.

C ○ Local access authentication protocols.

D ○ Local access key exchange protocols.

32 The "twofish" encryption algorithm:

A ○ Is an asymmetric block cipher.

B ○ Was the algorithm chosen for the Advanced Encryption Standard (AES).

C ○ Was a finalist for the Advanced Encryption Standard (AES).

D ○ Is a symmetric stream cipher.

33 One security issue associated with hoaxes is:

A ○ Too often people perform the instructions contained in them.

B ○ When opened they can spread a virus or worm.

C ○ They can infect a user's computer even if they did not open the message.

D ○ They can be spread via CD-ROM.

34 **The three types of fire detection systems are:**

A ○ Air, light, and smoke.

B ○ Air, flame, and smoke.

C ○ Heat, light, and smoke.

D ○ Heat, flame, and smoke.

35 **The level of security provided by S/FTP is:**

A ○ None.

B ○ Both authentication and encryption.

C ○ Encryption only.

D ○ Authentication only.

36 **Internet worms such as Code Red were successful because:**

A ○ Most organizations failed to disable unnecessary services.

B ○ Most organizations failed to apply security patches to their systems.

C ○ Most organizations failed to properly configure their firewalls.

D ○ ISPs failed to properly configure their firewalls.

37 **Opportunities for insider fraud can be reduced through:**

A ○ Mantraps.

B ○ Non-disclosure agreements and employment agreements.

C ○ Job rotation and separation of duties.

D ○ Employment agreements and job rotation.

38 **The goal of Business Continuity Planning is to:**

A ○ Prevent disasters from occurring.

B ○ Determine which disasters are likely to occur.

C ○ Restore damaged facilities.

D ○ Keep critical business operations running.

39 **Exigent circumstances refers to:**

A ○ The seizure of evidence that is about to be destroyed.

B ○ The reclassification of direct evidence to hearsay.

C ○ A lapse in the chain of evidence.

D ○ Evidence collected by an amateur.

40 **The two types of emergency response teams are:**

A ○ Personnel and property.

B ○ Salvage and recovery.

C ○ Natural and man-made.

D ○ Preventive and reactive.

41 **Password complexity is important because:**

A ○ Strong passwords resist SYN attacks.

B ○ It saves on valuable computer processing time.

C ○ They are more difficult for users to remember.

D ○ They are more difficult for intruders to crack.

42 **CD-R, CD-RW, diskette, and DVD-R are examples of:**

A ○ Optical storage media.

B ○ Read-write storage media.

C ○ Removable storage media.

D ○ Magnetic storage media.

43 **The best defense against viruses and worms is:**

A ○ Anti-virus software.

B ○ Keeping patches up-to-date.

C ○ Disconnecting systems from the network.

D ○ State-inspecting firewalls.

44 **A system which is used to automatically sense and block incoming attacks is known as a(n):**

A ○ Passive Intrusion Detection System.

B ○ Circuit level gateway.

C ○ Firewall.

D ○ Active Intrusion Detection System.

45 **PPP is:**

A ○ An encryption algorithm.

B ○ An encapsulation protocol.

C ○ An authentication protocol.

D ○ A digital signature algorithm.

46 **Public Key Cryptography is another term used for:**

A ○ Asymmetric cryptography.

B ○ Symmetric cryptography.

C ○ Shared secret cryptography.

D ○ Public domain cryptography.

47 **SSL provides:**

A ○ Digital signature.

B ○ Authentication.

C ○ Both authentication and encryption.

D ○ Encryption.

48 **Soda acid is rarely used for fire suppression in computer facilities because:**

    A ○ It is very expensive.

    B ○ It has been outlawed by the Montreal Protocol of 1987.

    C ○ It is highly corrosive.

    D ○ It is no longer effective.

49 **Anonymous FTP is so-called because:**

    A ○ No one knows who developed it.

    B ○ It is useful for transmitting confidential information.

    C ○ User identification is "double blind."

    D ○ The user who connects need not provide any identification.

50 **The best access control approach is:**

    A ○ Explicitly list all users who do not need access.

    B ○ Permit access only to users who need access, and deny all others.

    C ○ Permit access to all users, and deny all who do not need access.

    D ○ Explicitly list all users who do and do not need access.

Answers

1 **B.** Providing a userid constitutes identification. For review see Chapter 3: Access Control.

2 **A.** A router connects networks together and forwards packets to networks based upon IP address. For review see Chapter 9: Devices and Media.

3 **C.** A replay attack involves "playing back" sequences that were recorded earlier. For review see Chapter 4: Attacks and Malicious Code.

4 **D.** Packet filters block / permit traffic based on IP address and port number, both inbound and outbound. They must examine packet headers in order to do so. For review see Chapter 5: Remote Access.

5 **C.** RADIUS is a remote access authentication protocol. For review see Chapter 5: Remote Access.

6 **C.** Cryptography can be used to ensure integrity, authentication, and confidentiality. For review see Chapter 12: Cryptography Basics.

7 **A.** S/MIME (Secure Multipurpose Internet Mail Extensions), MOSS (MIME Object Security Services), and PEM (Privacy Enhanced Mail) are three mechanisms that are used to secure e-mail. For review see Chapter 6: E-Mail and Internet Security.

8 **B.** Fire, water, and smoke are three physical security threats - there are many others. For review see Chapter 14: Physical Security.

9 **D.** FTP authenticates users but does not encrypt anything (not even the authentication). For review see Chapter 7: File Transfer and Directory Services.

10 **C.** The primary reason for disabling an unused service is to reduce the risk of compromise to the system. A disabled service cannot be used to compromise a system. For review see Chapter 11: Security Baselines.

11 **B.** Security policies are categorized as informative, regulatory, mandatory, and advisory. For review see Chapter 16: Security Management.

12 **D.** The rule of best evidence states that only originals are acceptable in most cases. For review see Chapter 17: Computer Forensics and Incident Response.

13 **A.** The Business Impact Assessment describes the impact of a disaster on business operations. For review see Chapter 15: Business Continuity and Disaster Recovery.

14 **B.** Discretionary Access Control is asserted by the user or owner of an object. For review see Chapter 3: Access Control.

15 **C.** CAT-5 cable is rated to transmit data at a maximum of 100Mbps, which is the speed of Fast Ethernet. For review see Chapter 9: Devices and Media.

16 **D.** SYN floods are considered successful when they exhaust the target system's available resources. For review see Chapter 4: Attacks and Malicious Code.

17 **D.** A circuit-level gateway maintains a table containing the state of all current sessions, and uses this table to make future block/permit decisions. For review see Chapter 10: Security Topologies.

18 **A.** SSH is a drop-in replacement for Telnet and Rlogin. For review see Chapter 5: Remote Access.

19 **A.** Each pair of users would have to generate their own secret keys; this is impractical in all but the smallest groups of people. For review see Chapter 12: Cryptography Basics.

20 **C.** PGP (Pretty Good Privacy) is a tool used to encrypt, decrypt, and sign e-mail messages and text files. For review see Chapter 6: E-Mail and Internet Security.

21 **B.** Fingerprint, palm, and retina scans are just a few examples of biometrics. For review see Chapter 14: Physical Security.

22 **A.** TFTP provides no security whatsoever. For review see Chapter 7: File Transfer and Directory Services.

23 **D.** An audit trail is a list of events and transactions. For review see Chapter 11: Security Baselines.

24 **C.** Confidential and Unclassified are two examples of government data classification. For review see Chapter 16: Security Management.

25 **B.** Admissibility of evidence is based upon whether it is relevant, reliable, and if it was legally obtained. For review see Chapter 17: Computer Forensics and Incident Response.

26 **A.** The Criticality Assessment is a list of the organization's most critical business processes or functions. For review see Chapter 16: Security Management.

27 **C.** Mandatory Access Control (MAC) is centrally controlled by the system. For review see Chapter 3: Access Control.

28 **D.** UTP type cable is rated at a maximum of 100 meters in length. For review see Chapter 9: Devices and Media.

29 **B.** A brute force attack involves guess every possible combination of characters until the correct one is discovered. For review see Chapter 4: Attacks and Malicious Code.

30 **C.** A proxy server prohibits all direct communication between two computers, intercepting and examining all traffic before forwarding it on. For review see Chapter 10: Security Topologies.

31 **A.** CHAP, PAP, and EAP are remote access authentication protocols. For review see Chapter 5: Remote Access.

32 **C.** Twofish was an AES finalist; Rijndael was the chosen standard. For review see Chapter 12: Cryptography Basics.

33 **A.** A hoax is a technologically harmless message; the danger is that people too often obey the instructions contained in them and damage their systems. For review see Chapter 6: E-Mail and Internet Security.

34 **D.** The three types of fire detection systems are heat, flame, and smoke. For review see Chapter 14: Physical Security.

35 **B.** S/FTP provides both encryption and authentication. For review see Chapter 7: File Transfer and Directory Services.

36 **B.** The failure to install security patches creates opportunities for Internet worms to spread. For review see Chapter 11: Security Baselines.

37 **C.** Job rotation and separation of duties make it more difficult for employees to commit insider fraud. For review see Chapter 16: Security Management.

38 **D.** Business Continuity Planning is concerned with keeping critical business functions running during a disaster. For review see Chapter 15: Business Continuity and Disaster Recovery.

39 **A.** In exigent circumstances, evidence may be collected without a warrant if it is believed that the evidence is about to be destroyed. For review see Chapter 17: Computer Forensics and Incident Response.

40 **B.** The two types of emergency response teams are salvage and recovery. For review see Chapter 15: Business Continuity and Disaster Recovery.

41 **D.** Strong passwords are more difficult for intruders to crack. For review see Chapter 3: Access Control.

42 **C.** These are all removable storage media. For review see Chapter 6: E-Mail and Internet Security.

43 **A.** Anti-Virus software is still considered the best defense against viruses and worms. For review see Chapter 4: Attacks and Malicious Code.

44 **D.** An Active IDS automatically senses and dynamically blocks incoming attacks. For review see Chapter 10: Security Topologies.

45 **B.** PPP, or Point to Point Protocol, is a protocol used to encapsulate network packets. For review see Chapter 5: Remote Access.

46 **A.** Public Key Cryptography is the common term for asymmetric key cryptography. For review see Chapter 12: Cryptography Basics.

47 **C.** SSL, or Secure Sockets Layer, provides both authentication and encryption. For review see Chapter 6: E-Mail and Internet Security.

48 **C.** Soda acid is very corrosive and can damage computer equipment. For review see Chapter 14: Physical Security.

49 **D.** Anonymous FTP does not require a user to identify him/her. For review see Chapter 7: File Transfer and Directory Services.

50 **B.** The best access control approach is to deny access to everyone, and then to explicitly permit access only to those who require it. For review see Chapter 11: Security Baselines.

Appendix B

About the CD-ROM

● ●

*T*he CD-ROM that comes with this book contains test questions to help you prepare for the exam.

System Requirements

Make sure that your computer meets the minimum system requirements listed here. If your computer doesn't match up to most of these requirements, you may have problems using the contents of the CDs:

- ✔ A Pentium class PC with a 200MHZ or faster processor recommended.
- ✔ At least 32MB of total RAM installed on your computer. For the best performance, we recommend that people who want to use X Window System have at least 64MB and preferably 96MB of main memory.
- ✔ A CD-ROM drive.
- ✔ A 3¼-inch floppy disk drive and a blank 3¼-inch disk.

Using the CD with Microsoft Windows

To install the items from the CD to your hard drive, follow these steps:

1. Insert the CD into your computer's CD-ROM drive.
2. Click Start, Run.
3. In the dialog box that appears, **type D:\SETUP.EXE.**
4. Click OK.

   A license agreement window appears.

5. Read through the license agreement, then click the Accept button to continue the installation.

   The CD's Welcome screen appears. This interface shows you what's on the CD and guides you through the installations.

6. Click anywhere on the Welcome screen to enter the interface.

7. To install a program, click the corresponding Install button.

   The CD interface drops to the background while installing the program you've selected.

8. When you finish installing programs, click the Quit button to close the interface.

   You can now safely eject the CD.

What You'll Find on the CD

The following is a summary of the software included on this CD.

Boson Practice Tests for Security+

This demo included Practice Tests. For more information, check out www.boson.com.

Practice Test

The practice test contains 125 questions similar to what you'll find on the Security+ exam. You can select questions from any of the five content domains to focus on your weak areas or you can take the entire test. You can also randomize the questions to keep it interesting! Each correct answer includes a brief explanation and references the appropriate chapter for review.

Study Notes

For those of you with all the latest gadgets and matching utility belt - we've formatted the practice test questions for Pocket Word. Now you can download the questions to your PocketPC and use Pocket Word to study just about anywhere!

Flash Cards

For those of us that prefer more traditional learning techniques, we've also formatted the test questions to print out on 3x5 index cards!

If You Have Problems (Of the CD Kind)

We tried our best to test various computers with the minimum system requirements. Alas, your computer may differ. The likeliest problem is that you don't have enough RAM for the programs you want to use. If you have trouble with corrupt files on the CDs, please call the Wiley Customer Care phone number: 800-762-2974 (outside the United States: 317-572-3994) or e-mail at techsupbum@wiley.com. Customer service won't be able to help with complications relating to the program or how it works.

Index

• W •

• X •

Notes

Notes

Notes

Notes

Notes

Wiley Publishing, Inc.
End-User License Agreement

READ THIS. You should carefully read these terms and conditions before opening the software packet(s) included with this book "Book". This is a license agreement "Agreement" between you and Wiley Publishing, Inc."WPI". By opening the accompanying software packet(s), you acknowledge that you have read and accept the following terms and conditions. If you do not agree and do not want to be bound by such terms and conditions, promptly return the Book and the unopened software packet(s) to the place you obtained them for a full refund.

1. **License Grant.** WPI grants to you (either an individual or entity) a nonexclusive license to use one copy of the enclosed software program(s) (collectively, the "Software" solely for your own personal or business purposes on a single computer (whether a standard computer or a workstation component of a multi-user network). The Software is in use on a computer when it is loaded into temporary memory (RAM) or installed into permanent memory (hard disk, CD-ROM, or other storage device). WPI reserves all rights not expressly granted herein.

2. **Ownership.** WPI is the owner of all right, title, and interest, including copyright, in and to the compilation of the Software recorded on the disk(s) or CD-ROM "Software Media". Copyright to the individual programs recorded on the Software Media is owned by the author or other authorized copyright owner of each program. Ownership of the Software and all proprietary rights relating thereto remain with WPI and its licensers.

3. **Restrictions On Use and Transfer.**

    (a) You may only (i) make one copy of the Software for backup or archival purposes, or (ii) transfer the Software to a single hard disk, provided that you keep the original for backup or archival purposes. You may not (i) rent or lease the Software, (ii) copy or reproduce the Software through a LAN or other network system or through any computer subscriber system or bulletin- board system, or (iii) modify, adapt, or create derivative works based on the Software.

    (b) You may not reverse engineer, decompile, or disassemble the Software. You may transfer the Software and user documentation on a permanent basis, provided that the transferee agrees to accept the terms and conditions of this Agreement and you retain no copies. If the Software is an update or has been updated, any transfer must include the most recent update and all prior versions.

4. **Restrictions on Use of Individual Programs.** You must follow the individual requirements and restrictions detailed for each individual program in the "About the CD-ROM" appendix of this Book. These limitations are also contained in the individual license agreements recorded on the Software Media. These limitations may include a requirement that after using the program for a specified period of time, the user must pay a registration fee or discontinue use. By opening the Software packet(s), you will be agreeing to abide by the licenses and restrictions for these individual programs that are detailed in the "About the CD-ROM" appendix and on the Software Media. None of the material on this Software Media or listed in this Book may ever be redistributed, in original or modified form, for commercial purposes.

5. Limited Warranty.

(a) WPI warrants that the Software and Software Media are free from defects in materials and workmanship under normal use for a period of sixty (60) days from the date of purchase of this Book. If WPI receives notification within the warranty period of defects in materials or workmanship, WPI will replace the defective Software Media.

(b) WPI AND THE AUTHOR OF THE BOOK DISCLAIM ALL OTHER WARRANTIES, EXPRESS OR IMPLIED, INCLUDING WITHOUT LIMITATION IMPLIED WARRANTIES OF MERCHANTABILITY AND FITNESS FOR A PARTICULAR PURPOSE, WITH RESPECT TO THE SOFTWARE, THE PROGRAMS, THE SOURCE CODE CONTAINED THEREIN, AND/OR THE TECHNIQUES DESCRIBED IN THIS BOOK. WPI DOES NOT WARRANT THAT THE FUNCTIONS CONTAINED IN THE SOFTWARE WILL MEET YOUR REQUIREMENTS OR THAT THE OPERATION OF THE SOFTWARE WILL BE ERROR FREE.

(c) This limited warranty gives you specific legal rights, and you may have other rights that vary from jurisdiction to jurisdiction.

6. Remedies.

(a) WPI's entire liability and your exclusive remedy for defects in materials and workmanship shall be limited to replacement of the Software Media, which may be returned to WPI with a copy of your receipt at the following address: Software Media Fulfillment Department, Attn.: *Security+ Certification For Dummies,* Wiley Publishing, Inc., 10475 Crosspoint Blvd., Indianapolis, IN 46256, or call 1-800-762-2974. Please allow four to six weeks for delivery. This Limited Warranty is void if failure of the Software Media has resulted from accident, abuse, or misapplication. Any replacement Software Media will be warranted for the remainder of the original warranty period or thirty (30) days, whichever is longer.

(b) In no event shall WPI or the author be liable for any damages whatsoever (including without limitation damages for loss of business profits, business interruption, loss of business information, or any other pecuniary loss) arising from the use of or inability to use the Book or the Software, even if WPI has been advised of the possibility of such damages.

(c) Because some jurisdictions do not allow the exclusion or limitation of liability for consequential or incidental damages, the above limitation or exclusion may not apply to you.

7. U.S. Government Restricted Rights. Use, duplication, or disclosure of the Software for or on behalf of the United States of America, its agencies and/or instrumentalities "U.S. Government" is subject to restrictions as stated in paragraph (c)(1)(ii) of the Rights in Technical Data and Computer Software clause of DFARS 252.227-7013, or subparagraphs (c) (1) and (2) of the Commercial Computer Software - Restricted Rights clause at FAR 52.227-19, and in similar clauses in the NASA FAR supplement, as applicable.

8. General. This Agreement constitutes the entire understanding of the parties and revokes and supersedes all prior agreements, oral or written, between them and may not be modified or amended except in a writing signed by both parties hereto that specifically refers to this Agreement. This Agreement shall take precedence over any other documents that may be in conflict herewith. If any one or more provisions contained in this Agreement are held by any court or tribunal to be invalid, illegal, or otherwise unenforceable, each and every other provision shall remain in full force and effect.

FOR DUMMIES®

The easy way to get more done and have more fun

PERSONAL FINANCE

0-7645-5231-7

0-7645-2431-3

0-7645-5331-3

Also available:

Estate Planning For Dummies
(0-7645-5501-4)

401(k)s For Dummies
(0-7645-5468-9)

Frugal Living For Dummies
(0-7645-5403-4)

Microsoft Money "X" For
Dummies
(0-7645-1689-2)

Mutual Funds For Dummies
(0-7645-5329-1)

Personal Bankruptcy For
Dummies
(0-7645-5498-0)

Quicken "X" For Dummies
(0-7645-1666-3)

Stock Investing For Dummies
(0-7645-5411-5)

Taxes For Dummies 2003
(0-7645-5475-1)

BUSINESS & CAREERS

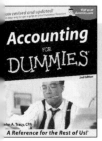
0-7645-5314-3

0-7645-5307-0

0-7645-5471-9

Also available:

Business Plans Kit For
Dummies
(0-7645-5365-8)

Consulting For Dummies
(0-7645-5034-9)

Cool Careers For Dummies
(0-7645-5345-3)

Human Resources Kit For
Dummies
(0-7645-5131-0)

Managing For Dummies
(1-5688-4858-7)

QuickBooks All-in-One Desk
Reference For Dummies
(0-7645-1963-8)

Selling For Dummies
(0-7645-5363-1)

Small Business Kit For
Dummies
(0-7645-5093-4)

Starting an eBay Business For
Dummies
(0-7645-1547-0)

HEALTH, SPORTS & FITNESS

0-7645-5167-1

0-7645-5146-9

0-7645-5154-X

Also available:

Controlling Cholesterol For
Dummies
(0-7645-5440-9)

Dieting For Dummies
(0-7645-5126-4)

High Blood Pressure For
Dummies
(0-7645-5424-7)

Martial Arts For Dummies
(0-7645-5358-5)

Menopause For Dummies
(0-7645-5458-1)

Nutrition For Dummies
(0-7645-5180-9)

Power Yoga For Dummies
(0-7645-5342-9)

Thyroid For Dummies
(0-7645-5385-2)

Weight Training For Dummies
(0-7645-5168-X)

Yoga For Dummies
(0-7645-5117-5)

Available wherever books are sold.
Go to www.dummies.com or call 1-877-762-2974 to order direct.

FOR DUMMIES®

A world of resources to help you grow

HOME, GARDEN & HOBBIES

0-7645-5295-3

0-7645-5130-2

0-7645-5106-X

Also available:

Auto Repair For Dummies
(0-7645-5089-6)

Chess For Dummies
(0-7645-5003-9)

Home Maintenance For
Dummies
(0-7645-5215-5)

Organizing For Dummies
(0-7645-5300-3)

Piano For Dummies
(0-7645-5105-1)

Poker For Dummies
(0-7645-5232-5)

Quilting For Dummies
(0-7645-5118-3)

Rock Guitar For Dummies
(0-7645-5356-9)

Roses For Dummies
(0-7645-5202-3)

Sewing For Dummies
(0-7645-5137-X)

FOOD & WINE

0-7645-5250-3

0-7645-5390-9

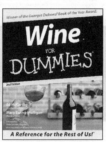

0-7645-5114-0

Also available:

Bartending For Dummies
(0-7645-5051-9)

Chinese Cooking For
Dummies
(0-7645-5247-3)

Christmas Cooking For
Dummies
(0-7645-5407-7)

Diabetes Cookbook For
Dummies
(0-7645-5230-9)

Grilling For Dummies
(0-7645-5076-4)

Low-Fat Cooking For
Dummies
(0-7645-5035-7)

Slow Cookers For Dummie
(0-7645-5240-6)

TRAVEL

0-7645-5453-0

0-7645-5438-7

0-7645-5448-4

Also available:

America's National Parks For
Dummies
(0-7645-6204-5)

Caribbean For Dummies
(0-7645-5445-X)

Cruise Vacations For
Dummies 2003
(0-7645-5459-X)

Europe For Dummies
(0-7645-5456-5)

Ireland For Dummies
(0-7645-6199-5)

France For Dummies
(0-7645-6292-4)

London For Dummies
(0-7645-5416-6)

Mexico's Beach Resorts Fo
Dummies
(0-7645-6262-2)

Paris For Dummies
(0-7645-5494-8)

RV Vacations For Dummie
(0-7645-5443-3)

Walt Disney World & Orlar
For Dummies
(0-7645-5444-1)

Available wherever books are sold. Go to www.dummies.com or call 1-877-762-2974 to order direct.

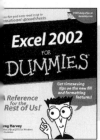

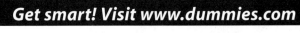

FOR DUMMIES®

Helping you expand your horizons and realize your potential

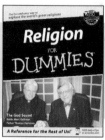
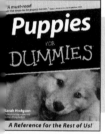

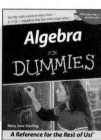

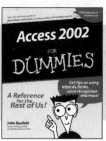